The Baptism of Disciples Alone

A Covenantal Argument for Credobaptism Versus Paedobaptism

Fred A. Malone, Ph.D.

Cape Coral, Florida
Founders Press
2003

Published by
Founders Press
Committed to historic Southern Baptist principles
P.O. Box 150931 · Cape Coral, FL 33915
Phone (239) 772-1400 · Fax: (239) 772-1140

Electronic Mail: founders@founders.org or www.founders.org

©2003 by Founders Press
All rights reserved.

Printed in the United States of America
ISBN 0-9713361-3-X

Unless otherwise indicated all Scripture quotations are taken from the New American Standard Bible, © 1960, 1962, 1963, 1968, 1971, 1972, 1973, 1975, 1977, by the Lockman Foundation. Used by permission.

The publication of this book is made possible by the encouragement and financial assistance of the Association of Reformed Baptist Churches of America.

P.O. Box 289 · Carlisle, PA 17013
Phone (717) 249-7473 · Fax (717) 258-0614
Electronic Mail: *arbca@reformedbaptist.com*
Website: *www.reformedbaptist.com*

Dedication

To my precious wife, Deborah, who followed me from the Baptist to Presbyterian to the Baptist ranks again with a sweet and trusting, though not blind, spirit. It always bothered her that it took a theologian (me) to explain to her the complicated arguments as to how infant baptism is biblical. As she put it, it was like having a priest tell her what she could not see in the Scriptures herself.

To pastors Steve Martin of the Heritage Church, Fayetteville (Atlanta), Georgia; Walter Chantry of the Grace Baptist Church, Carlisle, Pennsylvania; and fellow board members of the Southern Baptist Founders Ministries who urged me off square one to revise my journal article on this topic for book publication.

To Dr. Tom Ascol, my dear friend, who deserves "a star in his crown" for his encouragement, advice and editing on this project. Thanks also goes to Matthew Allen and Ken Puls for their help editing.

Special thanks to Ernest C. Reisinger, for taking a former Presbyterian to be his associate pastor in 1977, for taking me under his wing and making me answer right questions in many areas of theology, for being greatly used in the lives of many young men to better equip them for the gospel ministry, and for graciously writing the foreword to this work.

To the dear members of First Presbyterian Church (PCA), Eutaw, Alabama, who were so warm and encouraging when their pastor changed to a Baptist. They never made me feel like a traitor to them or to the Reformed faith, even though I often felt like a traitor to them.

To the people of Heritage Baptist Church, Fort Worth, Texas, and First Baptist Church, Clinton, Louisiana, for their encouragement toward my writing ministry. The latter dear people of

God graciously granted me a one-month sabbatical to finish the major portion of this work.

To my parents, Elton P. and Mary Davis Smith Malone, for taking me to church and helping me through many years of seminary training. My mother's difficult death in 1997 and my father's death in 1999 during the completion of a draft of this book make its completion a testimony to the sustaining grace of God to a poor sinner. My dear sister, Mrs. Don (Sandra) Cain, faithfully cared for my parents during this time, enabling me to substantially finish this work while living so far away from them.

Finally, to God be the glory.

Fred A. Malone
April 12, 2002
Clinton, Louisiana

Contents

Foreword		vii
Preface		xiii
Introduction	Why Write This Book?	xxiii
	The Covenantal Baptist Position Briefly Stated	xxxii
Section I	Preliminary Principles: Hermeneutics, Authority, and Baptism	1
Chapter 1	No Straw Men: John Murray's Case for Infant Baptism	3
Chapter 2	Biblical Principles of Interpretation and Infant Baptism	23
Section II	The String of Pearls: Covenant Theology, The New Covenant, and Baptism	49
Chapter 3	The Covenant Theology of the Bible (Part 1): Paedobaptist versus Baptist Views	51
Chapter 4	The Covenant Theology of the Bible (Part 2): New Covenant Fulfillment and Infant Baptism	81

Chapter 5	The Relationship between Circumcision and Baptism	111
Chapter 6	Household Baptisms, "the *Oikos* Formula," and Infant Baptism	127
Chapter 7	Answering the Infant Baptism Proof-Texts	137
Chapter 8	Jesus' Attitude Toward Children	151
Chapter 9	The Disjunction of John's and Jesus' Baptisms with Christian Baptism	157
Chapter 10	The Weight of Precept, the Argument of Silence, and the Regulative Principle of Worship	163
Chapter 11	The Argument of Expanded Blessings to "Covenant Children"	173
Chapter 12	The Testimony of Tradition and the Historical Argument of Silence	187
Chapter 13	What Difference Does It Make?	195
Chapter 14	Postlude: A Final Appeal to Build Baptist Churches	201
Appendix A	Spurgeon on Baptism	205
Appendix B	The Proper Mode of Biblical Baptism	223
Appendix C	Book Review of *The Biblical Doctrine of Infant Baptism*	245
Appendix D	Appendix to the *1689 London Baptist Confession*	253
Selected Bibliography		267

Foreword

THE AUTHOR: DR. FRED A. MALONE

Years ago I had to be in Washington, D. C., for a weekend. Since I did not know any churches in Washington, I called a friend who did. He mentioned two churches. Both had good ministers who were expository preachers. However, he recommended one above the other because one minister had blood and pain mixed with his convictions. Dr. Fred Malone is that kind of minister. He has blood and pain mixed with his convictions on the subject of baptism, and it comes through in this book.

It gives me real pleasure to write this foreword for three reasons. First, I know the author. Second, I witnessed some of his deep agony over this subject. Third, to a much lesser degree, I had some of the same struggles. A Philadelphia newspaper published the following announcement in January 1946:

> **Presbytery Names a Lay Preacher**
>
> The Carlisle Presbytery at its January meeting in the Second Presbyterian Church commissioned Ernest Reisinger of Carlisle as a lay preacher. It was probably the first such action taken anywhere in the denomination since the commissioning of laymen was authorized last May by the General Assembly.
>
> Under his commission, Mr. Reisinger, who is a member of the local construction firm of Reisinger Brothers, will be lay preacher at Biddle Presbyterian Chapel, East and North Streets, where he teaches a Sunday School class and conducts midweek prayer services. He was authorized to teach and preach, but cannot administer the sacraments or perform the marriage ceremony. Rev. Spencer B. Smith, Camp Hill moderator, presided.

Commissioning a lay preacher was a unique step for the Presbyterian church at the time. When questioned about baptism, I answered honestly that I was not settled yet on my own position. The presbytery further asked me if I would ever be inclined to preach against infant baptism, to which I replied that I would never preach against any issue about which I was still unclear. So, on that basis, I was commissioned by the Carlisle Presbytery as a lay preacher. I later became clear on the issue and became a Baptist.

I first met Fred Malone in the early 1970s at the Reformed Theological Seminary in Jackson, Mississippi. He was a student, and I was there to give a series of lectures on God-centered evangelism. Fred was a young Calvinist and a longtime Southern Baptist, still practicing shallow methods of evangelism. He was not very receptive to me or to what I was teaching. In fact, he was obviously upset at what I taught, even challenging my position in a discussion class. Later, while in seminary, he moved in the right direction by fully embracing Reformed views, including my views on evangelism. However, he took a wrong turn as well, embracing paedobaptism at the same time.

Fred, like many other young men, thought that in order to be a consistent Reformed minister, he had to be a paedobaptist. He did not know much about his Baptist fathers or his Baptist theological roots. Fred was ordained by the Associate Reformed Presbyterian Church (ARP) and called to pastor the First Presbyterian Church (PCA) of Eutaw, Alabama. Although he held to paedobaptism theologically, he told me later that his conscience screamed every time he sprinkled a baby. In 1977, he returned to his Baptist roots, becoming my associate pastor at North Pompano Baptist Church. He served as pastor from 1979 to 1980 before returning to seminary for doctoral work. During those years we spent together, I found him to be a man who loved God, God's Book and God's people. He was valiant for the truth. He is a faithful father, a loving husband and a loyal colleague in the ministry.

THE SUBJECT: BAPTISM

This subject has left many casualties and divisions; therefore, it must be approached with charity and a conciliatory spirit. A wise caution is found in the words of the late Dr. D. Martyn Lloyd-Jones:

> First, let us take the biblical doctrine of baptism. It is probably unnecessary for me even to mention the fact that this is a subject about which there has been great disputation. Whereas many people might, perhaps, have been comparatively ignorant about some of the other causes of dissension, I am sure that at some time or another, every professing Christian has been engaged in discussion on the question of baptism. And equally saintly, equally spiritual, equally learned, people are to be found holding the various opinions. Therefore it behooves us once more to say that not only must we approach the subject with caution, but still more importantly, in a Christian manner and in the Spirit which we claim we have received and to whom we submit ourselves. Never has it been more important to avoid mere labels, glib generalisations, and dogmatic pronouncements than when considering a subject like this. Is it not perfectly obvious, before we go any further, that this subject cannot be finally decided, that it is not one of those subjects concerning which you can give an absolute and unmistakable proof? If it could there would never have been all this controversy and there would not have been denominational distinctions.
>
> I would cite the example of Professor Karl Barth, the great Reformed theologian (though my citing him does not mean that I agree with his essential position). Barth was brought up in the typical presbyterian manner, but he has undergone a great change in his view of baptism. Having been brought up to believe in infant baptism, he has written a book to say that he no longer believes that, but believes in adult baptism. So it ill behooves us to be overdogmatic and to give the impression that there is only one possible point of view.
>
> As we saw in the last lecture, baptism is not essential to our salvation. No sacrament is essential to salvation: if you say it is, you are aligning yourself with the Roman Catholics. Protestants have always said that while baptism and the Lord's Supper are commands of the Lord, and we should therefore practise them, they are not essential. They do not add grace, they simply point to it and bring it to us in a special way. So we must approach the subject with this caution and with a Christian spirit (*The Church and the Last Things,* Vol. 3, of *Great Doctrines of the Bible,* CrossWay Books, Wheaton, IL, pp. 35–36).

THE BOOK

Some sermons are prepared by study and by research. A few sermons are born with tears and prayer (these are the best). This is also true of books—some are born. This book is born.

There is no end to books written on the subject of baptism. Most of them have been written by paedobaptists, and some are written about the differences they have among themselves. Ironically, it was the books and arguments of paedobaptists that convinced me to become a Baptist. Some paedobaptists believe in baptismal regeneration; others do not. The arguments and teachings of the Roman Catholic Church differ from those of the Lutherans and the Episcopalians, who differ among themselves. They both differ from the Presbyterians and the Christian Reformed. Most Protestant paedobaptists do not agree with the Greek Orthodox Church, which practices immersion of infants. Dr. Malone has done his homework in examining these arguments, and I am sure they contribute to making him a thoroughly convinced Baptist. This book is the fruit of serious study and examination of the biblical doctrine of baptism. It is long overdue, and I believe it will go down in history as a classic on the subject from a Baptist point of view.

At this point, I think I hear some paedobaptist saying, "What about the covenant?" Some paedobaptists seem to think when they say "covenant," a Baptist must surrender or run; this book will prove otherwise. Dr. Malone addresses the knotty questions of covenant theology, circumcision, and the sprinkling of infants.

The following experience was related to me by a Baptist pastor's wife. She was attending a ladies' Bible study held in a local Presbyterian church, and she was the only one in the study who was not a Presbyterian. The subject of children came up. The ladies were talking about "covenant children" when someone realized that there was a Baptist in the class. She began to apologize profusely for bringing up the subject of "covenant children" because, she asserted, she knew that Baptists did not believe in the covenant. This dear lady did not know that the prince of Baptist preachers, Charles Haddon Spurgeon, said, "the covenant is the marrow of Divinity." Dr. Malone's book will dispel such ignorance.

This book will provide an excellent tool for pastors and serious Christians. It is also an excellent apologetics resource to answer the well-trained paedobaptist who often overwhelms those who have never given serious study and examination to the subject. The motivated reader will learn the Reformed Baptist position on "covenant children" from this book; that is, they enter the covenant by circumcision of the heart, are sealed by the Holy

Spirit, and are revealed in a credible profession of faith, confessed publicly by baptism.

Dr. Malone states in his book that believer's [disciple's] baptism alone is the baptism instituted by our Lord and His apostles and the only baptism prescribed by the Holy Scriptures.

Neither this book, nor any other, will settle the long-standing difference among the best of God's true servants. However, it will give a thorough answer for the Baptist position and show that it is a viable and honorable position. It will also show that Reformed Baptists do believe in the covenant. There will be no question that our brother Malone has studied the Scriptures and history on this subject, and now many of the Lord's people will have the benefit of all the author's years of serious study. May it please our Great Redeemer to shower His blessing upon our brother's long and tedious efforts.

I pray that the reading and studying of this book will produce a conciliatory spirit among Baptists and our dear and respected paedobaptist friends. I also pray our differences on baptism will not hinder our mutual efforts to obey our Lord's clearest command, "Go into all the world and preach the gospel."

Ernest C. Reisinger
Christian Gospel Foundation
Cape Coral, Florida

Preface

MY PROBLEM WITH INFANT BAPTISM

As a former Presbyterian minister, I baptized two of my infants. I was sincere. It was meaningful. I believed that infant baptism (paedobaptism) was biblical. However, I was sincerely and biblically wrong.

Now, I am convinced that the baptism authorized by the Bible is the baptism of disciples. In fact, I believe the Bible authorizes the baptism of disciples *alone*. This position may also be called *credobaptism* from the Latin verb *credo,* meaning *believe or trust*. Other designations are *believer's baptism, confessor's baptism,* or *professor's baptism,* all synonyms describing the baptism of disciples alone. Hoping to be gracious toward my paedobaptist friends and mentors, the purpose of this book is to prove that the Bible authorizes only disciple's baptism. This book is also written, however, to help parents, pastors, and laymen better understand the Baptist position for credobaptism versus paedobaptism so they can decide which local church to join and serve in.

The subject of baptism is of great practical importance. Should Christian parents have their babies baptized (paedobaptism)? Or should they evangelize their children, pray for them, and wait for a disciple's profession of faith from them before baptism (credobaptism)? Is "repent and be baptized" a command that parents should obey for their children, or is it a command for their children to obey for themselves (Acts 2:38–41)?

Is paedobaptism so clear in Scripture that it would be sinful *not* to baptize one's babies? And if sinful, should not paedobaptist pastors exercise discipline against those church members who refuse to baptize their infants? Would Christian parents, who believe *sola Scriptura* (Scripture alone), find infant baptism so clear in Scripture that they would become convinced in their own conscience that they *must* have their infant baptized or else disobey God's revealed Word? Must they rely on "expert" theologians to explain their biblical duty toward their children for what they cannot see in Scripture for themselves?

This issue of parents coming to their own conviction about the baptism of their children is of great importance. This is especially true because most of the specific Scripture texts and theological arguments for infant baptism are the subject of dispute among major paedobaptist theologians. If infant baptism is biblical, then parents should be able to see this for themselves in Scripture in order to obey God by having their infants baptized. However, if credobaptism alone is biblical, then parents must not rob their children of the opportunity to obey a command of God for themselves, nor of having the joyful experience of confessing Christ in believer's baptism. If lettered paedobaptist theologians differ so vastly among themselves about infant baptism, should unlettered parents be pressured into baptizing their infants? They are the ones who will give account to God for what they do with their own children.

I see two basic problems with infant baptism, both of which I will cover in more detail in subsequent chapters. The problems are (1) the "regulative principle of worship," and (2) biblical hermeneutics.

THE PROBLEM OF THE "REGULATIVE PRINCIPLE"

Is infant baptism as clear in Scripture as other issues, like repentance before baptism (John 4:1–2; Acts 2:38, 41), or self-examination before the Lord's Supper (Acts 2:41–42; 1 Corinthians 11:27–29), or a woman's participation in the Lord's Supper (Exodus 12:1–4, 16; 1 Corinthians 11:18–22), or men only as elders (1 Timothy 2:12; 3:1–7), etc.? Obviously not. The latter issues at least are mentioned in Scripture and are settled by clear Scriptural commands following "the regulative principle of worship," an essential doctrine in both Baptist and Presbyterian churches.

The Reformed regulative principle of worship requires that elements of worship, including sacraments, be "*instituted* by God

Himself, ... *limited* by his own *revealed* will, and ... *prescribed* in holy Scripture" (*Westminster Confession of Faith* 21:5; 21:1; 1:6).[1] The regulative principle teaches that the elements of New Testament worship and church order should be "regulated" by Scripture and clearly instituted for New Covenant worship. In other words, elements of Christian worship must be instituted by God and prescribed by God, either in the way of commands or clear examples.

The Lutheran "normative principle" and the Roman Catholic "inventive principle" are different in that they also permit in worship things not specifically prohibited in New Testament Scripture. This may even include noninstituted worship practices erroneously deduced from other Scripture such as the existence of priests, altars, pageantry, incense, and priestly rituals for New Testament worship.

The Presbyterian *Westminster Confession of Faith* (1646) and *London Baptist Confession* (1689) both include baptism as an element of New Testament worship. Therefore, the meaning, mode, and subjects of baptism, as a sacrament acknowledged to be "ordained by Jesus Christ" (*WCF* 28:1) and "instituted by Christ" (*WCF* 21:5), must conform to the regulative principle of instituted worship, not to the normative principle of things not specifically prohibited. Because infant baptism is considered a biblical sacrament, one of the official elements of worship, shouldn't it, too, be "instituted" by Christ according to the same principle as the Lord's Supper? Yet, it is not so prescribed.

The regulative principle was a major issue to our Baptist forefathers, necessary to give biblical authority to infant baptism. This is made clear in "An Appendix" to the *1689 London Baptist Confession,* first published with the confession in 1677:

> Therefore we cannot for our own parts be persuaded in our own minds, to build such a practice as this, upon an unwritten tradition: But do rather choose in all points of Faith and Worship, to have recourse to the Holy Scriptures, for the information of our judgment, and regulation of our practice.... *All instituted worship*

---

[1] I will use the term "sacrament" in this book because it concerns a paedobaptist sacrament. The *1689 London Baptist Confession* prefers the term "ordinance."

receives its sanction from the precept, and is to be thereby governed in all the necessary circumstances thereof [emphasis mine].²

It is my belief that the regulative principle of worship, stated so clearly in the Presbyterian *Westminster Confession of Faith* and *1689 London Baptist Confession,* requires instituted revelation to authorize infant baptism. Because no such revelation exists, infant baptism is a violation of the regulative principle of worship.

Our Lord Jesus Christ established the regulative principle of Christian worship in His earthly teachings. He declared His authority over instituted Old Testament worship (Jerusalem) and noninstituted worship (Samaria) with these words to the Samaritan woman at the well:

> Woman, believe Me, an hour is coming when neither in this mountain, nor in Jerusalem, shall you worship the Father. You worship that which you do not know; we worship that which we know; for salvation is from the Jews. But an hour is coming, and now is, when the true worshipers shall worship the Father in spirit and in truth; for such people the Father seeks to be His worshipers (John 4:21–23).

This declaration of our Lord is a historical-redemptive statement of the highest meaning, which establishes Him and His teachings as the New Covenant authority for worship over Old Testament and noninstituted forms. Before He left earth, He affirmed this principle in His apostles' charge in the Great Commission: "teaching them to do all that I commanded you" (Matthew 28:20). We must assume from these statements that the earthly teachings of the Lord Jesus Christ and their later applications by His apostles form the content of instituted and commanded Christian worship. To resort to Old Testament forms by possibly erroneous inference or to practice noninstituted forms is a violation of His Lordship over Christian worship. The only instituted baptism in the New Testament by Christ and His apostles is credobaptism: the baptism of disciples alone.

---

²"An Appendix" in *The 1689 London Baptist Confession* (1677; facsimile edition, Auburn, MA: B&R Press, 2000), 109–142. This appendix is reproduced in Appendix D of this book.

THE PROBLEM OF BIBLICAL HERMENEUTICS

Baptists and Presbyterians agree with a basic Augustinian principle of biblical interpretation that "the New is in the Old concealed; and the Old is in the New revealed." This places an emphasis upon the New Testament revelation as the final determiner of instituted and regulated Christian worship versus Old Testament worship and forms continued by inference alone (Ephesians 2:20; 3:5). This principle, consistently applied, also argues against any notion of infant baptism grounded upon a supposed and possibly erroneous "good and necessary inference," which may be neither "good" nor "necessary."

Baptists and Presbyterians agree that there is no express command for or clear example of infant baptism in the Bible. Professor John Murray, for example, admits that no command or example of infant baptism exists in the New Testament. Hence, his main principle of interpretation used to establish infant baptism is "good and necessary inference":

> One of the most persuasive objections and one which closes the argument for a great many people is that there is *no express command* to baptise infants and *no record* in the New Testament of a clear case of infant baptism. . . . The evidence for infant baptism falls into the category of *good and necessary inference,* and it is therefore quite indefensible to demand that the evidence required must be in the category of express command or explicit instance (emphasis mine).[3]

Apparently, Murray holds to B. B. Warfield's position: "The warrant for infant baptism is not to be sought in the New Testament but in the Old Testament" by good and necessary inference.[4]

Murray's reference to good and necessary inference is based on the *Westminster Confession of Faith* 1:6, which says:

> The whole counsel of God, concerning all things necessary for his own glory, man's salvation, faith, and life, is *either expressly set down*

---

[3]John Murray, *Christian Baptism* (Nutley, NJ: Presbyterian and Reformed Publishing Company, 1970), 72.
[4]B. B. Warfield, *Studies in Theology* (1932; reprint, Grand Rapids, MI: Baker Book House, 1981), 399.

in scripture, or by good and necessary consequence may be deduced from scripture: unto which nothing at any time is to be added, whether by new revelations of the Spirit, or traditions of men. Nevertheless, we acknowledge the inward illumination of the Spirit of God to be necessary for the saving understanding of such things as are revealed in the word; and that there are some circumstances concerning the worship of God, and government of the Church, common to human actions and societies, which are to be ordered by the light of nature and Christian prudence, according to the general rules of the word, which are always to be observed [emphasis mine].

However, is good and necessary *inference* a safe hermeneutical principle to apply to a New Testament sacrament *instituted* by Christ? Is it really indefensible, as Murray claims, to base the practice of a New Testament instituted sacrament and element of Christian worship upon an express command or explicit instance in the New Testament, rather than upon possibly erroneous inferences from the Old Testament? This position is not generally held, according to the regulative principle, concerning other elements of New Testament worship, all of which are expressly set down in Scripture. Why is it held for infant baptism?

All agree that reason, logic, and deduction are involved in the interpretation of the Scriptures. However, one might argue that the word *consequence* in the *WCF* means an inescapable conclusion whereas Murray's substitution of inference leans simply toward a plausible case. The doctrine of the Trinity, for example, is certainly a good and necessary consequence deduced from Scriptures which speak of God as One yet in three Persons equally divine. However, some possibly plausible inferences from Scripture, when used to form a doctrine (a favorite tool of the cults), may be neither "good" nor "necessary," especially in light of the regulative principle of instituted sacraments. It is this use of possibly plausible or possibly erroneous good and necessary inference which must be rejected as the basis for building a case for an instituted sacrament. The elements of Christian worship must be clearly *"instituted* by God Himself, . . . *limited* by his own *revealed* will, and . . . *prescribed* in holy Scripture" (*WCF* 21:5; 21:1; 1:6). Plausible inferences do not attain to this level of certainty.

It would be easy to pass over the subject of infant baptism as a minor issue, but it is not. This is a controversial subject that necessarily separates Christian brethren and churches one from the other confessionally, sacramentally, and ecclesiastically.[5] Charity must govern each discussion. However, each pastor must settle this issue in order to determine which sphere of Christ's church he may serve with a clear conscience. Further, members must determine whether they have obeyed Christ's command for biblical baptism as well as which church they can join and serve as elders, deacons, and teachers with a clear conscience. It is my hope that this book will help those so struggling and will assist those pastors and laymen who need a resource to teach or defend *the baptism of disciples alone.*

I have chosen the designation "the baptism of disciples alone" to describe the only instituted and regulated baptism "expressly set down in Scripture." It is no more an unbiblical description of baptism in the Bible than are other principles of reformation theology: Scripture alone, grace alone, faith alone, Christ alone, and God's glory alone. That which is "expressly set down in Scripture" concerning an instituted, regulated sacrament is sufficient to earn the designation "alone."

A PERSONAL TESTIMONY

In 1977, as a Presbyterian Church in America (PCA) minister, I was forced by conscience to move from a paedobaptist (infant baptism) to a Baptist (disciple's baptism only) position. It was, and still is, one of the most traumatic experiences I have been through as a pastor and Christian. It is true that I had been raised a Baptist, but I adopted infant baptism in 1972 out of theological conviction while a student at the Reformed Theological Seminary (RTS) in Jackson, Mississippi.

---

[5] I am thankful for the charitable spirit that exists between paedobaptist and Baptist brethren at such places as the Banner of Truth Conference. In such fellowships, baptism does not often become the object of first discussion. I personally try never to bring up infant baptism first. Recently, in other circles, I have noticed a more aggressive attitude against the Baptist position. Confrontive comments place one on the defensive with such thoughts as these: Do I pursue the issue of baptism, which he has presented, possibly ending our fellowship in discord? Do I keep quiet as if I have no answer? Why can we not fellowship around what we have in common as did good John Bunyan and dear John Owen?

As I look back to those blessed days at RTS (1970 to 1974), when I was a sincere and searching student, I believe that I accepted infant baptism with a clear conscience before God. Yet I sometimes wonder if I searched out the truth concerning infant baptism as sincerely as I thought I did. In the warm fellowship of my paedobaptist brethren, coupled with the suspiciousness of Baptists about my choice of seminary, it is more than possible that I allowed subjective feelings and wonderful opportunities for paedobaptist ministry to influence my study of infant baptism.

I do not believe that I am the only Baptist who became a Presbyterian under those circumstances. In fact, I have come to believe that our good Presbyterian assemblies have a lot of Baptists sitting in their pews out of frustration with local Baptist churches. Further, it might be surprising to discover how many Presbyterian pastors were once Baptists. I receive regular reports of Baptist seminary students who have accepted the Reformed theology of our Baptist forefathers, often taught it by Baptist pastors, then subsequently accept a job in a paedobaptist church as a paedobaptist. Often the reported accounts express "no opportunities and too much opposition to Reformed theology in Baptist churches" as a major reason for the switch.

Oh, that we had more Baptist "pioneers" willing to endure hardship to build new churches or to reform our established Baptist churches! Where will Reformed Baptists of conscience worship in coming generations if we do not take up the cross now?

As time passed happily while serving paedobaptist churches, I re-examined my position on infant baptism in 1977 and found many inconsistencies that, for whatever reasons, I did not find in seminary. At that time, I composed a journal entitled *A String of Pearls Unstrung* to explain my change to a Baptist position for my presbytery and for interested friends. Recently, that journal was updated and reprinted as a small booklet by Founders Press of Cape Coral, Florida.[6] At the urging of friends helped by the journal, I have expanded that booklet into this larger book. It is intended to be read easily by pastors, students, and motivated laymen. Footnotes and a bibliography will point out additional resources for those so inclined.

I have endeavored to let most of my work be as original as possible. However, two books which helped me years ago to confirm my

---

[6]Fred A. Malone, *A String of Pearls Unstrung* (Cape Coral, FL: Founders Press, 1998).

study are *Should Babies Be Baptized?* by T. E. Watson and *The Children of Abraham* by David Kingdon.[7] I highly recommend these works to paedobaptist and Baptist friends alike. Also, I have included Charles H. Spurgeon's fine treatise on baptism in Appendix A and a critical review of Pierre Marcel's classic work defending infant baptism in Appendix C. Appendix D is the original appendix to the *1689 London Baptist Confession* defending the baptism of disciples alone.

The reader also will find that I have dealt mainly with the subjects of baptism in this work. This is because who is to be baptized is a more important question than how it is to be done. With respect to the mode of baptism, John Calvin himself believed that the Bible word *baptizo* means *to immerse* and taught that the early church practiced immersion:

> But whether the person being baptized should be wholly immersed, and whether thrice or once, whether he should only be sprinkled with poured water—these details are of no importance, but ought to be optional to churches according to the diversity of countries. Yet *the word 'baptize' means to immerse, and it is clear that the rite of immersion was observed in the ancient church* [emphasis mine].[8]

I accept Calvin's analysis, even though he was inconsistent in allowing other modes of baptism. Appendix B is dedicated to a brief defense of immersion as the biblical mode of the baptisms of John, Jesus, the apostles, and the early church, contrary to John Murray's sprinkling or pouring view.

As I cover each point of theology, I hope (as do we all, I am sure) to give glory to God by letting His infallible Word be the absolute and final authority of each conclusion. My continual prayer is for the Holy Spirit to illumine my mind and the mind of the reader as we gaze together into the mind of God on the written page.

---

[7]Thomas E. Watson, *Should Babies Be Baptized?* (London: Grace Publications Trust, 1995); David Kingdon, *Children of Abraham,* (Sussex: Carey Publications, 1973). I also recommend Paul K. Jewett, *Infant Baptism and the Covenant of Grace* (Grand Rapids, MI: William B. Eerdmans Publishing Co., 1978). Although Jewett's work was available, I did not study it at the time. However, I have come to appreciate his work as a fair and effective rejection of infant baptism. His work on the early church and the Reformation in regard to baptism is invaluable.

[8]John Calvin, *Institutes of the Christian Religion,* ed. John T. McNeill, trans. and indexed by Ford Lewis Battles (Philadelphia, PA: The Westminster Press, 1967), 4:15:19 (1320).

Introduction

WHY WRITE THIS BOOK?

There are at least four good reasons for writing this book, and all are related to the growing reformation and revival among Baptists in America, England, and South Africa. The acceptance of infant baptism by Baptists is often related to their growing acceptance of the broader Reformed faith once held by our Baptist forefathers, as outlined in the *1689 London Baptist Confession* and its American iterations, the *Philadelphia* and *Charleston Baptist Confessions*. The following reasons justify this work.

Baptist Ignorance

First, in my experience as a Baptist, I have found that many fellow Baptists are ignorant of both the Baptist and paedobaptist positions. Such ignorance often makes Baptist pastors, ministerial students, and church members easy targets for a well-trained paedobaptist apologist. When discussing the doctrine of baptism with Baptist ministers, I have found many who are ignorant of covenant theology and unable to answer paedobaptist arguments from that position. This is an indictment against Baptist theological education which, by God's grace, has recently seen the beginnings of a much-needed reformation.

In addition, many Baptists during the last century have imbibed classic dispensational views. This new development in Baptist theology gradually replaced views that had been very covenantal up to that point.⁹ I will explain in chapter two why classic dispensationalism has a difficult time arguing against infant baptism based upon Old Testament inference. One needs to remember that many leading dispensationalists in England and America have been paedobaptists. Dispensationalism by no means refutes infant baptism. Therefore, Baptists who have imbibed dispensational views are often confused by a studied paedobaptist covenantalist because they are unversed in the biblical covenants.

Pastoral Losses

Second, Baptists have lost a number of pastors and seminary students to Presbyterianism (although they are not thereby lost to the kingdom of God!). There is a growing resurgence of Reformed theology among Baptist pastors and laymen in America, with many returning to the Reformed faith which our Baptist forefathers generally held.¹⁰ However, in the process of rediscovering our Baptist and Reformed roots, some fine Baptist pastors have become Presbyterian by accepting infant baptism.¹¹ It is very

---

⁹One example of the covenantal view of Baptists is R. B. C. Howell, *The Covenants* (Charleston, SC: The Southern Baptist Publication Society, 1855). R. B. C. Howell served as president of the Southern Baptist Convention from 1851 to 1857. He was well-known as a defender of the baptism of disciples alone from a covenantal perspective. Other evidence of Baptist covenantalism is seen in the *London Baptist Confession* (1689), and in the works of J. L. Dagg, James P. Boyce, Charles H. Spurgeon and many others.

¹⁰The resurgence of Baptists to their Reformed roots is evident in the increased number of Baptist churches in America that have adopted the *1689 London Baptist Confession;* i.e., the Association of Reformed Baptist Churches in American (ARBCA) and many Southern Baptist Churches. Other indications include the return of many Southern Baptists to the Reformed theology of their founders (W. B. Johnson, Basil Manly, J. L. Dagg, James P. Boyce, John Broadus, Basil Manly, Jr., etc.), as exemplified in the Southern Baptist Founders Conference and Founders Ministries.

¹¹As I was completing this introduction, I received notice of another Baptist friend who was called to pastor a PCA church. A number of former Southern Baptists who learned Calvinism from our Baptist forefathers now serve in Presbyterian churches. Also, I have received inquiries from several PCA laymen who are Baptists in background. They have been asked to be officers in their PCA churches, but they are struggling over infant baptism. Further, I have heard of at least one Presbyterian seminary which has had at least 40 percent Baptists in their entering student body, many of whom became pastors in the PCA and other Presbyterian denominations upon graduation.

Introduction xxv

tempting to follow wonderful Reformed teachers such as John Murray, Charles Hodge, John Owen and R. C. Sproul down the path of infant baptism.[12] Can they be right on so many vital issues and so wrong on this? It is hard to believe so.

It is also very tempting as a Baptist pastor to savor the warm fellowship and opportunities of Presbyterian denominations where the Reformed faith is more widely spread and more readily accepted than among modern-day Baptists. Many Baptist pastors have suffered persecution and rejection while trying to teach Baptists the Reformed faith, which most early Baptists originally believed. It is easy to convince oneself that infant baptism is a minor issue when compared to many major agreements with paedobaptists in other matters. This is especially true when one considers the joyful prospect of warm-hearted Reformed fellowship, service, and opportunities in paedobaptist churches.

However, the issue of the sacraments (ordinances) is not minor by any stretch of the Reformed imagination. Along with infant baptism come issues regarding the nature of the church and church membership, the evangelism of "covenant children," church discipline, and so forth. For example, the original PCA *Book of Church Order* presents an entirely different approach to evangelizing infant-baptized children than do those churches that establish membership of any age only upon a confession of faith as evidence of a regenerate heart:

> By virtue of being born of believing parents, children are, because of God's covenant ordinance, made members of the Church, but this is not sufficient to make them continue members of the Church. When they have reached the age of discretion, they become subject to obligations of the covenent [sic]: faith, repentance, and obedience. They then must make public confession of their faith in Christ, *or become covenant breakers, and subject to the discipline of the Church* [emphasis mine].[13]

Although PCA ministers are cautioned to use "liberty" and "godly wisdom" when applying the extract just quoted, one wonders

---

[12]I am not accusing any of blindly following. However, even a sincere conscience in deciding for infant baptism may be strongly affected by the overwhelming testimony of such good men.
[13]*The Book of Church Order,* printed for the General Assembly of the Presbyterian Church in America (Montgomery, AL.: Committee for Christian Education and Publications, 1975), chap. 57, par. 4.

what is the age of discretion. Sixteen? Twelve? Ten? Pierre Marcel, whose views are very influential among modern Presbyterians, believes that it is twelve.[14] Further, what kind of pressure do children at that age feel under the threat of church discipline? Premature confessions of faith are necessarily encouraged by this system.

This is a very different approach to child evangelism than is practiced in Baptist churches that are Reformed in theology. It is an approach that could easily degenerate into a pressured decisional regeneration error like that practiced in many Arminian Baptist churches via the high-pressure invitation system at the so-called age of accountability. "Communion classes" for 11 to 12-year-olds have degenerated in some paedobaptist denominations to an expected admission to the Lord's Supper upon satisfactory completion of the course, thereby displacing admission based upon the elders' confidence that evangelical repentance and faith are evident. In any case, I do not think that many PCA church members would look favorably upon the discipline of their infant-baptized children who refuse to be influenced by possible church censure to confess Jesus Christ as Lord. In fact, I doubt many church members even know that this is in their *Book of Church Order*.

The first generation of reformers who establish a purer paedobaptist denomination may not live to see the long-range effects of the error in their sacramental teaching. But what of the second, third, and future generations? The proper administration of the sacraments was at the heart of the Reformation and is one of the marks of a true church. It is unworthy of one's vows before a presbytery to minimize them for the sake of peace or opportunity. This issue is not the same as one's practice of Christian liberty or view of eschatology. It is much more fundamental and necessary to church order and practice.

We Baptists are not so narrow that we do not realize that the kingdom of God grows across denominational lines. We love and respect our paedobaptist brethren. We are much indebted to our Presbyterian divines. However, our Baptist corner of Zion has lost valuable leadership because of the acceptance of infant baptism. It is my hope that this work will help to "plug the leak in the dike" and will, at least, give pause to those pastors who are

---

[14]Pierre Marcel, *The Biblical Doctrine of Infant Baptism,* trans. Philip Edgcumbe Hughes (London: James Clarke & Co. Ltd., 1959), 99.

Introduction xxvii

ready to downplay differences between Baptists and paedobaptists on the ordinance of baptism. We Baptists cannot afford to lose one faithful pastor unnecessarily for the cause of reformation and revival.

Membership Losses

Third, Baptists have lost not just pastors but also valuable members to presbyterianism when those members are vitally needed in the cause of reformation and revival in Baptist churches.[15] It is my hope that this work can be a resource book for pastors who have members tempted to forsake Baptist reformation for presbyterian stability.

More than one Baptist church has lost faithful members to its Presbyterian counterpart. I personally have recommended that Baptist brethren (including my own children and church members) consider a good PCA, Associate Reformed Presbyterian Church (ARP), or Orthodox Presbyterian Church (OPC) church when there is no Baptist church in town that teaches the historic Baptist and Reformed faith. However, there are a growing number of historic Baptist pastors and ministerial students who have no place to serve or who have been removed from Baptist churches because of their sound Baptist theology. What if we could conserve our Baptist church members and/or start new Reformed and Baptist works instead of losing them (in an ecclesiastical sense) to presbyterianism? The cause of reformation, revival, and conscience among Baptists is worth the personal sacrifice that necessarily accompanies such labors. This pioneer spirit, which characterized many of our Baptist forefathers, needs to be rekindled today.

Baptist churches have often lost members not because there is no Reformed and Baptist church in town but because of the trials of bringing biblical reformation to a Baptist congregation. There are times when the efforts toward restoring a Baptist church to its historic, Reformed theological roots, church discipline,

---

[15]I am convinced by my own experiences and by the testimonies of others that a significant number of members of PCA churches are from Baptist backgrounds and are still unsure of or still reject infant baptism. However, in the absence of a good Reformed and Baptist church, they have been attracted to the sound Reformed doctrines, elder rule, and no altar call of the PCA.

and spiritual life can be very trying. Opposition from friends and family can prove very difficult, frustrating, and painful. Why not go down the street to a fellowship that more readily accepts Reformed theology without all the trials of Baptist reformation—especially if that church does not require the acceptance of infant baptism to join?[16]

The answer to that question is very simple: for the cause of biblical truth now and in future generations. The error of infant baptism may seem minuscule right now compared to other theological and practical errors in many present-day Baptist churches, but if one of the sacraments is in error, it will inevitably affect one's spiritual life and the spiritual life of one's children and grandchildren. We must not forget that the proper administration of the sacraments is one of the marks of a true church and therefore no small issue.[17] Baptists need to conserve the results of reforming efforts and keep our members faithful to the churches that taught them the Reformed faith that they now love.[18]

The Real Issue

Fourth, the real issue is whether infant baptism is a practice based upon the Scripture alone that can be substantiated by standard hermeneutical principles. If it is, then Baptists are guilty of refusing to submit to God's revealed Word in this mat-

---

[16] Many Baptists have told me that they did not have to accept infant baptism to join a Presbyterian church. Their disciple's baptism by immersion was accepted. However, some Catholics have reported that they asked Presbyterian pastors to baptize them by immersion when they were converted and yet were denied—a real inconsistency. Amazingly, their Catholic infant baptism was acceptable!

[17] If we agree with historic Reformed teaching that the three essential marks of a true church are (1) the preaching of the Word of God, (2) *the proper administration of the sacraments,* and (3) church discipline, then the issue of infant baptism can never be relegated to a minor issue. This is not to say that there cannot be a true church where a sincere error in baptism exists, but we all must agree that this is not a minor issue. Further, the spiritual condition of children is involved. Some who practice infant baptism are opposed to the evangelizing of their children as unbelievers.

[18] It is a common report among reforming pastors that members and visitors sometimes receive great help from their ministries but then join other churches because of the pressures of family, friends, or the demands of faithful membership.

ter and denying children a sacrament. However, if it is not based upon the authority of Scripture alone, then those who practice it are guilty of denying God's people a sacrament, adding to God's Word, and binding many consciences to a man-made doctrine. Further, if it is not based on the authority of Scripture alone, then the erroneous hermeneutical principles that establish it can only be damaging to the cause of *sola Scriptura*. R. B. C. Howell, a Southern Baptist Reformed scholar of the nineteenth century and president of the Southern Baptist Convention (SBC) numerous times, listed nineteen dangers of infant baptism which ultimately will weaken evangelism and church life.[19]

Every sincere Bible-believing Christian and pastor should want to know the answer to these questions about infant baptism. If God has so instructed us about such a major issue as a Christian sacrament (or ordinance), then the decision of whether to practice it or not is not a matter of Christian liberty.

Although I do not subscribe to the overstatement of his second consideration, the great Presbyterian and Princeton president, Archibald Alexander, recognized the importance of correctly practicing baptism while he wrestled with becoming a Baptist in 1797:

> Two considerations kept me back from joining the Baptists. The first was that the universal prevalence of infant baptism, as early as the fourth and fifth centuries, was unaccountable on the supposition that no such practice existed in the times of the apostles. The other was, that *if the Baptists are right, they are the only Christian church on earth, and all other denominations are out of the visible church* [emphasis mine].[20]

I will deal with Alexander's untenable first reason later, but his second reason, though extreme, ought to shock those who relegate baptism to a secondary doctrine while determining which church to serve and to join.

Elders, like Archibald Alexander, take ordination vows that they sincerely believe and will teach the sacraments according to their respective confessions. As he finally was, so also must every

---

[19] R. B. C. Howell, *The Evils of Infant Baptism* (1852; reprint, Watertown, WI: Baptist Heritage Press, 1988), 302–310.
[20] J. W. Alexander, *The Life of Archibald Alexander* (Reprint, Harrisonburg, VA: Sprinkle Publications, 1991), 205.

man be convinced in his own conscience and not by the conscience of others. However, the following statement accurately summarizes comments expressed to me by both Presbyterian elders and laymen:

> When I read the Baptist side of the argument, it sounds convincing. When I read the paedobaptist side, it also sounds convincing. I could go either way. Great minds have wrestled for centuries over this issue. Who am I to settle it? Can such great paedobaptist minds be so right on so much and so wrong on this? Because of such great men, I lean toward the paedobaptist side. And since I consider it a minor issue, compared to the major doctrinal problems in Baptist churches today, I will practice it until I am convinced otherwise.[21]

One problem with this statement is that a sacrament is not a "minor issue." Another is that believers (especially church leaders) are to come to their beliefs with their *own* convictions, not the convictions of "great men." Pastors are called to be "experts" on the essentials of church life in their local congregations. This is why Paul said to a young pastor, "Be diligent to present yourself approved to God as a workman who does not need to be ashamed, handling accurately the word of truth" (2 Timothy 2:15). Whether a Baptist or paedobaptist pastor, to be unable to hold or defend one's practice of a sacrament from Scripture alone with sincere conviction is a violation of conscience, one's own confession, and ministerial ordination vows.

Leonard T. Van Horn, a PCA teaching elder and personal friend to whom I am much indebted, has lamented the waning lack of seriousness concerning ordination vows today. Though dealing with vows concerning the Doctrines of Grace and other issues such as women's ordination, Madison Avenue tactics, and so forth, Dr. Van Horn's conclusion applies just as truly to those who take vows concerning infant baptism without personal biblical conviction:

> The writer, who is now retired from the ministry, urges all pastors of Reformed churches to show integrity regarding their ordination vows. It is not biblically ethical to leave out certain doctrines in our preaching and teaching. If a preacher no longer believes

---

[21]I will not divulge confidences here, but suffice it to say that this summarized statement has come to my hearing ten or more times.

them, he should inform the appropriate church court; they must deal with it. To be "Reformed" is not a matter of convenience. It is a matter of eternal importance once one has taken vows and subscribed to them.[22]

Dr. Van Horn's call to integrity concerning ordination vows is much needed for all churches today, both Baptist and paedobaptist. Ordination vows are not a matter of convenience. We all must hold to and teach our doctrines with personal and sincere biblical conviction, not the convictions of others.

Another problem with the previously quoted summarized statement of Presbyterian elders and laymen is stated in Romans 14:22–23, a warning about disagreed-upon practices:

> The faith which you have, have as *your own conviction* before God. Happy is he who does not condemn himself in what he approves. But he who doubts is condemned if he eats, because his eating is not from faith; and *whatever is not from faith is sin* [emphasis mine].

In this passage, Paul is talking about disagreed-upon practices in Christian liberty. How much more should we be careful with disagreed-upon practices concerning a sacrament? It is much safer for conscience and truth to be conservative in practice rather than to add an uncertain practice. Whatever is not of faith is sin. We give account to God for what we do (James 3:1).

Most of us sincerely believe that we are basing our position upon the Scriptures. However, one side or the other is wrong about this matter—and it does make a difference. It has implications regarding the nature of the New Covenant, the doctrine of the church, the evangelism of children, assurance of salvation, the administration of the Lord's Supper, church discipline, and other important matters.[23]

---

[22]Leonard T. Van Horn, "The Reformed Pastor and His Vows," *The Banner of Truth* 412 (January 1998): 19. I owe much to Dr. Van Horn's charity, patience, and wise leadership when I changed my view of baptism in Warrior Presbytery (PCA) in 1977.
[23]Such issues include whether to preach the gospel to covenant children or not, whether they should receive communion as infants by virtue of infant baptism, what it takes to be a covenant breaker in the unbreakable New Covenant (Hebrews 8:8–12), whether the church is to be made up of professing Christians only or not. Jonathan Edwards had to deal with the deadening generational

In summary, it would have been easy for me to have passed over this controversial topic and to continue in my previous sphere of service in the Presbyterian Church (Presbyterian Church U.S.A., ARP, PCA). It still saddens my heart that my vows required me to withdraw myself voluntarily from that sphere with its wonderful fellowship and opportunities. However, our conscience and practice must be ruled by Christ alone through the guidance of His written Word alone and by no man, tradition, or dubious logical extension.

THE COVENANTAL BAPTIST POSITION BRIEFLY STATED

I have come to believe that the only proper subjects of Christian baptism are defined biblically as disciples. The following summary of the covenantal Baptist position was believed and taught by early Southern Baptist theologians such as Basil Manly Sr., William Bullein Johnson, James P. Boyce, P. H. Mell, R. B. C. Howell, and John L. Dagg, as well as by the English Baptist, Charles Haddon Spurgeon.

The following points are consistent with the *1689 London Baptist Confession*. I believe:

1. That before the foundation of the world, God the Father, Son, and Holy Spirit entered into a Counsel of Peace, or Covenant of Redemption, to save an elect people from their sins (Ephesians 1:1–14; Titus 1:9). That within the decrees of God, only two covenant heads were designated, Adam and Christ. That God the Father decreed to create the world, including Adam as the covenant head of humanity, that He decreed to permit the fall of Adam by his own free choice, and that He decreed to send His Son as the covenant Head to rescue an elect people from their sins and death. That all men whoever were to be born had Adam designated as their head in his Covenant of Works and that all of God's elect people had Christ designated

---

effects of infant baptism in the Half-Way Covenant. He dealt with infant-baptized adults who had never expressed a conversion experience nor were admitted to the Lord's Supper. Yet their children were infant baptized but not admitted to the Lord's Supper until a profession. This practice filled the churches with baptized, yet unconverted members for generations.

Introduction   xxxiii

as their Head in the Covenant of Redemption. That every person at any time in history is either in Adam or in Christ (Romans 5:12–19), but never in both or neither.

2. That the so-called Covenant of Grace with God's elect is His historical working out of that eternal Covenant of Redemption in Christ.

3. That Adam was created upright and placed in a relationship with God that would continue perpetually if he kept God's commands, variously called the Covenant of Works or Covenant of Life (Ecclesiastes 7:29; Hosea 6:7). As the covenant head of all humanity, his fall into sin brought sin, death, and condemnation upon the entire race (Romans 5:12–19).

4. That God did reveal historically the "promise of grace" in Genesis 3:15, commonly called the Covenant of Grace, successively revealing its future fulfillment in Jesus Christ's New Covenant through the historical "covenants of promise" (Ephesians 2:12). Thus, salvation by grace through faith in the coming "seed of the woman" as covenant Head was revealed and offered from the fall of man throughout the Old Testament "covenants of promise."

5. That the New Covenant of Jesus Christ is the prophesied fulfillment of what has been called the historical Covenant of Grace, revealed in the "covenants of promise" since the fall, and is the fullest and final historical manifestation of that eternal Covenant of Redemption to save God's elect (2 Timothy 1:8–10).

6. That the New Covenant is an effectual covenant of realized blessings, not like the Sinai Covenant which it abrogates (Galatians 3:19), with an effectual Mediator as its covenant Head, writing the law on every member's heart as individuals (Jeremiah 31:27–34; 32:40), giving them the true knowledge of God, and forgiving their sins (Hebrews 8:8–12; 10:15–17).

7. That Jesus Christ is the seed of the woman (Genesis 3:15), the final physical seed of Abraham to whom the promises were made (Galatians 3:16, 19), the effectual Mediator of the New Covenant (Romans 5:12ff.), and the covenant Head whose "of faith" seed become joint-heirs with Him, members of the New Covenant, children of Abraham, the

true circumcision, the true Jew, "the Israel of God," and the fulfillment of the promises to Abraham (Galatians 3:14, 6:15–16; Romans 2:28–29, 4:16).[24]

8. That all who repent of sins and believe in Jesus Christ, Jew or Gentile, shall be saved and, as evidence of their New Covenant membership and heart-circumcision, should be baptized as disciples who have professedly entered the New Covenant by repentance and faith alone.
9. That John baptized disciples alone who repented of sin (Matthew 3:6). That Jesus and His disciples "made and baptized more *disciples* than John" (John 4:1). The disciples were first made, then baptized. That all who were baptized had to decide to be baptized for themselves, not by another's decision for them (as in circumcision).
10. That there is no stated abrogation of the only subjects of Jesus' baptism, disciples alone, in the New Testament.
11. That the Great Commission commands us to "make disciples of all the nations (individuals from all nations, not the national entities), baptizing *them* (the "made" disciples) . . . teaching *them* (the baptized disciples) to do all that I commanded you" (Matthew 28:19–20). Luke corroborates this understanding: "and that repentance and remission of sins should be preached in His name to all nations, beginning at Jerusalem" (Luke 24:47).
12. That this is exactly what happened at Pentecost. Only those who "received [Peter's] words were baptized" (Acts 2:41), not the infant children of believers.
13. That, amidst the debates about whether infant-baptized children of believers are included in the New Testament church visible, it is often overlooked that the common designation for the church visible in Acts is "the disciples" (Acts 1:15; 6:1f.; 9:19, 26, 28; 11:29; 13:52; 14:20, 22,

---

[24] O. Palmer Robertson, *The Israel of God* (Phillipsburg, NJ: Presbyterian and Reformed Publishing Company, 2000), 43–45. Robertson reserves the title "the Israel of God" (Galatians 6:15–16) in the New Covenant only for Jews and Gentiles who are justified by faith and are members of the universal church. This is exactly the Baptist position when identifying the members of the New Covenant. Only the regenerate are members, not believers and their seed.

28; 15:10; 18:23, 27; 19:9, 30; 20:1, 7, 30; 21:4, 16): "And it came about that for an entire year [Saul and Barnabas] met with *the church,* and taught considerable numbers; and *the disciples* were first called Christians in Antioch" (Acts 11:26). The church is called "the disciples" because it was made up of those who had repented of their sins, publicly confessed faith in Christ, and followed Him as committed "learners." These disciples were first called Christians at Antioch, and only disciples were called Christians in Antioch. There is no room in these designations for the children of believers to be called church members or Christians simply by organic relation. The church visible is an assembly of disciples, whether adults or children.

14. That baptism is a sign of the subject's cleansing from sin, his union with Christ by his faith, his union with the body of Christ, and his commitment to a new life in Christ from thenceforth (Romans 6:4–5; 1 Corinthians 12:13; Ephesians 4:4–6).

15. And, finally, as stated in the *Westminster Confession* and the *London Baptist Confession* (1689), baptism and the Lord's Supper, including their subjects, are "sacraments instituted by Christ." That they are included as elements of worship under the regulative principle of worship positively instituted by God and "limited by His own revealed will" (*WCF* 20:1, 5). The elements of Christian worship governed by the regulative principle are all "expressly set down in Scripture," not deduced "by good and necessary inference." The only form of baptism which fits this principle is that which was "instituted" and "prescribed in the Holy Scripture"; that is, the baptism of disciples alone, not of infants by additional and supposed "good and necessary inference." Baptism is for disciples alone (John 4:1; Acts 2:38–41): *solis discipulis.*

Section I

PRELIMINARY PRINCIPLES
HERMENEUTICS, AUTHORITY, AND BAPTISM

This section is dedicated to preliminary principles that must govern the study of baptism. The hermeneutical principles necessary to settle the question are usually agreed upon by both Baptists and paedobaptists. However, all honest students of the Bible know that they are not perfect in their application of these principles; none of us are omniscient. Therefore, this section offers a presentation of infant baptism by one of its most influential proponents of the twentieth century, the late Professor John Murray of Westminster Theological Seminary.

Following this presentation is a fuller discussion of proper hermeneutical principles. What I hope to demonstrate is that the hermeneutical error that establishes infant baptism is also found in dispensationalism, modern-day Theonomy, and a normative view of worship that misunderstands and misrepresents the regulative principle. What they all have in common is a misapplication of the rule of "good and necessary consequence." By building their case on neither "good" nor "necessary" inferences from Scripture, these other errors, so similar in their hermeneutics to paedobaptism, serve as a caution to building the case for infant baptism upon the same principle of supposed good and necessary inference. A corrective to these hermeneutical errors is offered that establishes the baptism of disciples alone, the communion of disciples alone at the Lord's Supper, a rejection of dispensational and theonomic views, and a call to reform the worship of the church by the historic regulative principle.

Chapter 1

No Straw Men: John Murray's Case for Infant Baptism

What is the case *for* infant baptism? Before critiquing the doctrine, I want to summarize the case for it as honestly as I can. Christian love and integrity require that we avoid building "straw men" when representing the views of those with whom we differ. To do this, I will be using *Christian Baptism* by John Murray, widely regarded as a standard work by paedobaptist scholars.[25] To preserve continuity in Murray's argument, I will not include the position of Pierre Marcel. Instead, I refer the reader to Appendix C, which contains a critique of his classic work, *The Biblical Doctrine of Infant Baptism*.[26]

In the pages that follow, Murray is allowed to speak for himself as much as possible. My objections are largely relegated to the footnotes and will be expanded in later chapters. The concluding section will include a brief evaluation of what I perceive to be the central error of Professor Murray's position.

JOHN MURRAY'S VIEWS

Professor Murray's arguments can be outlined in seven points, which are his chapter titles: (1) the import of baptism, (2) the mode of baptism, (3) the church, (4) infant baptism, (5) objections to infant baptism, (6) whose children are to be baptized, and (7) the efficacy of baptism.

---
[25] John Murray, *Christian Baptism* (Nutley, NJ: Presbyterian and Reformed Publishing Company, 1970).
[26] Pierre Marcel, *The Biblical Doctrine of Infant Baptism,* trans. Philip Edgcumbe Hughes (London: James Clarke and Company, Ltd., 1959).

The Import of Baptism

Murray begins with the explanation that the baptism being considered is Christian baptism, that of the Great Commission alone (Matthew 28:19–20), as opposed to the baptisms of John the Baptist and Jesus.[27]

Claiming that John's baptism and ministry was only preparatory to Jesus', Murray concludes:

> We may no more identify the baptism of John with the ordinance instituted by Christ than we may identify the ministry and mission of John with the ministry and mission of Christ. Hence we cannot derive from the nature of John's baptism, the precise import of the ordinance of Christian baptism.[28]

According to Murray, the meaning of John's baptism must not be identified with later Christian baptism in any way. Although both involved water and the forgiveness of sins, the separation between John's baptism and Trinitarian baptism (Matthew 28:19–20) must remain.[29]

Second, Murray retains a distinction between the baptism of Jesus' apostles and later Christian baptism:

> [W]e do not have warrant by which to identify this baptism during Jesus' earthly ministry with the ordinance of Matthew 28:19, 20. The latter is baptism in the name of the Father, and of the Son, and of the Holy Ghost. We have no warrant to suppose that the earlier rite took this form. It is quite reasonable to believe that there was a very close relation between these two rites both in the mind of Jesus himself and in the recognition of the disciples. Indeed, so

---

[27] This position has surprised many laymen who have asked me about infant baptism. They assumed that perhaps John the Baptist's and certainly Jesus' baptism (practiced by His disciples, John 4:1ff.) are Christian baptism. It is noteworthy that many paedobaptists do not agree with Murray on this point, revealing one of their many internal debates on this issue.

[28] Murray, *Baptism*, 5. Murray points out that he disagrees with Calvin (*Institutes*, 4:15:7-8 and 4:16:27) and others on this point. Calvin believed that John's and the apostles' baptisms were the same as the Great Commission's. This is just one example of the significant disagreement among paedobaptists on almost every point and ground of infant baptism. See *Should Babies Be Baptized?* by T. E. Watson for a comparative list of contradictory positions on each point by paedobaptists.

[29] Murray, *Baptism*, 5.

close may have been the relation that baptism in the name of the triune God was the necessary development of the earlier rite. But we are compelled to recognise the distinctiveness of the rite enunciated and embodied in the great commission. It is from the terms of this institution and from subsequent references in the New Testament that we are to derive the precise import of this ordinance.[30]

Again, by maintaining the distinction between Jesus' baptism and later Christian baptism, Murray has removed the data of the Gospels from consideration concerning the meaning and subjects of Great Commission baptism. We will examine this position in detail in Chapter 9.

Third, even though purification is the central meaning behind John's and Jesus' baptism, Murray denies that purification is the central import of Christian baptism. Rather, "baptism signifies union with Christ in his death, burial, and resurrection . . . of this union baptism is the sign and seal."[31] Yet later, Murray also states that "baptism is the circumcision of the New Testament" (Colossians 2:11, 12), thus symbolizing purification from defilement. His summarizing statement is: "baptism signifies and seals union with Christ and cleansing from the pollution and guilt of sin."[32] Murray appears to be inconsistent with his own statements on this issue.

---

[30]*Ibid.* This approach is difficult to maintain. Further, Murray's own hermeneutical principle is that the inclusion of infants in the Abrahamic Covenant by circumcision has not been explicitly revoked or repealed, thus proving the inferred continuance of the covenant privilege of baptism to infants, 52–53, but he also argues that John's and Jesus' baptisms have no connection to Christian baptism because there is no positive "warrant" to connect them. This is inconsistent. According to Murray's own hermeneutic of good and necessary inference, the connection should continue because there is no explicit revocation or repeal of their baptisms prior to or after the institution of the Great Commission. Further, Murray's position contradicts the Great Commission itself, which teaches the apostles to teach the church to do all that Jesus commanded; this includes His institution of the baptism of disciples alone.

[31]*Ibid.*, 6. Suffice it to say now that baptism is never called a "seal" of the New Covenant; rather, regeneration by the Holy Spirit is so called (Ephesians 1:13; 2 Corinthians 1:22).

[32]*Ibid.*, 9. Baptists believe that the New Testament antitype to Old Testament circumcision is heart circumcision, not baptism directly (Colossians 2:11–12; Philippians 3:3; Romans 2:28–29; Galatians 6:15–16). In the Old Testament, circumcision is prospective of the need of regeneration; in the New Testament, baptism is retrospective of regeneration received.

The Mode of Baptism

Murray's argument concerning the mode of baptism concludes that *baptizo* does not mean to immerse. Rather, appealing to word studies in the Septuagint, it means *to pour* or *to sprinkle*.[33] As noted in the Preface, this view puts Murray at odds with Calvin who understands *baptizo* to mean immerse.

The Church

Murray next discusses the relationship between baptism and the church. He opens this discussion with the statement that "baptism is the sign and seal of membership in the church."[34] Then he asks: What is the church?

The Church as Invisible

First, he considers "the church as invisible." That is, there is an aspect of invisibility to the church:

> ... it is comprised of those who are sanctified and cleansed by the washing of water by the Word, the company of the regenerate, the communion of saints, the congregation of the faithful, those called effectually into the fellowship of Christ.[35]

Because regeneration and faith are both spiritual and invisible, "no man or organisation of men is able infallibly to determine who are regenerate and who are not, who are true believers and who are not."[36]

Murray makes the point that only God can determine which persons are true and false believers (John 8:31; 15:1–8). Therefore, it must be admitted that not everyone in the church visible is necessarily regenerate. This aspect of invisibility cannot be

---

[33]*Ibid.*, 9–33; and Duane Spencer, *Holy Baptism: Word Keys Which Unlock the Covenant* (Tyler, TX: Geneva Ministries, 1984). Murray's explanation of certain texts such as Mark 1:9 does not do justice to the grammar. Though a detailed study of the mode of baptism is beyond the narrow scope of this work, Appendix B outlines a brief refutation of John Murray's views, along with those of another paedobaptist, Duane Spencer.
[34]Murray, *Baptism*, 34.
[35]*Ibid.*
[36]*Ibid.*

finally determined by fallible men, but "the Lord knows them that are His."[37]

The Church as Visible

Second, although the church has an invisible aspect, it is not an invisible entity:

> Union with Christ and the faith through which that union is effected, though in themselves invisible and spiritual facts, are nevertheless realities which find expression in what is observable. Faith always receives registration in word and action.[38]

As a result, a visible organization is implicit in the very nature of what constitutes a church, whether in a house, city, province, the whole world, or of all history.

Because human agency is at work in a church, "there is government and discipline in Christ's church and such are administered by men, in accordance with Christ's appointment."[39] How then shall these fallible men include or exclude members in the church? Murray says:

> What we find in the New Testament is that the constituting bond of communion was common faith in Christ and that the condition of admission to the fellowship was this same common faith (cf. Acts 2:38–42; 8:13, 35–38; 10:34–38; 16:14, 15, 31–33). This faith, however, did not have any automatic way of evidencing itself and, consequently, could become effective in gaining admission to the fellowship of the saints only by confession or profession.[40]

Because a profession or confession of faith could be made by those who do not have true faith, we are faced with the problem

---

[37]*Ibid.*, 35–36. Baptists agree with Murray on this point, but he uses it to justify infants in the church and to criticize the Baptist goal of a regenerate membership. Baptists baptize upon profession of faith, not infallibly determined regeneration (*London Baptist Confession,* 19:2). Paul often gave the benefit of the doubt as to who were true Christians by profession and freely designated them so till proven otherwise (Philippians 1:5–7).
[38]*Ibid.,* 37.
[39]*Ibid.,* 38.
[40]*Ibid.* This is exactly the Baptist position. Murray correctly references Acts 2:38–42 for this position yet, inconsistently, uses it as a proof for infant baptism in other contexts.

that the visible church may include individuals who do not really belong to the invisible body of Christ.

According to Murray, there are two dangers to avoid based on this problem of unregenerate church members. The first danger is to accept only an intellectual and historical faith as required for church membership. This can be avoided if church leaders make it plain to confessors that "only the regenerate can truly make the profession required."[41] The second danger is to accommodate the definition of the church to include as members the obviously unregenerate. This can be avoided by putting those who prove to be profane and not disciples outside the church.[42]

Baptism then is the sign and seal of membership in the church, based upon confessed faith in Jesus. It is an essential mark of discipleship. The person who refuses baptism is not to be considered a member of Christ's body, the church.[43]

The Church Generically One

The form of the church is different under the Old Testament and the New Testament. The fullness of the form in the New, however, must not remove the generic unity between the church in both dispensations,[44] nor must it be forgotten that the New Testament form is founded upon the Abrahamic Covenant (Galatians 3:9, 14, 17; Romans 11:16–21; Ephesians 2:12–20):

> New Testament believers of all nations are Abraham's seed and heirs according to promise. . . . In terms of the covenant union and communion the church is but the covenant people of God in all ages and among all nations.[45]

---

[41]*Ibid.,* 40–41.

[42]*Ibid.,* 43–44; and R. C. Trench, *Notes on the Parables of Our Lord* (Grand Rapids, MI: Baker Book House, 1971), 35. By misinterpreting the parable of the wheat and the tares (Matthew 13:24–30), some paedobaptists have justified the inclusion of unregenerate infants in the church. However, the field is not the church, as some claim, it is the world (cf. Matthew 13:38). We are not knowingly to allow the unregenerate into the church.

[43]Murray, *Baptism,* 45.

[44]*Ibid.,* 46. Murray argues for "generic unity" between the "church in the wilderness" and the New Testament church as an argument for infant baptism's parallel to circumcision. However, he overlooks that the church in the wilderness did not circumcise their infants.

[45]*Ibid.,* 47. Baptists agree with Murray's statement that only New Testament believers are Abraham's seed. However, this very fact is the reason we reject

In summary, Murray argues for a New Testament church built upon a confession of Jesus Christ as evidence of regeneration. This is exactly the Baptist position. He recognizes that false professors will enter in, but he argues that we cannot accommodate that fact by diminishing the definition of the church as God's people. The New Testament church is tied to the Old Testament church by the covenant with Abraham, by which the promises come. Thus, he concludes, the relationship between Abrahamic circumcision and infant baptism is preconditioned by "generic unity."

Infant Baptism

Murray introduces this chapter by claiming that the import of baptism must be the same for infants as for adults: "Baptism is the sign and seal of membership in Christ's body, the church." He then summarizes:

> The basic premise of the argument for infant baptism is that the New Testament economy is the unfolding and fulfillment of the covenant made with Abraham and that the necessary implication is the unity and continuity of the church.[46]

First, he argues for the inclusion of infants in the Abrahamic Covenant as evidenced by the sign of circumcision. This circumcision is more than external privilege. It is the sign and seal of the covenant in its "deepest and richest significance." It is the removal of the defilement of infants with which they enter this world.[47] And it is the seal of the righteousness of faith. Therefore,

---

infant baptism as the fulfillment of circumcision. Only Abraham's faith-seed in Christ should receive the sign of baptism (Galatians 3:16, 19).

[46]*Ibid.*, 48. In this attempt to make the meaning of baptism the same for infants and adults, Murray overlooks the *Westminster Confession's* statement that baptism "is unto *the party baptized* into the visible church . . . also to be unto *him* a sign and seal of the covenant of grace, of *his* ingrafting into Christ, of regeneration, of remission of sins, and of *his* giving up unto God through Jesus Christ to walk in newness of life. . . . "[*WCF* 28:1; emphasis mine]. One wonders how an infant can benefit from this meaning of baptism in the same way as an adult who consciously understands.

[47]One has to wonder what Murray means by this. Does this mean that the baptized infant is no longer defiled by original sin, is no longer under the Covenant of Works, and is not condemned, as Marcel says (Marcel, *Infant Baptism*, 50)? And if he is not under the Covenant of Works, can he then be under the

"Circumcision, signifying what in principle is identical with that signified by baptism, was administered to infants who were born within the covenant relation and privilege."[48]

Second, Murray asserts that this privilege continues under the New Testament economy as the fulfillment of the Abrahamic Covenant. Because the denial of this privilege would be a complete reversal of the Old Testament economy, there would have to be an explicit revocation of the practice in order to refuse baptism to the infants of believers. The absence of such an explicit revocation, together with certain positive evidence in favor of its continuance, as well as the expected expansion of New Covenant blessings, require that we accept its continuance.[49] This is Murray's primary argument.

Third, the significance of infant baptism requires its practice. Like circumcision, it represents more than admission to external covenant privilege. Even though false professors will manifest themselves in infant baptism (as with professor's baptism), this does not diminish its internal meaning. However, the ground of infant baptism is simply God's call to give to the infant seed of believers the sign and seal of the Covenant of Grace. Presumptive election or regeneration is not the ground.[50] Instead, it is the simple fact of divine institution.[51]

Fourth, corroboratory evidence provides positive support for infant baptism. Although Murray candidly admits that there is

Covenant of Grace and later return to the Covenant of Works if nonelect? And if he is still under that Covenant of Works, can he also be under the Covenant of Grace at the same time? Such language is very confusing and must ultimately mislead the recipient as to his spiritual condition. Marcel seems to say the same thing, that baptized infants are a third category of people, no longer condemned under the Covenant of Works yet not necessarily saved under the Covenant of Grace (see Marcel, *Infant Baptism,* 109–110, 147, 190).
[48]Murray, *Baptism,* 50–51.
[49]*Ibid.,* 53. The positive institution of disciple's baptism alone and the revocation of circumcision (Acts 15; Galatians 6:15–16) are not enough for Murray to reject giving infant baptism to the physical seed of covenant members. Even though infant baptism is never mentioned in Scripture, in order to reject it, Murray seems to take the absurd position of requiring an explicit statement in Scripture rejecting it. This is a violation of the regulative principle of worship.
[50]*Ibid.,* 56–57. Although Murray denies baptismal regeneration and presumptive regeneration, many paedobaptists (i.e., the Church of England) do hold this view.
[51]*Ibid.,* 61.

"no express statute authorising the baptism of infants," he argues that five points of corroboration support the practice.

1. He argues that Jesus' attitude toward the children (Matthew 18:1–6; 19:13–14; Luke 18:15–17) supports the practice of infant baptism. He concludes that Jesus' statement, "of such is the kingdom of heaven," means that the membership of little children in the kingdom of God cannot be restricted to children who are of sufficient age to be capable of intelligent understanding and faith. Because this is possible, it is good and necessary inference to conclude that they cannot be denied the covenant sign. However, Murray adds that this applies only to those children within the covenant relations.[52]
2. Murray next contends that the New Testament's instructions to children addresses them as saints (Ephesians 6:1, 4; Colossians 3:20–21). Because they were addressed in the body of believers, they were considered as saints and were entitled to the covenant sign.[53]
3. He then asserts that the teaching of 1 Corinthians 7:14 places the children of believers into a "holy" status by virtue of their parental relations. This connection and privilege is "consonant" with the basis for infant baptism.[54]
4. He next argues that the household baptisms hold presumptive evidence of infant baptism (Acts 10:47–48; 11:14; 16:15, 33–34; 1 Corinthians 1:16). Murray states that "we cannot prove conclusively that there were infants in these households." However, he adds, the fact that there are fewer than twelve instances of baptism

---

[52]*Ibid.*, 65–66. The question remains: Then why did Jesus not baptize these children? The answer cannot be that circumcision was still in force, because He instituted baptism while circumcision was in force, nor can it be because Matthew 18 occurred before Pentecost, because only disciples were baptized at Pentecost and after (Acts 2:41). If Jesus instituted baptism, then why did He not apply the sign to the children of disciples according to the Abrahamic requirement?

[53]*Ibid.*, 66–67. The appeal is to the Fifth Commandment, to which all children are responsible. All are responsible to obey all of God's commands whether they repent or not, or whether they are "saints" or not (Romans 2:1–16; Acts 17:30).

[54]*Ibid.*, 67–68. This position, rejected by some paedobaptists, will be discussed at length in Chapter 7.

(not counting John's and Jesus'), of which three were households, would indicate that household baptisms were very common:

> If so, it would be practically impossible to believe that in none of these households were there any infants. It would be unreasonable to believe so. The infants in the households belonged to the households and would be baptised. Presumption is, therefore, of the strongest kind, even though we do not have an overt and proven instance of infant baptism.[55]

5. Murray also contends that children were addressed at Pentecost in coordination with their parents (Acts 2:38–39). When Peter stated that "the promise is to you and to your children," he was doing more than just promising the same blessing upon repentance and baptism to children as well as to parents. Rather, "the promise is to the children as well as to the parents and that, in respect of this property, the children are included with their parents."[56]

Murray adds that, when one bears in mind the Abrahamic Covenant, one can understand Peter to recognize that "there was no suspension or abrogation of that divine administration whereby children are embraced with their parents in God's covenant promise." It is on this basis that the baptism of infants is established.[57]

Objections to Infant Baptism

Murray then lists seven objections to infant baptism and gives his best attempt at refuting each one.

---

[55]*Ibid.*, 68–69. This is inconsistent with Murray's later argument that we do not have enough instances of New Testament baptism to let the overwhelming examples of "professors only" establish the norm (73). Here he relies upon the much fewer instances of household baptisms to establish the practice of infant baptism on the basis of silence and inference.

[56]*Ibid.*, 70. Acts 2:41 contradicts Murray's claim. Only those who received Peter's word were baptized—of any age.

[57]*Ibid.*, 71. Murray's position refuses to depend upon the divine institution of a sacrament under a new covenant to abrogate previous sacramental arrangements. This places a demand upon God and, at the same time, violates the regulative principle.

1. The first objection is that there is no express command or clear case of infant baptism in the New Testament. Murray agrees that this is true but argues that express command and clear example are not the only kind of evidence sufficient to establish a doctrine:

   > What by good and necessary inference can be deduced from Scripture is of authority in the church of God as well as what is expressly set down in Scripture. *The evidence for infant baptism falls into the category of good and necessary inference, and it is therefore quite indefensible to demand that the evidence required must be in the category of express command or explicit instance.* In other words, the assumption upon which this objection rests is a false assumption and one which cannot be adopted as the norm in determining what Christian doctrine or Christian institution is [emphasis mine].58

   Further, Murray argues that there are only a few instances of Christian baptism in the New Testament, which in his view diminishes the argument that infant baptism was not practiced. He declares it "unreasonable to suppose that there were no infants" in the household baptisms or to suppose that they were refused baptism.59

2. The second objection is that the instances of baptism recorded in the New Testament "presuppose a credible and intelligent profession of faith" which infants cannot fulfill. His main argument against this position is that it is uncertain a profession of faith was required in cases of household baptisms.60

   According to Murray, even if the demand of repentance and faith were practiced, it would only be in reference to the adults present. Therefore, such a demand would not necessarily make infants ineligible because they may

---

58*Ibid.*, 72. Amazingly, what Murray characterizes as a "false assumption" actually describes the regulative principle of instituted worship. The regulative principle is not "indefensible."
59*Ibid.*, 73. Murray's argument from numerical instances is weak. The fact is that there are many thousands of baptisms of disciples alone (Acts 2:41) while the few instances of household baptism mention no infant baptism. To adopt a practice from silence is not the same as rejecting a practice never mentioned. The former is the normative principle, the latter is the regulative.
60*Ibid.*

experience salvation without a psychological capability of repentance and faith.

3. The third objection addressed by Murray involves the difficulty of being able to discern if infants are regenerate. Murray believes this objection does not stand because even adult baptism is not based upon sure regeneration but only upon a credible profession of faith. The basis of infant baptism is divine institution, not apparent regeneration.[61]

4. The fourth objection is that infants cannot understand the meaning of baptism. Murray says this is not valid because God's blessings and means of grace are not contingent upon the understanding of the recipient. The little children did not understand Christ's blessing of them, yet who would say that it was of no avail? To Murray, then, this objection misconstrues the nature of God's grace and means.[62]

5. The fifth purported objection against infant baptism addressed by Murray involves the evidence of failed lives of those baptized as infants. Murray responds that this is no argument against the institution, for the same objection could be made against adult baptism.[63]

6. The sixth asserted objection is that circumcision and baptism are simply different. For starters, circumcision was given only to males whereas baptism is given to male and female. Murray says this objection does not stand because the meaning is essentially the same, as Colossians 2:11–12 demonstrates. Further, the expansion of blessings under the new economy to include females in the covenant sign does not show disparity but extension of privilege.[64]

7. Seventh, "it is objected that paedobaptists are strangely inconsistent in dispensing baptism to infants and yet

---

[61]*Ibid.*, 74. The basis for infant baptism is not divine institution, but human inference.
[62]*Ibid.*, 74–75.
[63]*Ibid.*, 75.
[64]*Ibid.*, 76. How do we know that baptism is extended to females except from commands and examples in the New Testament? Murray uses such evidence to argue for extended privilege to infants yet rejects commands and examples for disciples alone as sufficient evidence to reject infant baptism.

refusing to admit them to the Lord's table."⁶⁵ The accusation is that circumcised infants received the Old Testament Passover but, inconsistently, infants are not allowed to take the Lord's Supper after infant baptism.

Murray responds that to assume that circumcised infants took the Passover does not follow. There is no evidence they did and it is "unreasonable" to assume so with such an unsuitable diet for infants. The children who asked questions of the supper were not infants and paedobaptists do not refuse "children of sufficient age and understanding to know the meaning of the Lord's supper."⁶⁶

Murray then states, if it were true that paedobaptists were inconsistent at this point, there is another way of resolving the issue besides prohibiting infant baptism:

> It could be resolved by going in the other direction, namely, that of admitting infants to the Lord's supper. And when all factors entering into this dispute are taken into account, particularly the principle involved in infant baptism, then far less would be at stake in admitting infants to the Lord's supper than would be at stake in abandoning infant baptism.⁶⁷

Murray does not adopt paedocommunion because he claims to identify sufficient differences between baptism and the Lord's Supper to justify the inclusion of infants in one and not the other. To him, baptism represents salvation and union with Christ whereas the Lord's Supper signifies that which is consequent to salvation. That is, the Lord's Supper requires intelligent understanding because it is a remembrance, communion, and discerning of the body. Thus, in his view, it is appropriate to give baptism to infants, but not the Lord's Supper.⁶⁸

---

⁶⁵*Ibid.*, 76.
⁶⁶*Ibid.*, 77.
⁶⁷*Ibid.* Such reasoning is dangerously pragmatic when forming the practice of an instituted sacrament of Jesus Christ.
⁶⁸*Ibid*, 77–78. Baptism also requires the intelligent remembrance and repentance of sin, the remembrance of Christ crucified and risen, and the promise to walk in newness of life. Murray's argument is very weak on this point.

Other differences between the two sacraments include the frequency of observance (once versus many) and the difference in the elements (water versus bread and wine). These two differences show suitability toward infants in baptism but not in the Lord's Supper. Thus, baptism is the rite of initiation into the body of Christ, suitable to infants as was circumcision, whereas the Lord's Supper represents abiding responsibility, something not suitable to infants. Murray concludes that this objection does not stand.[69]

Whose Children are to be Baptized?

According to Murray, only those who are united to Christ and members of His body have a right to present their children for baptism. This is because the basis of infant baptism is the covenant of God with His people. Those who were baptized as adults and have professed faith in Christ can present their children. However, those who were baptized as infants must make a public profession of faith before they can present their children.

If the parents refuse to confess Christ and be eligible for the Lord's Supper by that same confession, then discipline may be exercised. This may include the refusal to baptize their children.[70]

The Efficacy of Baptism

The efficacy of baptism is explained by Murray as having the same meaning for infants and adults.[71] According to Murray,

---

[69]*Ibid.*, 78–79. There is just as much abiding responsibility following baptism as the Lord's Supper.

[70]*Ibid.*, 80–85. One wonders how many parents may have given a false profession to get their infants baptized. Some parents will believe or do almost anything for their children's benefit.

[71]*Ibid.*, 88–89. In his explanation, Murray differs with William Cunningham, who maintains that the confessional meaning and efficacy of baptism apply only to confessing "adults" and cannot apply to infants. See William Cunningham, *The Reformers and the Theology of the Reformation* (Edinburgh: The Banner of Truth Trust, 1967), 244, 247, 249, 262–265, 271, 280. Cunningham teaches that the efficacy of adult baptism urges adults to the implications of baptism while that of infant baptism is a prospective seal which they may have afterwards. Baptists ask: "What efficacy? Where is this even mentioned of baptism in the Scriptures?"

baptism is not the same as the grace which it signifies and seals; neither does it confer nor convey grace. Rather, baptism advertises the great truth of God's grace and guarantees the reality and security of that covenant grace.[72] Therefore, it carries the same efficacy for adults and infants. It is "the divine testimony to their union with Christ and the divine certification and authentication of this great truth."[73]

When asked what comfort may be derived from baptism, Murray answers that "we may never divorce the faith of God's covenant grace from the discharge of those obligations which adhere in the covenant relation."[74] Confidence in covenant grace can never be derived from the sacrament of baptism apart from faith. That would be presumption:

> Hence the sign and seal of baptism can be no pledge or guarantee to us of that which baptism signifies except as we are mindful of God's covenant, embrace its promises, discharge its obligations, and lay hold in faith upon the covenant faithfulness of God.[75]

What then is the comfort that can be derived from infant baptism? Murray says it is that God saves not in an individualistic, atomistic way, but that "God deals savingly with men in their organic corporate relationships" (Exodus 20:6; Psalm 103:17, 18). This does not mean that parents can have assurance or a guarantee "that the children concerned are without condition the partakers of the grace signified and sealed by baptism." The degree of assurance of such grace is in proportion to the extent that the parents are faithful to God's requirements in raising children.[76]

---

[72] Murray, *Baptism,* 86–87.
[73] *Ibid.,* 90.
[74] *Ibid.*
[75] *Ibid.,* 91.
[76] *Ibid.,* 92. See also Douglas Wilson, *Standing on the Promises* (Moscow, Idaho: Canon Press, 1997), 21–32. Such language is confusing at best and presumptuous at worst. It appears to promise parents their children's salvation if they are faithful *enough.* Douglas Wilson offers an extreme view that places such a conditionalism upon parental faithfulness that the sovereignty of God in the covenant family of Isaac loses its lesson (Romans 9). Wilson's extreme view will be examined in Chapter 11.

Therefore, it is in the family and the church that God primarily fulfills His saving purposes:

> The efficacy of infant baptism principally consists in this, that it is to us the certification or seal that God works in accordance with this covenant provision and fulfills His covenant promises.[77]

A PRELIMINARY EVALUATION OF MURRAY'S "GOOD AND NECESSARY INFERENCE" ARGUMENT

As stated earlier in this chapter and in the Preface, Murray's central argument for infant baptism is based upon his understanding of good and necessary inference from the *Westminster Confession* (*WCF* 1:6):

> The whole counsel of God, concerning all things necessary for his own glory, man's salvation, faith, and life, is either *expressly set down in Scripture,* or by *good and necessary consequence may be deduced from Scripture:* unto which nothing at any time is to be added, whether by new revelations of the Spirit, or traditions of men [emphasis mine].

Murray says of this paragraph:

> One of the most persuasive objections and one which closes the argument for a great many people is that there is *no express command* to baptise infants and *no record* in the New Testament of a clear case of infant baptism.... The evidence for infant baptism falls into the category of *good and necessary inference,* and it is therefore quite indefensible to demand that the evidence required must be in the category of express command or explicit instance [emphasis mine].[78]

Murray's dependence upon good and necessary inference as sufficient to institute infant baptism together with his declaration that it is indefensible to demand an express command or explicit instance to justify the practice, are errors in his hermeneutics.

---

[77]Murray, *Baptism,* 92–93. According to Murray, this efficacy is not a promise of salvation to any individual who is baptized. It is simply a promise that God saves through covenant relations and will save through His covenant.
[78]*Ibid.,* 72.

Murray fails to recognize that New Testament sacraments must be expressly commanded and explicitly instituted by Christ according to the regulative principle of worship.

The *Westminster Confession of Faith* 1:6 teaches that things may be "deduced from Scripture" by "good and necessary consequence" when trying to determine "the whole counsel of God." However, that which is "expressly set down in Scripture" is specifically distinguished by the Westminster divines from good and necessary consequence. They are not the same things. The former is instituted revelation; the latter is human deduction from instituted revelation.

To be sure, we all use human deductive reasoning to determine that which is expressly set down in Scripture. For instance, "I do not allow a woman to teach or to rule over a man" is clear enough through consistent logic to deduce that a woman cannot serve in the church as an elder. Or, the requirement that an elder must be a "one-woman man" clearly implies that he cannot be a polygamist. However, these examples of explicit application from a text are a far cry from the use of human deductive reasoning to infer a doctrinal principle from Scripture when that principle is not plainly stated in the text. For example, drawing the conclusion that the phrase "one-woman man" prohibits a former widower or a man formerly divorced for biblical grounds from serving as an elder is an erroneous inference beyond the text.

No, the Westminster divines distinguished the obvious practice of deduction used to explain that which is expressly set down in Scripture from that kind of deduction which draws an inference beyond that which is expressly set down by words. It then calls that inferential reasoning a good and necessary consequence of what Scripture plainly and directly teaches. Some today try to make the human deduction of good and necessary consequence always attain the same level of certainty as the human deductive reasoning that identifies those things expressly set down in Scripture. Again, there is a difference between the two.

For the sake of clarity, the reader should understand that it is a valid hermeneutical method to draw inferences from Scripture. Drawing good and necessary inferences is required to draw up confessions, to do systematic theology, and to engage in pastoral applications to people. Yet no one would claim that all deductions or inferences are equally clear, good, necessary, and authoritative. There is such a thing as "poor and unnecessary inference." In fact, using poor and unnecessary inferences is a primary strategy of the cults; i.e., the baptism for the dead. How does one distinguish between the two? One must distinguish between inferences that are possibly *plausible* and those that are consequentially *necessary*. The Scriptural basis for any inference must be very good and clearly necessary, conforming to standard rules of hermeneutics to be authoritative. Even if the case for paedobaptism were potentially plausible, it still is unwise to form a doctrine of an instituted sacrament by inference alone when never mentioned or expressly set down in Scripture. Inference, even if one concludes it good and necessary, cannot be used to invent sacraments or subjects of sacraments, as do the Roman Catholics.

Further, there is a warning in the *Westminster Confession* against adding to Scripture by the traditions of men, even if those traditions are asserted to be deduced from Scripture, as did the Pharisees in their erroneous deductions (*see* Matthew 15:1–10). They often followed the "string-of-pearls" method of stringing Scriptures together out of context to invent new laws by inference.

To summarize, there is a limit to the practice of good and necessary consequence in its application. The limitation is this: *Inference cannot contradict other instituted Scripture or sound hermeneutical principles that govern one's deductions from Scripture.* For sacraments in particular, under the regulative principle of worship, good and necessary consequence cannot be used to institute any sacrament or the subjects of sacraments.

It is interesting as a historical matter that the early Particular Baptists, who adopted the *Westminster Confession* as their own, with modifications, left out "by good and necessary consequence" from the identical paragraph in the *London Baptist Confession,* substituting the phrase: "or necessarily contained in Scripture" (*LCF* 1:6). Likely they did this in order to distinguish true good and necessary consequence, which should always be limited by the containment of Scripture, from the abuse of good and necessary consequence as logical inference alone, which is used by paedobaptists to establish infant baptism by instituting the subjects of a sacrament never contained in Scripture. This is a defective use of inference (or good and necessary consequence). It goes beyond the containment of Scripture and sound hermeneutical principles, and violates the regulative principle of instituted sacraments.

An example of this error is Andrew Sandlin's extreme, unqualified statement that good and necessary consequence, which can be based upon erroneous inferences, always *is as binding as Scripture* itself. The binding power of good and necessary consequence totally depends upon the hermeneutical validity of the inferences that could be neither "good" nor "necessary." He says:

> The most frequent and obvious objection to the Reformed view of infant baptism is that no obvious, explicit reference to it is found in the Scriptures. . . . But those who hold the Reformed faith do not agree that infant baptism should be rejected on the grounds that *it is not taught obviously and explicitly in the Holy Scriptures,* for they do not hold that a doctrine or practice need be expressed in obvious, explicit terms to be valid. *Supporting as they do the assertion of the* Westminster Confession *that those teachings which "by good and necessary consequence" can be deduced from Scripture are as binding as those taught plainly and explicitly (chapter 1, section 6)*, they deduce from the relation between circumcision and baptism, from the covenantal character of the gospel and the Christian faith, and from statements regarding household salvation and baptism, the practice of paedobaptism [emphasis mine].[79]

In this statement, Sandlin unqualifiedly asserts something that the *WCF* 1:6 does not say, that things deduced from Scripture "are as binding as those taught plainly and explicitly." He does not distinguish the actual necessary consequences that are contained in the fabric of Scripture from his own possibly erroneous conclusions as to what those are. What he concludes to be good and necessary may possibly be nothing more than erroneous deductions. If erroneous deductions are regarded as binding as Scripture, they then become erroneous additions to revelation. Thus, such an absolute, unqualified statement by Sandlin takes a decisive step toward the Roman Catholic position that theological inference and church tradition are as authoritative as Scripture itself, even regarding the institution of a sacrament never mentioned in Scripture! This position undermines *sola Scriptura.* The *WCF* warns against adding invented traditions of men as authoritative. There are limits to good and necessary consequence as a basis for

---

[79]Andrew Sandlin, "A Support for Reformed Paedobaptism (with a Reformed Baptist Reply by Fred Pugh)" Tms [photocopy], position paper (Painesville, OH: The Church of the WORD, 1996), 8.

confessional doctrine. Rather, confessional doctrine should be necessarily contained in Holy Scripture.

Good and necessary consequence can be valid only when deduced from written revelation and not contrary to other written revelation; in other words, the analogy of faith. Neither can it be used to violate standard hermeneutical principles or the regulative principle of worship, because the correct interpretation of Scripture never contradicts itself. Scripture must interpret Scripture by sound hermeneutical principles. Even if one could infer infant baptism as a plausible consequence of certain Scriptural teachings, as pearls strung on a string, it would still contradict all that the Scripture positively institutes, instructs, and provides as examples concerning the subjects of baptism which is expressly set down in Scripture. Good and necessary inference is not a valid hermeneutic when defining the subjects of a sacrament supposedly instituted by Christ (*WCF* 21:5).

What principles of biblical interpretation, then, should we employ to determine whether or not infants should be baptized? What hermeneutical principles are valid to employ for something so important as one of the sacraments? And what principles provide such a degree of certainty that *not* to follow them is ignorance at best or sin at worst? I will explore these issues in the next chapter, which discusses the issue of hermeneutics in more detail to determine which are the appropriate principles to govern our doctrine of baptism. For now, the bottom line is that Murray's dependence upon "good and necessary inference" to regulate a sacrament "instituted by Christ" is, in fact, indefensible according to Scripture and the *Westminster Confession* itself.

Chapter 2

Biblical Principles of Interpretation and Infant Baptism

When I reexamined infant baptism in 1977, I discovered a thorny hermeneutical problem that troubled my paedobaptist flesh. As I attempted to clarify the biblical principles of interpretation needed to settle my uncertainties about the subject, and, accordingly, to remain a Presbyterian pastor, it soon became apparent that some very basic evangelical and Reformed principles of interpretation, or hermeneutics, drove me further away from infant baptism rather than closer toward it.

The thorny problem that bothered me was that all children of the household, especially those circumcised, seemed to partake of the Passover as well (Exodus 12:24, 43–51). Because there was no command prohibiting their participation, then it seemed good and necessary to infer that they did in fact participate, thus opening the way for paedocommunion. However, neither I nor many other Presbyterian pastors practiced paedocommunion, even though it was being discussed in my denomination at the time (1972 to 1977). This inconsistency forced me to reexamine the hermeneutical principles underlying both paedobaptism and paedocommunion.

This chapter outlines my search for consistent biblical principles of interpretation to apply to Christian baptism under four headings: (1) my original hermeneutical questions, (2) a statement of basic evangelical and Reformed hermeneutics, (3) the inconsistent hermeneutics of infant baptism stated and refuted, and (4) proper biblical hermeneutics for Christian baptism.

MY ORIGINAL HERMENEUTICAL QUESTIONS

My original questions concerning the biblical basis for infant baptism revealed several hermeneutical holes in the answers of paedobaptists, which caused me to search out a more consistent foundation for infant baptism. As we will see, I did not find any—much to my disappointment then as a happy Presbyterian minister.

My change of view began as I read Exodus 12 as part of my devotions. Surely I had read it many times before, but this time I felt unrest in my soul. I read about the institution of the Passover, "And you shall observe this event as an ordinance for *you and your children* forever" (Exodus 12:24). This was the same phrase used by Peter in Acts 2:38–39 to refer to baptism: "For the promise is *for you and your children. . . .*" Questions flooded my mind! Did children in the household participate in the Passover as covenant children? If they did, at what age did they begin? And, further, if they participated at any age as covenant children, what does this have to say about our infant-baptized children's participation in the Lord's Supper, which has its roots in the Passover?

As I meditated on the children's participation, I wondered if this might not be simply a command to continue the ordinance from parent to child in unbroken generations. "And you shall observe this event as an ordinance for you and your children *forever*" (Exodus 12:24). Certainly this thought is included. However, after much study, I decided that the text suggests both the participation of the household children in the feast and the giving of a command to continue the ordinance forever.

That the word *forever* in the text implies the perpetuity of the ordinance is obvious, but in the covenant household context, the *vav* conjunction (and) seems to include the children of the household, as well as the adults (including women), as participants in the Passover. The inclusion of children in the meal is clear because there were no other leavened breads and meats allowed to be present in the household (12:19, 29, 28). Except for infants still on the breast, there literally was nothing else for the children to eat but the Passover meal!

John Murray proposes that the children's question about the meal (12:26) indicates their lack of participation in it up to that point. He also assumes that their questioning indicates an ability to understand the answer, thus excluding infants but admitting small children.[80] However, there is nothing in the text to

---

[80]Murray, *Baptism,* 77. Such a position would seem to equate the children's question as equivalent to the self-examination requirement before partaking of the Lord's Supper. This is a bit of a stretch for me. Questions do not equal a good profession.

prohibit the children's participation and there are several positive indications that they did so. Applying the good and necessary inference that establishes paedobaptism, one must also examine the possibility that infant-baptized children of all ages be admitted to the Lord's Supper (paedocommunion).

In thinking about these questions, I found it disturbing that Louis Berkhof and John Murray understood this issue differently. I had uncovered a hermeneutical disagreement among paedobaptists that I had not understood before. Berkhof, for example, states:

> Children, though they were allowed to eat the Passover in the days of the Old Testament, cannot be permitted to partake of the Table of the Lord, since they cannot meet the requirements for worthy participation.[81]

While admitting that the Old Testament children participated in the Passover, Berkhof excludes them from the Lord's Supper because the New Testament revelation positively institutes self-examination and the discerning of the body (1 Corinthians 11:28).

Here Berkhof shows the inconsistency of his hermeneutic. Infants must not take communion even though they could participate in the equivalent in the Old Testament, he says, because the New Testament revelation positively prescribes self-examination and conscious faith. Yet, inconsistently, Berkhof holds to infant baptism, noting that the positive commands and examples in the New Testament to repent and believe before baptism do not override the Old Testament Abrahamic command to apply the covenant sign to infants. Berkhof's position was my position and that of most of my Presbyterian pastor friends. It is still the majority position of the PCA.[82] Inconsistently, he is trying to have it both ways.

Murray, on the other hand, discounts the interpretation that infants and small children participated in the Passover. He asserts

---

[81]Louis Berkhof, *Systematic Theology* (Grand Rapids, MI: William B. Eerdmans Publishing Co., 1941), 656.
[82]*See* "Report of the Ad-interim Committee to Study the Question of Paedocommunion Majority Report" (General Assembly of the Presbyterian Church in America, 1986). The majority report rejected paedocommunion. The minority report, penned by Robert S. Rayburn, affirmed it.

two grounds for this conclusion: (1) there is no mention of infants in the text, and (2) the diet was not suitable for infants.

The problem with Murray's first objection is that the same reasoning may be consistently applied to the silence concerning infants in New Testament household baptisms. If, as he says, there is no mention of infants in the Old Testament household taking the Passover, then he cannot assume that there were infants in the New Testament household and that they were baptized. Again, he cannot have it both ways. In addition, his contention that participating children were of an age where they were able to understand the meaning of the Passover when they asked what it meant, is entirely speculative. How many times have our own small children asked questions about Christ or the Lord's Supper when they were able to take the elements yet not able to understand the answers? My children started asking these kinds of questions by one and one-half to two years of age.

Second, Murray does not seem to know or recognize that infants under one year are capable of ingesting unleavened bread and meat (wine is not mentioned).[83] This kind of reasoning is speculative and uninformed, not of the kind worthy of determining who should be allowed to participate in a sacrament. His two objections do not stand up to close examination.

Therefore, I conclude with Berkhof, after examining the text, context and supporting Reformed comment on Exodus 12, that the children of the household who were capable of ingesting meat and unleavened bread partook of the Passover feast simply by their covenant position in the household and by their circumcision (Exodus 12:24, 43–51).

IMPLICATIONS

What are the implications of this conclusion? I soon found out. The next month I read an article in a denominational newsletter reaching the same conclusion I had reached supporting the idea of covenant children's communion. The author sought to allow infant-baptized children entrance to the Lord's Table as soon as they are able to take the elements in a worship service! The line of argument supporting the transformation of circumcision into

---

[83]Murray, *Baptism,* 76–79.

infant baptism by good and necessary inference was used as the principle for transforming the subjects of the Passover into the subjects of the Lord's Supper.[84]

As I began to assimilate and analyze this article, several arguments against its conclusions came to mind. The two clearest were that the New Testament commands one to examine himself before participating in the Lord's Supper and the New Testament does not positively command or provide an example of including infants and small children in the supper. The first is an argument of instituted precept, and the second an argument of silence and inference. The second may also be used in a negative way, as it is by paedobaptists, to state that there is no prohibition of infants from baptism either. However, the latter argument must rely upon supposed good and necessary inference from the Old Testament when interpreting a New Testament sacrament instituted by Christ, rather than depending upon New Testament revelation to institute and define New Testament sacraments and delineate participation in them. Simply put, true good and necessary inference cannot overrule that which is expressly set down in Scripture. If it does, then it cannot truly be a logically *necessary* inference. Further, it occurred to me, as Walter Chantry has observed, that to ignore a practice such as infant baptism because the Scripture is silent about it is *not the same* as adopting a practice when the Scripture is silent about it. The former silence conforms to the regulative principle, the latter to the normative principle.

I concluded that both the New Testament command and example dictate that the subjects for the Lord's Supper observance be only believers who are capable not only of understanding the meaning of the supper but also of examining their inward spiritual motivation in taking it. I concluded, along with many Reformed paedobaptist theologians, that these two arguments are sufficient to show the error of infant or covenant communion. This led me to additional questions:

1. If children in the Old Covenant were allowed to participate in the Passover feast as soon as they were able to consume the elements, but children in the New Covenant are not allowed to participate until a professed faith and

---

[84]Robert T. Henderson, "Is the Lord's Supper a Passover Feast for [the] Whole Congregation?" *The Open Letter:* 8, no. 1 (January 1977):1, 4.

self-examination are evidenced, is there also an inconsistency with infant baptism? What hermeneutic must determine consistently the subjects both of baptism and the Lord's Supper?
2. What has changed in the application of the covenant family concept from the Old Covenant administration to the New Covenant administration?
3. Why does the covenant child participate in the Passover and not in the Lord's Supper?
4. Why is paedocommunion not required of all Presbyterians when paedobaptism is required, though both are based upon Old Testament good and necessary inference?
5. Why is New Testament precept and example sufficient to deny paedocommunion but insufficient to deny paedobaptism?
6. Why can Presbyterian pastors have "liberty" on paedocommunion but none on paedobaptism? Should liberty not be allowed for both?
7. Has the New Covenant child of believers less blessings than the Old Covenant child?
8. What *exactly* are the covenant blessings for the New Covenant child of believers?

These questions were answered by going back to basic principles of evangelical and Reformed hermeneutics.

BASIC EVANGELICAL AND REFORMED HERMENEUTICS

There are certain principles of interpretation generally accepted and followed by most evangelical and Reformed scholars.[85] According to Bernard Ramm, the explanation of differences between evangelical scholars is not that of different hermeneutics but of inconsistent application.[86] The following ten principles are generally accepted on all sides.

---
[85]The *Chicago Statement on Biblical Inerrancy* and the *Chicago Statement on Biblical Hermeneutics* are examples of such unity on basic principles of biblical interpretation.
[86]Bernard Ramm, *Protestant Biblical Interpretation* (Grand Rapids, MI: Baker Book House, 1970), ix, 10, 224.

The inspiration and inerrancy of Scripture. Although there are wide differences among evangelical scholars about the meaning of certain Scripture passages, there is wide agreement upon the verbal, plenary inspiration of Scripture. That is, both the Old and New Testaments are fully inspired by God and kept from error in the original autographs, though God used human authors to write the text.

The literal-grammatical-historical method. Most evangelical scholars agree that Scripture is to be interpreted:

- *literally,* according to the ordinary meaning of words in current use, unless the text and context places a different import upon the meaning; this includes the use of lexicons, expert language studies, secular sources, and contemporary use, balanced with a thorough examination of how God authoritatively uses each word in Scripture. For example, Louis Berkhof recognizes that such etymological and contemporary use studies must depend to some degree upon experts;[87]
- *grammatically,* with strict attention to the grammar of the original languages, including the ordinary use of grammar from secular sources; this also includes the use of etymology and the current use of words as just mentioned; and
- *historically,* with regard to the historical backgrounds of the text; this includes the secular and biblical resources that enlighten historical events, customs, language usage, and so forth.

---

[87]Louis Berkhof, *Principles of Biblical Interpretation* (Grand Rapids, MI: Baker Book House, 1950), 67–68. Scriptural usage has the final word, but Scripture was not inspired in a vacuum. The grammar and vocabulary of the Greek New Testament were drawn from secular, SEPTUAGINT and Koine Greek. To determine the meaning of Greek words in Scripture without referring to normal secular usage is to deny the human side of inspiration, including such issues as an author's education, personality, upbringing, culture. Such a view would actually close the meaning of many Scripture words (*hapax-legomena*) and create a redefinition of many words which would change doctrine.

Berkhof explains: "As a rule it is not advisable that the interpreter should indulge very much in etymological investigations. This work is extremely difficult, and can, ordinarily, best be left to the specialists. Moreover, the etymological meaning of a word does not always shed light on its current signification. *At the same time, it is advisable that the expositor of Scripture take notice of the established etymology of a word, since it may help to determine its real meaning and may illumine it in a surprising manner*" [Berkhof, *Principles*, 67–68, emphasis mine].

Though agreeing on these things, sincere scholars differ on how the Scripture interprets itself literally, especially in regard to such issues as prophecy and fulfillment, typology, parables, and metaphors.

The analogy of faith. This means that the final authoritative interpreter of a specific Scripture is the rest of Scripture, i.e., the whole counsel of God. Scripture interpreting Scripture is the best friend of the literal-grammatical-historical method. This places Scripture over man's tradition, church history, science, or ecclesiastical pronouncements. It also limits the unbounded paedobaptist application of good and necessary inference when it contradicts God-given revelation concerning an instituted sacrament.

The perspicuity of Scripture. This means that Scripture is sufficiently clear upon essential matters of faith and practice, even in modern language translations, to guide the common Christian in faith and life. This does not deny the need of gifted teachers to explain God's Word, but it does affirm that the Scripture is clear enough that the common Christian should be convinced of their beliefs from the Scripture alone without blindly following respected teachers. As the *Westminster Confession* says:

> All things in Scripture are not alike plain in themselves, nor alike clear unto all; yet those things which are necessary to be known, believed, and observed, for salvation, are so clearly propounded and opened in some place of Scripture or other, that not only the learned, but the unlearned, in a due use of the ordinary means, may attain unto a sufficient understanding of them (*WCF* 1:7).[88]

The unity of Scripture. The Old and New Testaments together are not contradictory but complementary, having the Holy Spirit as their common Divine Author. Both are necessary to discover God's will.

---

[88] One problem with infant baptism, which often bothered me as a Presbyterian pastor, is that it is not sufficiently clear in the Scriptures for ordinary Christian parents to determine their duty of infant baptism without "help" from pastors and complicated theological studies. Many have expressed to me: "If it is a command to obey, why is it not more clear in Scripture?"

The diversity of Scripture. "The New is in the Old concealed; the Old is in the New revealed." God's progressive revelation in history necessitates a distinction to some degree between the Old Testament and the New Testament; otherwise the New would never have been given.

The finality and clarity of the New Testament. The New Testament is the final and clearest revelation of God to man, and men must not add to it by alleged further revelations. The New Testament is clearer than the Old Testament because it finally and authoritatively interprets Old Testament types and shadows, not because the Old Testament was unclear as a revelation of God.

The priority of the New Testament. Because "the Old is in the New revealed," there must be a final dependence upon the New Testament revelation to determine how the Old Testament is fulfilled in it. This is a necessary corollary to the concept of progressive revelation and biblical theology and is an essential prerequisite to a sound systematic theology. When defining the principles of interpretation concerning the relationship between the Old and New Testaments, Berkhof offers several principles:

- The Old Testament offers the key to the right interpretation of the New.
- The New Testament is a commentary on the Old.
- The interpreter should beware of minimizing the Old Testament.
- The interpreter should guard against reading too much into the Old Testament.[89]

These are sensible principles to which all evangelicals adhere. However, it is this second principle, that "The New Testament is a commentary on the Old," that is often inconsistently applied. The New Testament has priority to teach how the Old is fulfilled in it as the inspired commentary on the Old Testament. This is why the Lord Jesus Christ declared His authority over

---
[89]Berkhof, *Principles,* 137–138.

Old Testament and noninstituted forms of worship (John 4:21–24), charging His apostles to teach the church to do what He actually commanded (Matthew 28:20). The priority of the New Testament for interpreting how the Old Testament is fulfilled is fundamental. The teachings of Jesus and His apostles are the standard of Old Testament interpretation (Ephesians 2:20).

The typology of Scripture. Typological exegesis is a necessary principle to understand when interpreting Old Testament prophecy and New Testament fulfillment, i.e., the New Covenant prophecy of Jeremiah 31:31–34. This is true especially when good and necessary inference from the Old Testament is the justification for a New Testament instituted sacrament. According to Bernard Ramm, typology has been a major area of disagreement between dispensational and covenantal scholars.[90]

Classically, dispensationalists have required an Old Testament prophecy to be fulfilled in the exact literal form of the prophecy, thus projecting elements unfulfilled exactly and literally in the New Testament into a future millennium containing a future temple with sacrifices in Jerusalem (Ezekiel 37:26–28). More covenantal interpreters understand the New Testament quotations of Old Testament prophecies as biblically fulfilled literally in the New Testament if there is a historical correspondence and a heightened fulfillment. For instance, Jesus literally fulfilled and abrogated the temple sacrifices, then entered the better heavenly tabernacle, negating the necessity for another earthly one (Hebrews 9). Also, the church fulfills the Ezekiel 37:26–28 prophecy, according to literal New Testament revelation (2 Corinthians 6:16), thus eliminating the inferred need for another physical temple to fulfill the prophecy. God dwelling in His people is a heightened fulfillment far superior to the building of another physical temple on earth.

However, paedobaptist covenantalists make the opposite error. They erroneously attempt to make the Old Testament "church in the wilderness" virtually identical to the New Testament church. This includes the placement of the covenant sign upon infants, ignoring principles of typological exegesis, as well

---

[90]Ramm, *Protestant*, 239–241.

as ignoring the fact that infants were not circumcised in the wilderness. The church in the wilderness is simply the typological shadow of the New Testament revealed form, not requiring literal correspondence in every element, as dispensationalists require. After all, one should remember that dispensationalists often interpret the church in the wilderness as evidence for the "carnal Christian" doctrine of the modern day.

Typological exegesis places the priority upon the New Testament as the final authoritative interpreter of the Old, rather than turning to the Old as the final interpreter of its own New Testament fulfillment.

Priority between hermeneutical principles. Dan McCartney, a professor of New Testament at Westminster Theological Seminary, and Charles Clayton explain that the meaning of Scripture is one and that no part of Scripture contradicts another. However, because men are fallible, some guidelines in the application of hermeneutical principles are necessary to identify those areas where the interpreter is likely to go wrong. They list five general priorities in the application of biblical hermeneutics:

1. *The near context is more determinative of meaning than the far context.* A statement of Paul should be related to other statements of Paul before being compared to statements of Matthew or Isaiah. . . .
2. *A didactic or systematic discussion of a subject is more significant for that subject than a historical or descriptive narrative.* It should be obvious that when a historical narrative reports something as happening under some specific circumstance, one cannot draw theological conclusions from it. . . .
3. Related to number 2 is *the principle that explicit teaching is more significant than supposed implications of a text.* . . .
4. *Literal passages are more determinative than symbolic ones.* . . .
5. *Later passages reflect a fuller revelation than earlier.* The most obvious application of this principle is that the New takes precedence over the Old. Again, there is no real

conflict between the testaments when properly understood in their whole biblical and redemptive historical contexts, but the later revelation is fuller and clearer and occurs in our own redemptive historical context.[91]

All of these priorities are important in the discussion of baptism. However, I believe several of these priorities are ignored in certain arguments of paedobaptists. The clearest examples are the paedobaptists' violations of numbers 3 and 5. They agree in principle that an explicit teaching takes precedence over supposed implications of a text, but they fail to realize that the texts instituting New Testament baptism as a sacrament for disciples alone cannot be overruled by supposed Old Testament inferences regarding infant circumcision. They agree that the New Testament takes precedence over the Old Testament as the final, clearest revelation of God and that it is the interpreter of how the Old is fulfilled in it. However, paedobaptists ignore the priority of this principle when using possibly erroneous inference from an Old Testament administration to establish infant baptism over New Testament administration and institution. These priorities of hermeneutics must be followed at all times, but especially when establishing the institution, meaning and subjects of a sacrament. Old Testament inference cannot overrule explicit New Testament institution of a sacrament.

These ten basic hermeneutical principles provide a consistent framework for the discussion of baptism.

THE INCONSISTENT HERMENEUTICS OF INFANT BAPTISM

The priority of the New Testament must be maintained in order to determine how the Old Testament is fulfilled in it, not vice versa. Understanding this principle is essential to refuting the paedobaptist claim for the authority of infant baptism upon good and necessary inference from the Old Testament.

The paedobaptist principle that whatever is in the Old Testament continues unless it is specifically abrogated in the New

---

[91]Dan McCartney and Charles Clayton, *Let the Reader Understand* (Wheaton, IL: Victor Books, 1994), 195–197.

Testament actually negates the hermeneutical principle that the New Testament is the final, clearest revelation of God that has final authority to determine how the Old is fulfilled in it (John 4:21–24; Matthew 28:20; Ephesians 2:20). It negates the only instituted baptism expressly set down in Scripture, that of disciples alone, by an illegitimately applied good and necessary inference from the Old Testament. It places the burden of proof upon those who hold to New Testament finality and priority as if such a position is untenable when, in reality, all profess to hold to that principle. This inconsistency is why liberty is given to Presbyterian pastors on the issue of New Testament priority for disciple's communion alone, but, through inconsistency, no liberty is given to those who hold to New Testament priority regarding disciple's baptism alone.

Before I apply the correct principle of New Testament priority to infant baptism, let me illustrate how this principle is violated in several ways unrelated to baptism. The principle of New Testament priority is violated by dispensationalists, proponents of normative worship, and theonomists. Each of these positions holds to the same hermeneutical error violated by proponents of infant baptism. This error is the granting of a final priority upon the Old Testament to determine how it is fulfilled in the New rather than a priority upon the New to determine how the Old is fulfilled in it.

The Dispensational Error

The dispensational error is this: If any element of an Old Testament prophecy is not literally fulfilled in a one-to-one fashion in the New Testament, then one must assume that it awaits a further literal fulfillment in the future millennium. This hermeneutical tenet explains why dispensationalists normally wait for a future literal rebuilding of the Temple in Jerusalem, rather than being satisfied that the New Testament church is the greater fulfillment of that prophecy as the New Testament testifies (Ezekiel 37:26–28; 1 Corinthians 3:16–17; 2 Corinthians 6:16; Ephesians 2:19–22). John Wilmot states the difference in hermeneutics this way:

> Mr. B. W. Newton, maintaining a rigidly literal outlook, writes that "the prophecies of the New Testament cannot be interpreted in opposition to those of the Old Testament," that "they are professedly

supplemental to those already given in the Old Testament," and "it is important to receive the instruction of the prophets if we wish to apprehend the additional lessons of the apostles." The rule would be sound if the Testaments were reversed, that is to say, *the prophecies of the Old Testament must not be interpreted in opposition to the New Testament* [emphasis mine] . . . to quote Charles Hodge of Princeton: "The quotations given in the New Testament from the Old Testament are not *mere* quotations, but authoritative expositions. The apostles, in their use of Old Testament passages, tell us what the Holy Spirit *meant*."[92]

Wilmot's statement that the Old Testament prophecies must not be interpreted in opposition to the New Testament applies equally well to infant baptism: *The revelation of the Old Testament must not be interpreted in opposition to New Testament revelation.*

For instance, the Old Testament's institution of circumcision must not take precedence over how the New Testament defines the meaning and fulfillment of circumcision, whether one understands that to be baptism or regeneration. The New Covenant itself is a prophecy from the Old Testament (Jeremiah 31:31–34; 32:40), but it must not be interpreted in opposition to the New Testament explanation (Hebrews 8:8–12; 10:16–17). The New Testament is the authoritative exposition of what the Holy Spirit meant in the Old Testament prophetic passages. As written revelation, it carries a higher weight and priority than a supposed good and necessary inference deduced from the Old Testament.

In other words, by refusing to allow the New Testament to have final priority to determine the subjects of New Testament baptism, paedobaptists commit the same hermeneutical error as dispensationalists. If only Hodge had applied his same hermeneutic to infant baptism!

---

[92] John Wilmot, *Inspired Principles of Prophetic Interpretation* (Swengel, PA: Reiner Publications, 1965), 12, 22. Dr. Lloyd-Jones wrote the introduction to this book.

The Normative Worship Error

As mentioned in the Introduction, the *Westminster Confession of Faith* and *London Baptist Confession* (1689) describe "the regulative principle of worship" as follows:

> ... the acceptable way of worshipping the true God, is *instituted* by himself; and so *limited by his own revealed will,* that he may not be worshipped according to the imaginations, and devices of men, or the suggestions of Satan, under any visible representations, or any other way, not *prescribed in Holy Scripture* [emphasis mine, *WCF* 21:1].

The regulative principle requires that the elements of worship, including the sacraments be "instituted by God . . . limited by his own revealed will . . . and prescribed in Holy Scripture."

The broader "normative principle" requires what is commanded in Scripture *and* additionally permits whatever is not prohibited. This is why the Lutherans, Episcopalians, Methodists, and others who hold to this principle draw upon the Old Testament priesthood and the use of vestments, utensils, altars, and so forth, in their worship by erroneous inference. Roman Catholics have done this in an extended way. Today, even conservative Baptists, Presbyterians, and others follow the normative principle under the name of "creative worship practices," adding drama, dance, movies, puppets, and such. Often, justification for such noninstituted practices comes from erroneous inferences from the Old Testament.

However, the Presbyterian (and Baptist) "regulative principle" is limited by revelation only to what is instituted or prescribed by God Himself in the Scripture. It favors those elements of worship that are "expressly set down in Scripture." This is why the *Westminster Confession* only recognizes New Testament elements of worship such as the reading of Scripture; preaching; prayer; hearing the Word of God; and teaching and admonishing one another in psalms, hymns, and spiritual songs, as well as the proper administration of baptism and the Lord's Supper. The sacraments are specifically designated as those "instituted by Christ" (*WCF* 21:5). Baptists agree.

This dependence upon New Testament priority for worship elements instead of continuing or permitting what is not specifically abrogated from the Old Testament through the illegitimate use of good and necessary inference is the same principle violated in infant baptism. The administration of baptism is an element included under the regulative principle, which is supposed to be instituted by, limited by, and prescribed by Holy Scripture, not by illegitimately applied good and necessary inference. Yet, there is no written revelation commanding or illustrating the baptism of infants, but only that of professing believers or disciples. Thus, disciples-alone baptism describes the only instituted baptism in the entire Bible.

David Kingdon has noted this inconsistency of paedobaptists regarding their general adoption of the regulative principle and their violation of it by arguing from silence for the practice of infant baptism:

> It is interesting to note that Paedobaptists employ the argument from silence in exactly the opposite way when in controversy with the Church of Rome. For example, Boettner writes: "Since the priesthood occupied such an important place in the Old Testament dispensation and in the thinking of the Jewish people, *it is inconceivable that had it been continued in the New Testament dispensation, God would have made no mention of it* at all . . . ?" (L. Boettner: *Roman Catholicism,* Presbyterian and Reformed, Philadelphia, 1962, p. 48; my [Kingdon's] italics). Thus against Rome Paedobaptists insist: There is no positive command to continue the Old Testament priesthood, therefore it is *not* in force, whereas against the Baptists they declare that though there is no positive command to baptise infants, the Old Testament command to circumcise infants still holds good, and provides a warrant for infant baptism.[93]

Kingdon's critique of the inconsistent application of the regulative principle by paedobaptists to infant baptism reveals a major hermeneutical flaw in that doctrine's hermeneutical foundation.

In his *Paedobaptism Examined* (1787), the eighteenth-century English Baptist Abraham Booth has provided a lengthy compendium of paedobaptist quotations that depend upon the regulative principle to refute the Roman Catholic multiplication

---

[93]Kingdon, *Children of Abraham*, 48, fn. 3.

of sacraments. He correctly points out that their same quotations may be used against the illegitimate use of good and necessary consequence to establish infant baptism. One quotation from the Anglican Bishop Burnet, in his exposition of the Thirty-Nine Articles, suffices to illustrate the contradiction inherent in the paedobaptist hermeneutic:

> Sacraments are positive precepts, which are to be measured ONLY by the institution, in which there is not room left for us to carry them any farther.[94]

To apply this quotation against Roman Catholic sacraments yet to ignore its application to infant baptism is the height of inconsistency. All sacraments, including baptism, must be instituted by positive precepts according to the regulative principle, not by an erroneously applied good and necessary inference.

John Frame, a Presbyterian professor at Reformed Theological Seminary, wrote an excellent paper explaining and defending the regulative principle of worship. He accurately identified the appropriate elements of worship (preaching, reading Scripture, prayer, sacraments, etc.; *WCF* 21:5). However, in his explanation of the "circumstances" of worship common to human society (ordinarily pews, songbooks, order, air-conditioning, time, etc.; *WCF* 1:6), he allowed sacred dance and drama to be "circumstances" (not elements) appropriate for New Testament worship, even though nothing of the sort is mentioned in the New Testament. How did he arrive at his position? By referring back to Old Testament forms and examples of worship through an illegitimate use of good and necessary consequence, even though it is clear that these forms were not part of synagogue or Christian worship in the New Testament.[95] This violates the regulative principle of worship and New Testament priority.

In his later book, *Worship in Spirit and Truth,* Frame changed his position, placing dance and drama under "applications" of the general elements of worship, rather than under circumstances as

---

[94]Abraham Booth, *Paedobaptism [Infant Baptism] Examined* (1787; reprint, Choteau, MT: Gospel Mission, 1980), 5.
[95]John M. Frame, "The Lordship of Christ and the Regulative Principle of Worship" Tms [photocopy], class handout provided by a student from Westminster Theological Seminary West, 1995, 39–40, 43–44.

before. Thus, drama becomes an "application" under the general command to preach. Dance becomes an application of praise.[96] Such rationalization actually constitutes a return to the normative principle of permitting that which is not prohibited, rather than following the regulative principle of doing only that which God institutes. Again, this erroneous use of good and necessary consequence violates the regulative principle of worship and New Testament priority.

Pierre Marcel considers infant baptism to be an application of the general rule of baptism by "normative principles" of application in exactly the same way that Frame justifies drama and dance in worship by application.[97] However, using normative principles of application, a legitimate principle in pastoral care, to invent new worship practices simply is not justified by the regulative principle. Such thinking becomes a clear example of how good and necessary inference, the basis for infant baptism, can be misapplied over instituted revelation and opens the door to other unbiblical normative practices that have the potential to change the definition of what is Reformed and regulated worship.

A clear dependence upon New Testament finality and priority would prohibit such unfettered inferences with respect to instituted elements of worship. This error is exactly the same kind of thinking about worship and Scripture that infiltrated liberal Presbyterianism and, in response, provoked the rise of Westminster Seminary, the OPC and eventually the PCA.[98] It is against stated Reformed and Presbyterian doctrine to adopt a normative principle and abandon the regulative principle governing New Testament elements of worship through the use of supposed "good and necessary consequence" from Old Testament elements. Why, then, is the same error permitted for infant baptism?

---

[96]John M. Frame, *Worship in Spirit and Truth* (Phillipsburg, NJ: Presbyterian and Reformed Publishing Company, 1996), 92–94.
[97]Marcel, *Infant Baptism,* 190.
[98]When I was a pastoral intern at First Presbyterian Church, Rock Hill, South Carolina, from 1972 to 1973, one of the many events that upset our elders about the P.C.U.S. was the use of dance in one of the worship services of another Presbyterian church in town. To them, it was an illustration of how far the P.C.U.S. had moved from the Scriptures and the regulative principle of Scripture. Now, such worship elements are being advocated by someone of the stature of Dr. Frame from the misuse of the principle of good and necessary consequence. Where will such good and necessary consequence end? One can only imagine.

The Theonomic Error

A third example of an erroneous priority of the Old Testament over the New may be illustrated by the rise of theonomy. This movement advocates the continued authority and necessity of the Mosaic case laws to be applied to church and society. As the late Greg Bahnsen, a primary advocate, explains:

> ... our attitude must be that all Old Testament laws are presently our obligation *unless* further revelation from the Lawgiver shows that some change has been made.
> The *methodological* point, then, is that we presume our obligation to obey any Old Testament commandment unless the New Testament indicates otherwise.[99]

This presumption of continuance from the Old Testament by good and necessary inference places upon the New Testament an artificial requirement of stated abrogation for each law before "any Old Testament commandment" (including case laws) can be considered no longer in force. Thus, Bahnsen determines what evidence from the New Testament he will accept other than instituted commands and examples. This is exactly John Murray's hermeneutical argument for paedobaptism: the command to circumcise infants, placing the covenant sign upon infant seed, continues in infant baptism by good and necessary inference, because there is no stated prohibition of infant baptism in the New Testament.

Although claiming to depend upon the New Testament revelation to determine how the Old Testament is fulfilled in it, Bahnsen still returns to the Old as the final arbiter of what continues in the New by a misuse of good and necessary inference. His interpretation of Matthew 5:17–20 describes the "commandments" in the kingdom that apply to Christians as well as magistrates as including all the Old Testament case laws. Yet the

---

[99] Greg Bahnsen, *By This Standard* (Tyler, TX: Institute for Christian Economics, 1985), 3. There is no argument with the truth that the Old Testament case laws contained moral principles based upon the Ten Commandments. However, the penal punishments of those case laws were unique to the Israelite theocracy as a physical nation of God's elect people. No such arrangement is possible in the only God-instituted theocracy that exists today, Christ's church. This is why Calvin disagreed with a predecessor to Bahnsen's position in his day.

word commandments (*entolay*) is used in the New Testament primarily to refer to the moral law, which includes the two great commandments (Matthew 19:17; 22:36–40), the new commandment (John 13:34), the teachings of Jesus (John 14:15), apostolic commands (1 Timothy 6:14), and the Ten Commandments (Romans 7:8, 13:9). Jesus Himself illustrated this with the Sixth and Seventh Commandments (Matthew 5:21ff). An exception is Ephesians 2:15 where Paul mentioned the abolishment of "the law of commandments (*entolay*) contained in ordinances," the ceremonial laws clearly distinguished. However, to conclude, as Bahnsen does, that Matthew 5:17–20 advocates the case law of Moses as obligatory in the present kingdom (including penal consequences) is poor exegesis at best. The New Testament revelation rejects such erroneously applied good and necessary inference by its own positive institution and prescription. Many paedobaptists who object to theonomy use New Testament priority for their rejection, yet they will not do the same for infant baptism.

A similar error by Bahnsen is illustrated in the Great Commission. There he seems to interpret "nations" as geopolitical entities that are to be taught the law of God by the church, rather than understanding the text to require disciples to be made from all nations and to be taught to obey Christ's instituted commands. He says instead, "The Great Commission laid upon the church by Christ calls for us *to teach the nations whatsoever Christ has commanded*" (Matthew 28:18–20).[100]

The Great Commission actually says "make disciples of all the nations, baptizing *them* in the name of the Father, and of the Son and of the Holy Spirit, teaching *them* to do whatsoever I have commanded you." Obviously, this means to take the gospel to all the geo-ethnic-political nations and to make disciples of all kinds of people from them, baptizing those made disciples and teaching *them* to do all that Jesus commanded. The *them* of Matthew 28:19 are the "disciples," not the "nations." Luke corroborates this understanding of the Great Commission as a calling of individuals from the nations to repentance for the remission of sins (Luke

---

[100]*Ibid.,* 34. To support his argument, Bahnsen then quotes John Murray, *Principles of Conduct* (Grand Rapids, MI: William B. Eerdmans Publishing Co., 1957), 154. The only problem is that Murray conscientiously disagrees with Bahnsen's position. This is questionable scholarship, using your opponent to support your case when the reader is led to believe that your opponent agrees

24:47). This is why the rest of the New Testament records the activity of Peter and Paul and the other apostles as teaching disciples, instead of their teaching earthly kings to obey Mosaic case laws or organizing the churches to do so politically.[101]

Theonomy simply assumes that Old Testament law continues unless specifically abrogated. Thus, it actually reinterprets the New Testament to fit preconceived ideas of Mosaic obligation. This is relying upon the Old Testament to determine how it is fulfilled in the New, rather than relying upon the final, clearer New Testament to determine how the Old is fulfilled in it. Theonomy is unsound because it accepts an erroneous good and necessary inference that overrides that which is expressly set down in the New Testament.

If paedobaptists who disagree with theonomy wish to reject it, I humbly suggest that they must also reject the misuse of good and necessary inference from the Old Testament as the basis for infant baptism. Both doctrines are based upon unfettered Old Testament good and necessary inference which artificially requires a specific New Testament prohibition to reject them both. However, those who hold to New Testament priority to determine how the Old is fulfilled in the New accept the positive instruction of the New as sufficient warrant to reject such questionable doctrines.

Summary

It is odd that dispensationalists, paedocommunionists, normative worshippers, and theonomists should be hermeneutical bedfellows, but they all share the same conclusion with paedobaptists that good and necessary inference from the Old Testament can overrule clear New Testament instituted revelation. Each of these examples shows the error of an Old Testament priority for final New Testament doctrine.

---

with you. Bahnsen does the same with John Calvin and Samuel Bolton, misrepresenting their views as agreeing with his own. The truth is that Calvin, *Institutes,* 4:20:14–16, and Samuel Bolton, *The True Bounds of Christian Freedom* (London: The Banner of Truth Trust, 1964), self-consciously rejected precursors of Bahnsen's view as unbiblical.

[101]It is no theological accident that theonomy has influenced the modern-day emphasis of using the church and pulpit for political mobilization, contrary to New Testament commands and practice.

And one error will lead to another. I believe that this is why our Presbyterian brethren are struggling over theonomy, paedo-communion, and normative worship practices. The acceptance of paedobaptism inevitably opens the door to these other errors. This also explains why many Baptists, ignorant of New Testament priority and the regulative principle of worship, have adopted normative worship practices and have lost many to paedobaptist churches. Both paedobaptists and Baptists who violate the principle that "the Old is in the New *revealed*" are quickly led down other paths.

BIBLICAL HERMENEUTICS FOR CHRISTIAN BAPTISM

We come now to state appropriate principles of interpretation for Christian baptism. Once again, we affirm that logical inference is necessary to interpret and apply the Scriptures. However, some of what is called good and necessary inference is neither "good" nor "necessary." The use of inference must always be bounded by several hermeneutical principles to make sure that our conclusions are contained in Scripture and not contradictory to that which is "expressly set down in Scripture." These principles follow.

An affirmation of the unity of Scripture. We must not become "New Testament–only" Christians. Paul affirmed the Old Testament as inspired of God and profitable for rebuke, correction and training in righteousness that the man of God (Christian) may be equipped for every good work (2 Timothy 3:15–17). He did the same in 1 Corinthians 10:1–13 where the Old Testament is full of examples for our instruction. "The New is in the Old concealed . . . " in the sense that the Old describes and prophesies the New that is to come. Not only that, but the New also affirms the authority of the Old Testament for the Christian, describing exactly how it continues with authority in the life of the believer. This is seen especially in the continuance of the Moral Law (Matthew 5–7, Romans 13:11ff.) and examples of faith (Hebrews 11).

The New Testament also describes the unity between the two testaments in terms of typological promise and fulfillment. Thus, through Jesus Christ, born-again Christians (circumcised and uncircumcised) become the fulfilled children of Abraham (Galatians 3), the true Jew and circumcision (Romans 2:29, Philippians 3:1–3, Colossians 2:11–12), the new temple of God (1 Corinthians 3:16–17, Ephesians 2:19ff.) and, therefore, the new Israel of God (Galatians 6:16, Jeremiah 31:31–34).[102]

This unity between the testaments must be affirmed over and over, especially when exploring the question of infant baptism.

An affirmation of the diversity of Scripture. There is a difference between the testaments and the covenants under which they are administered: "The Old is in the New revealed . . . " The continuance of the Old Testament is limited in certain ways by the New Testament. E. J. Young, a paedobaptist scholar, applied this principle to Old Testament interpretation:

> . . . the Old Testament is a preparation for the New, and the proper interpretation of the Old Testament is found in the New. If, then, one disregards the New Testament, he will never properly explain the Old. The prophecies, for example, can to a certain extent be understood from the Old Testament, but they can never be grasped in their fulness as they should be, unless we take into consideration the further revelation which God has given us in the New Testament. . . . Neglect of this principle simply leads to false interpretation.[103]

Perhaps a better way to state our principle is this: "The New which was in the Old concealed finally has been revealed by the New, explaining in a final authoritative way how it was concealed in the Old."

For instance, we can study Hebrews and see how the Old Testament sacrificial system was glorious and typological of Christ's work, thereby understanding His work better. However, the same book declares the abolition of the Old Covenant system through a typologically greater fulfillment in Christ (Hebrews 10:1–17). We must study both testaments for a full view of His work. However, we must admit the final authority of the New Testament as

---

[102]Robertson, *Israel of God,* 43–45. Robertson takes exactly this position in his new work. The Israel of God is all of the elect.
[103]E. J. Young, *Genesis Three* (Edinburgh: The Banner of Truth Trust, 1966), 57.

the last, fullest, and clearest revelation of God to man. Diversity between the testaments favors the New Testament for final priority and interpretation. This follows from the fact of progressive revelation and the additional fact that the discipline of biblical theology is the foundation for systematic theology.

The final authority of the New Testament to describe, institute and explain the New Covenant fulfillment of the Old Testament prophecies and types. If the New Testament clearly prescribed or instituted infant baptism as the greater fulfillment of Old Testament circumcision, we would have to practice it. However, if the New Testament describes something else other than infant baptism as the fulfillment of Old Testament circumcision, which it does in heart circumcision, then we must rest there.

It is this presupposed hermeneutic that separates Baptists from paedobaptists, in consistent application if not in theory. In fact, one of the finest statements of this hermeneutic is by Greg Bahnsen, a paedobaptist, in his defense of theonomy:

> Given the progress of revelation, we must be committed to the rule that *the New Testament should interpret the Old Testament for us;* the attitude of Jesus and the Apostles to the Mosaic law, for instance, must be determinative of the Christian ethic.... What *is* maintained is that our obligation to God's Old Testament law should be interpreted and qualified by the New Testament *Scripture*....[104]

I could not agree more. The difference between Bahnsen and myself is in consistent application of this agreed-upon "rule." He misinterprets certain New Testament passages, giving them a novel teaching, in support of his theonomy. Yet this is because in practice he allows the misuse of Old Testament good and necessary inference to color plain New Testament statements and exegesis.

Let us, then, consistently apply the New Testament priority, on which we agree, to the issue of Christian baptism and particularly to the subjects of baptism—and let us consistently apply the principle that the explicit teaching of Scripture takes prece-

---

[104]Bahnsen, *By This Standard,* 4.

dence over inference from Scripture. If we follow these principles consistently, we must conclude that supposed "good and necessary inference" from the Old Testament cannot carry more weight than the New Testament command and example expressly set down in Scripture, especially for the "sacraments instituted by Christ" Himself.

Section II

THE STRING OF PEARLS
COVENANT THEOLOGY, THE
NEW COVENANT, AND BAPTISM

In 1977, when I recognized that paedobaptists disagree as to whether Old Testament children participated in the Passover by covenant position, there remained in my mind a growing curiosity to reexamine the biblical basis for infant baptism. I believed that perhaps God was guiding me to re-study the doctrine. On the one hand, if I affirmed the concept, at least I would have confirmed in my own mind that my acceptance of infant baptism while in seminary had not been influenced by subjective considerations. On the other, I reasoned that, if I came to be a Baptist, I would have nothing to lose in accepting the truth of God's Word. Either way, I would be stronger in the end, even if my ecclesiastical service would become more complicated.

Although all paedobaptist theologians that I have read heartily agree that there is no positive command to baptize covenant infants, there does seem to be an impressive number of individual pearls that can be strung together upon good and necessary inference as a beautiful and unified necklace. In fact, a PCA pastor friend of mine once stated to me that "the individual arguments for infant baptism are weak, but taken together they present a strong argument." Yet this reasoning is extremely faulty. How can a strong chain be made of weak links?

What then are the pearls on the string of erroneous paedobaptist good and necessary inference? Here are the pearls covered in Section II whose beauty once caused me to add them to my own string:

1. The covenant theology of the Bible
2. The relationship between circumcision and baptism

3. The proof-texts concerning baptism
4. Jesus' attitude toward children
5. The disjunction of the baptism of John and Christian baptism
6. The argument of silence
7. The argument of expanded blessings
8. The testimony of tradition

Again, I have not dealt with the proper mode of baptism in the text, but have relegated it to Appendix B because I consider the issue of subjects of baptism to be the most important question.

Chapter 3

The Covenant Theology of the Bible (Part I): Paedobaptist Versus Baptist Views

Paedobaptist covenant theology was perhaps the most influential element in my former acceptance of infant baptism. It was the brightest and most beautiful pearl on my string of good and necessary inferences that convinced me of its truth. Indeed, voices from both Baptist and paedobaptist ranks shout that if one accepts covenant theology in principle, then one has to go all the way and accept infant baptism.[105] However, nothing could be further from the truth.

It is my contention that paedobaptists have gone beyond biblical bounds to produce an erroneous form of covenant theology. This explains why there are such significant differences between major proponents of paedobaptist theology. The moment a doctrine is based upon supposed good and necessary inference beyond or opposed to that which is expressly set down in Scripture, it is inevitable that its proponents will have major disagreements among themselves.

On the other hand, some Baptists have overreacted to certain inconsistent errors of covenant theologians (such as paedobaptism, paedocommunion, or theonomy) and have "thrown the baby out with the bathwater." As I read the covenants of the Old and New Testaments, only a Baptistic covenant theology holds consistently to the New Testament's interpretation of how the Old Testament is fulfilled in it.[106]

---

[105] It is obvious that paedobaptists believe this. However, some Baptist voices erroneously teach that the acceptance of covenant theology in principle requires one to accept infant baptism as well. Theirs is a reactionary theology that Reformed Baptists do not accept.

[106] This issue was the subject of my doctoral dissertation. *See* Fred A. Malone, *A Critical Analysis of the Use of Jeremiah 31:31–34 in the Letter to the Hebrews*

A brief summary of where covenantal Baptists agree and disagree with covenantal paedobaptists follows. The *London Baptist Confession* of 1689 further explains such agreements and disagreements. Of course, there is much agreement between Baptists and classic covenantal theologians such as Louis Berkhof, O. Palmer Robertson, and others. That point should not be minimized even though, here, I focus on the differences between us. In addition, I will not presume to speak for all baptistic theologians. However, the following survey provides a theology of the covenants adopted by many historically Reformed and covenantal Baptists, including the founders of both northern and southern Baptists in America.

BAPTIST AGREEMENTS AND DISAGREEMENTS WITH PAEDOBAPTIST COVENANTAL THEOLOGY

Agreements

First, along with paedobaptist covenantalists, covenantal Baptists believe in the decrees of God and the Covenant of Redemption before the foundation of the world. The Covenant of Redemption is the unified plan between the Father, Son, and Holy Spirit to redeem the elect from their sins (2 Timothy 1:9). The Father created the plan of redemption as Head of the Trinity, the Son agreed to come into the world as the Redeemer of God's elect, and the Holy Spirit agreed to regenerate the hearts of God's chosen people in time (Ephesians 1:3–14). Some identify the Covenant of Redemption with another covenant, the so-called Covenant of Grace. There is little difference between the two positions.[107]

Second, Covenantal paedobaptists and covenantal Baptists both believe in the Covenant of Works that God made with Adam as our federal head. Adam broke this covenant and brought all mankind into a state of sin, death, condemnation, and misery (Hosea 6:7; Romans 5:12–21). We believe that all people are born under the condemnation of the failed Covenant of Works and

---

(doctoral dissertation, Southwestern Baptist Theological Seminary, 1989). Available from University Microfilms Inc., Ann Arbor, Michigan.

[107]John L. Giradeau, *The Federal Theology: Its Import and Its Regulative Influence,* ed. J. Ligon Duncan (Greenville, SC: Reformed Academic Press), 16–18.

remain "under law," until they are transferred into the Covenant of Grace (Romans 3:19–20; 6:14).

Covenantal paedobaptists and Baptists also both believe in the historical Covenant of Grace that God made with His elect. The Covenant of Grace is the fulfillment of that eternal Covenant of Redemption, worked out in history through its covenant Head, Jesus Christ (Romans 5:12ff.). It began with the promise of grace in Genesis 3:15, when Eve was promised a "seed" who would crush Satan on the head, even though He would be bruised on the heel. We believe that God's promise in Genesis 3:15 was carried on in history through variously administered "covenants of promise" with Noah, Abraham, Moses, and David. It was fulfilled in the final New Covenant of Jesus Christ when He came to earth and delivered the fatal blow to Satan upon the cross, thereupon rising from the dead. We believe that His death effectually purchased salvation for all those whom He represented as their covenant Head (i.e., the particular redemption of all the elect in all of history through His New Covenant).

Covenantal paedobaptists and Baptists both believe that the way of salvation has been by grace through faith in God's provision of that "seed of the woman" since the fall of man. The Sinai Covenant was never given as a renewed Covenant of Works for salvation, although it was mistakenly so interpreted by the Pharisees in Jesus' day.[108] It was "added for the sake of transgressions" (Galatians 3:19) to the Abrahamic Covenant in a subordinate or supplementary way *until* the seed of the woman and of Abraham came to whom the promises had been made (Galatians 3:16, 19). The conditional elements of the Sinai Covenant referred to Israel's possession of the land of Canaan as long as God's commandments were obeyed, not to a personal salvation of works (Galatians 3:21). As a result, that Sinaitic Covenant ended historically at the coming of the seed to whom the promises were made, namely, Jesus Christ.

Finally, Covenantal paedobaptists and Baptists both believe that the New Covenant of Jesus Christ is the fulfillment of the Abrahamic Covenant and is the clearest and final fulfillment of the historical Covenant of Grace. The New Covenant is therefore the fulfillment of that eternal Covenant of Redemption to save God's elect people (2 Timothy 1:8–10).

---

[108] A. T. Robertson, *The Pharisees and Jesus* (1920; reprint, Eugene, OR: Wipf and Stock Publishers, 1999), 22–23.

Disagreements

Having agreed with our paedobaptist brethren on many aspects of covenant theology as just set forth, we differ with them on the interpretation of several New Testament texts concerning those who constitute the fulfilled "seed" of Abraham today and about whether our physical seed (that is, our children) are entitled to baptism in the same way that Abraham's children were entitled to circumcision.

By erroneous inference, covenantal paedobaptists go beyond the teaching of the New Testament and transfer the promises given to Abraham and his seed automatically to believers and their seed in the New Covenant administration, making believers "little Abrahams." This is because of the tendency of paedobaptists to make the Abrahamic Covenant with its organic element almost identical to the Covenant of Grace and, thus, the New Covenant administration. As Berkhof said of the Abrahamic Covenant, "This covenant is still in force and is essentially identical with the 'new covenant' of the present dispensation."[109] This belief that the New Covenant is "essentially identical" to the Abrahamic Covenant is what enables the paedobaptist to erroneously infer that the Abrahamic circumcision of infants carries over into the New Covenant in infant baptism, even though the latter is never commanded, instituted, or described in Scripture.

In contrast, covenantal Baptists believe that the New Covenant is the only historical, covenantal administration in force (except for the Covenant of Works). Further, they believe that the Abrahamic promises are fulfilled in Jesus Christ Himself, Abraham's final physical seed and only little Abraham, and in His New Covenant members, who are His elect seed of faith alone (Isaiah 53:10; Galatians 3; Hebrews 8:8–12). The Abrahamic Covenant was a covenant of promise (Ephesians 2:12). It promised the New Covenant to come, but the New Covenant is superior because it is the purest and final revelation of the eternal Covenant of Redemption (2 Timothy 1:8–10). The Abrahamic Covenant and the New Covenant are not identical in every way. The latter fulfills the former and replaces it as the only redemptive covenant administration in force.

Furthermore, we believe that the promises to Abraham, which are fulfilled in the New Covenant, are *not* the passing on of covenant

---

[109] Berkhof, *Systematic Theology,* 633.

signs to infant seed, but the promised outpouring of the Holy Spirit upon his elect Jew and Gentile seeds through faith in Christ (Galatians 3:2–5, 8–9, 14, 29). These seed promises to Abraham are completely fulfilled in Christ, Abraham's final physical seed, and in Christ's elect seed of faith in union with Him. Thus, Abraham is "the father of us all" who believe (Romans 4:13–16). These "Christ-seed" alone are the children of Abraham, members of the New Covenant, and the only ones entitled to the New Covenant signs of baptism and the Lord's Supper.[110] Therefore, New Covenant baptism must be applied only to those who express faith in Christ, following "in the steps of our father, Abraham" (Romans 4:12), in other words, disciples alone. Not surprisingly, this is why the book of Acts usually refers to the church as "the disciples" (Acts 11:26).

Having summarized our agreements and disagreements with paedobaptist brethren regarding the high points of covenant theology, the remainder of this chapter and all of the next will present a more detailed analysis of paedobaptist covenant theology. This will be followed by a counterpoint presentation of a baptistic covenant theology that supports only the baptism of professing believers or disciples in the New Covenant.

The topics of covenant theology to be examined are the definition and content of a biblical covenant and the unity and diversity between the biblical covenants. The next chapter will continue this examination of covenant theology by examining the New Covenant fulfillment and its implications for disciple's baptism versus infant baptism.

THE DEFINITION AND CONTENT OF A BIBLICAL COVENANT

Point 1: Paedobaptist Views of a Covenant

Paedobaptist covenantal theology begins with the concept that God has chosen to reveal Himself and to relate to men by way of

---

[110] Robertson, *Israel of God,* 45–49. While arguing against a physical people who may be called "Israel" today, Robertson reserves the term "the Israel of God" only for those justified by faith and who are a "new creation." This position argues against the inclusion of infants on the basis of birth in the New Covenant "Israel." The New Covenant Israel is the universal church, according to Robertson. This is nothing less than the covenantal Baptist position.

covenants. The primary Old Testament Hebrew word for covenant is *berith* while the primary New Testament Greek word is *diatheke*. These two words begin the definition of a covenant.

According to Louis Berkhof, *berith* has its idea either in the Hebrew *bara,* meaning "to cut," or *beritu,* meaning "to bind." The New Testament *diatheke,* meaning "a will or testament," adds to the unilateral idea of a covenant.[111] O. Palmer Robertson defines a covenant as follows:

> A long history has marked the analysis of the covenants in terms of mutual compacts or contracts. But recent scholarship has established rather certainly the sovereign character of the administration of the divine covenants in Scripture. Both biblical and extra-biblical evidence point to the unilateral form of covenantal establishment. No such thing as bargaining, bartering, or contracting characterizes the divine covenants of Scripture. The sovereign Lord of heaven and earth dictates the terms of his covenant.
>
> The successive covenants of Scripture may emphasize either promissory or legal aspects. But this point of emphasis does not alter the basic character of covenantal administration. Whatever may be the distinctive substance of a particular covenant, the mode of administration remains constant. *A covenant is a bond-in-blood sovereignly administered* [emphasis mine].[112]

Here Robertson combines various etymological and biblical ideas (bond, promise, cut, will, etc.) into a "bond-in-blood sovereignly administered" definition.[113] He also states that each covenant "may emphasize either promissory or legal aspects," depending upon the revelatory "substance of a particular covenant." In other words, one must be careful not to assume elements of one covenant for another. Specific written revelation must define each covenant.

---

[111]Berkhof, *Systematic Theology,* 262–64. The ordinary Greek word for covenant, *suntheke,* implies a mutual agreement between equals. The New Testament use of *diatheke* instead is more unilateral in origin in that it describes a "will" or "testament" instituted by a sovereign to a recipient.

[112]O. Palmer Robertson, *The Christ of the Covenants* (Phillipsburg, NJ: Presbyterian and Reformed Publishing Company, 1980), 15.

[113]I have great sympathy with this basic definition of Robertson, though I would emphasize the "bond" part of the definition a bit more. Not every divine covenant in Scripture carries the "in blood" part of the definition, though most include that element in the historical covenants.

Others, like Robert R. Booth, expand their definition of a covenant to go beyond the basic etymological and exegetical definition by generalizing from contextual elements found in particular covenants. In his book, *Children of the Promise,* Booth (a former Reformed Baptist) expands the definition of a covenant to go far beyond that of a simple bond, oath, promise, or pledge, defined further by specific revelation concerning each particular covenant. Booth says:

> If we are to rightly understand the Bible, we must understand the concept of a covenant. A covenant, when formed between a superior and an inferior, is a "conditional promise." A reward is promised, on the condition of obedience, and punishment is threatened for disobedience. For example, "whosoever believes shall be saved, whosoever believeth not shall be damned." The covenant is not only law, but also grace. It is only by the ill-deserved favor of God (i.e., grace) that he chooses to covenant with sinful men. Another writer (Robertson) adds to this definition that a covenant is *"a bond in blood sovereignly administered.* When God enters a covenant relationship with men, he sovereignly institutes a life-and-death bond. A covenant is a bond in blood, or a bond of life and death, sovereignly administered."
>
> We should, therefore, understand a covenant between God and man to be a conditional promise, sealed by blood, sovereignly administered by God, with blessings for those who obey the conditions of the covenant and curses for those who disobey its conditions.[114]

Thus, instead of establishing the basic definition of a covenant and then determining each covenant's content by written revelation, Booth adds elements to some covenants by inferences never articulated in Scripture. To go beyond the basic definition of a covenant to include physical descendants, conditional promises, curses and blessings in every covenant literally is to put words in the mouth of Scripture. This is a violation of basic hermeneutics and biblical theology. By this error, Booth makes every covenant conditional and breakable. He automatically assumes that all covenants are conditional upon man's obedience and that there is a curse for all individuals who break

---

[114]Robert R. Booth, *Children of Promise* (Phillipsburg, NJ: Presbyterian and Reformed Publishing Co., 1995), 24–25.

covenant with God. Booth therefore teaches erroneously that the New Covenant is a conditional and breakable covenant for real members of that covenant. Booth's presuppositions cloud his exegesis of the text.

In the New Covenant, our Lord Jesus Christ removed the curse of the Covenant of Works for all members of the covenant by His perfect life and death for sin. In the New Covenant there is no curse for covenant breaking (Jeremiah 31:27–34; 32:40). The reason is that, in the New Covenant, God guarantees each covenant member a heart to keep the new and everlasting covenant (Jeremiah 32:40). This is why there are curses for covenant breaking in some Old Testament "covenants of promise" but none in the New Covenant texts. The New Testament warns against false conversion, or false professed membership in the New Covenant, but not against covenant breaking. The New Covenant has promises for blessing those in it but no curses for covenant breakers. Why not? Because apparent covenant breakers remain cursed in Adam's Covenant of Works (Romans 5:12ff.). However, no participant in the New Covenant can ever break it. In this sense, the New Covenant is unconditional.

On the other hand, the New Covenant may be called conditional in the sense that it requires the death of a mediator to establish it and repentance and faith as conditions for entering it at a historical point in time. The fact that it has conditions in a sense does not mean, however, that it is breakable. Herman Ridderbos, a paedobaptist, commenting on Jesus' words from Jeremiah 31 at the Last Supper, says:

> This reference to Jeremiah 31 is so important because according to this prophecy, the Lord God himself will accomplish the fulfillment of the condition for the maintenance of the new covenant. For he will write his law in the hearts of his people. To this end he will forgive their former iniquity and will no longer remember their sins (Jer. 31:33, 34). According to these words at the last Supper, this fellowship of grace between God and his people is guaranteed by God himself and is consequently *unbreakable,* and finds its foundation and strength in Christ's substitutive suffering and death [emphasis mine].[115]

---

[115]Herman Ridderbos, *The Coming of the Kingdom* (Philadelphia, PA: The Presbyterian and Reformed Publishing Co., 1962), 201.

Berkhof agrees. God sovereignly provides the repentance and faith to each New Covenant member to ensure that the New Covenant will not be broken (Jeremiah 32:40).[116] Robertson certainly has a "bond in blood" definition with life and death as the basis of the covenant bond (i.e., the curse death of Jesus Christ in the New Covenant establishment). However, this is not the same as asserting that all New Covenant members have a conditional blessing and curse framework upon them and can really break the unbreakable New Covenant.

Each covenant must be defined by revelation beyond the basic definition of a bond, pledge, oath, or promise. One is hard pressed to find the covenants of Noah, Abraham, David, and the New Covenant, as stated in Scripture, containing curses for breaking the conditions of those covenants once entered. In fact, the breaking of the Abrahamic Covenant is defined as refusing to enter it by circumcision, not as breaking it once entered (Genesis 17:14). Booth's maximalist approach to defining a covenant imposes his definition upon all biblical covenants instead of allowing revelation to determine each covenant's content. Thus, Booth defines a covenant by erroneous inference, not exegesis.

In summary, classic paedobaptist covenantalists believe that the Covenant of Grace is the historical outworking of the Counsel of Redemption. Further, they believe that the Covenant of Grace of necessity includes a conditional curse and an organic element often included in some Old Testament covenants. This *a priori* assumption extends such elements into the New Covenant by an erroneous inference against that which is expressly set down in Scripture. The following counterpoint shows where Baptist covenantalists disagree with paedobaptists concerning the definition of a covenant.

Counterpoint 1: Baptistic Views of a Covenant

In order to compare the just stated paedobaptist views with a Baptistic covenantal theology, we must examine how Scripture overturns the paedobaptist concept of a covenant and its content.

Sinclair Ferguson, a paedobaptist, has verbalized John Owen's excellent approach to the hermeneutics of covenant theology with

---

[116]Berkhof, *Systematic Theology*, 280–81.

two statements. The first is Ferguson's summary statement of Owen's position:

> ... the exposition of each species of covenant theology is invariably dependent upon the definition of covenant it employs.[117]

The second quotation is Owen's:

> It is therefore certain that where God speaks of his covenant, we cannot conclude that whatever belongs unto a perfect, complete covenant is therein intended ... *what is intended by it must be learned from the subject-matter treated of, seeing there is no precept or promise of God but may be so called* [emphasis mine].[118]

To summarize these two hermeneutical principles, (1) one's definition of what is a covenant will determine one's final covenant theology, and (2) the content and form of each covenant must be determined from actual revelation concerning its precepts and promises, not from supposed good and necessary inference from other covenants. With these two principles I heartily agree.

Definition of a Covenant

The idea of a covenant in the preceding paedobaptist discussion centered on the words *berith* and *diatheke*. The Hebrew root of *berith* or *barah* carries the idea "to eat, to cut." The Akkadian words *birit* [among, between], *baru* [to choose, fix, or pledge] and *biritu* [to bond, clasp, or fetter] all carry the idea of *promise, bond,* or *pledge,* between parties. For this reason, I believe that the biblical idea of a covenant has promise, bond, or solemn oath at its very root meaning, whether human or divine.

For example, Noah's covenant did not include a "bond in blood" element in the covenant itself, nor a curse should Noah break that covenant. It was simply a unilateral sovereign promise to save Noah and his family and never destroy the world by water again. God Himself even supplied the "sign" of the

---

[117]Sinclair Ferguson, *John Owen on the Christian Life* (Edinburgh: The Banner of Truth Trust, 1987), 21–22.
[118]*Ibid.,* 21. Ferguson quotes John Owen, *See* John Owen, *An Exposition of the Epistle to the Hebrews,* ed. W. H. Gould, vol. 2, *Introduction* (Grand Rapids, MI: Baker Book House, 1980), 81.

covenant (Genesis 6:18–22; 9:8–17). Man could do nothing to break the covenant so that God would destroy the world by water again as a curse. Thus, the simple definition of a divine covenant as a "promise" or "bond by oath" must be maintained in the Noahic Covenant. This very comparison between the Noahic Covenant and the New Covenant is so stated by Isaiah:

> For this is like the days of Noah to Me; *when I swore* that the waters of Noah should not flood the earth again, so *I have sworn* that I will not be angry with you, nor will I rebuke you. For the mountains may be removed and the hills may shake, but *My lovingkindness will not be removed from you, and My covenant of peace will not be shaken,"* says the Lord who has compassion on you [Isaiah 54:9–10; emphasis mine].

Once again, we must rely on actual revelation to explain the content of each covenant.

An important example that a covenant is a promise, bond by oath, or solemn oath is found in Hebrews 6:13–20 where the word *diatheke* is not even used to explain the Abrahamic Covenant in the context:

> For when God made the *promise* to Abraham, since He could swear by no one greater, He swore by Himself, saying, "I will surely bless you, and I will surely multiply you." And thus, having patiently waited, he obtained the *promise*. For men swear by one greater than themselves, and with them an *oath* given as confirmation is an end of every dispute. In the same way God, desiring even more to show to the *heirs of the promise* the unchangeableness of His purpose, *interposed with an oath,* in order that by two unchangeable things, in which it is impossible for God to lie, we may have strong encouragement, we who have fled for refuge in laying hold of the hope set before us. This hope we have as an anchor of the soul, a hope both sure and steadfast and one which enters within the veil . . . [Hebrews 6:13–19; emphasis mine].

Here God explains His covenant with Abraham as being His promise to Abraham, sworn additionally by an oath, even though the word covenant is not used. Certainly God established His covenant with Abraham, but the central idea to this covenant was His solemn promise or oath.

The word *diatheke* ("testament or will") was chosen in the Septuagint (the Greek Old Testament; LXX) to translate *berith*.

Further, it was used in the New Testament most often because, as a will, it revealed a more unilateral, sovereign pledge or promise than did *suntheke,* a word reflecting an equilateral agreement between two or more equal persons.[119] Thus, the idea that a covenant is a unilateral promise from a sovereign to his lesser is strengthened.

This explanation has led me to understand that the idea of a divine covenant is simply a sovereign bond, promise, oath, or pledge of God to man. This very position is affirmed by John Owen when commenting upon the "better promises" of the New Covenant:

> And we may observe,—(1) That every covenant between God and man must be founded on and resolved into "promises." Hence essentially a promise and a covenant are all one; and God calls an absolute promise, founded on an absolute decree, his covenant, Gen. ix. 11. And his purpose for the continuation of the course of nature unto the end of the world, he calls his covenant with day and night, Jer. xxxiii. 20. The being and essence of a divine covenant lies in the promise. Hence, they are called "the covenants of promise," Eph. ii. 12;—such as are founded on and consist in promises [emphasis mine].[120]

Thus we come to a covenantal Baptist definition of a covenant: a biblical and divine covenant is a solemn promise or oath of God to man, each covenant's content being determined by revelation concerning that covenant. Any other position adds to revelation by an erroneous inference.

Another hermeneutical error by paedobaptists when defining a covenant is the assumption that the covenant idea, including the one Covenant of Grace, must automatically have a genealogical or organic element that always includes believers and their seed. This is because some of the historical Old Testament covenants of promise included a physical seed that yields forth that final physical seed, Jesus Christ. This is why the Covenant of Grace is dually defined by classic covenantalists. The covenant is made with the "elect only," yet it is also made with believers and

---

[119] John Murray, *The Covenant of Grace* (Grand Rapids, MI: Baker Book House, 1954), 8–11.
[120] John Owen, *An Exposition of the Epistle to the Hebrews,* ed. W. H. Gould, vol. 6, *Hebrews 8:1–10:39* (Grand Rapids, MI: Baker Book House, 1980), 65.

their seed. The Scriptures, however, that describe the Counsel of Redemption and its historical Covenant of Grace (Ephesians 1:3–14; Titus 1:1–3, 2 Timothy 1:9–10) refer only to the elect.

William Hendriksen, a representative of this dual definition of the Covenant of Grace, wrestles with these two ideas:

> Honesty demands that we admit the element of truth in both views. In one sense we can and must say that *only the elect are covenant members.* To deny this means to deny Scripture. In another sense we can and must maintain, *as has been done all along in this book,* that *believers and their children without exception are in the covenant.* Everything depends on just what is meant by "being in the covenant." . . . When the question is asked, "Who are in the covenant?" this may mean, "Who enjoy the friendship, the lovingkindness, which God has promised to give in the way of covenant obedience?" The only answer which can be given to the question thus understood is, "only believers are in the covenant." But when the same question is asked, namely, "Who are in the covenant?" meaning, "Who are duty-bound by the terms of a divine arrangement to seek 'the friendship of Jehovah'?" then the only answer that can be given is, "Believers and their children without exception" [emphasis mine].[121]

This dual explanation by Hendriksen reveals the arbitrary way paedobaptists often reach and stretch, searching for explanations to sustain the inclusion of infants in the New Covenant. It is one thing to say that the Old Testament covenants of promise included believers and their seed as they awaited the time when the final "seed of the woman . . . seed of Abraham . . . seed of David" was to be born in Bethlehem. However, it is another thing automatically to include, by definition, believers and their seed in the Covenant of Grace with the elect, manifested in the New Testament.

Furthermore, Hendriksen asks, "Who are duty-bound by the terms of a divine arrangement to seek 'the friendship of Jehovah'?" His answer is "believers and their children." However, according to the Scriptures, all men are duty-bound to seek the friendship of Jehovah as His creatures who have broken the

---

[121] William Hendriksen, *The Covenant of Grace* (Grand Rapids, MI: Baker Book House, 1984), 51–52.

Covenant of Works in Adam. God is now commanding that all men everywhere repent (Acts 17:26–31).

The Covenant of Grace is what God does to save the elect from their justly deserved condemnation in the Covenant of Works. Each historical covenant of promise contains to a lesser or greater degree the promises of the Covenant of Grace, each one being administrations of that Covenant of Grace and having certain external features attached (i.e., the temporary Sinai Covenant). To project the administratively attached elements of the historical covenants back into eternity past by an erroneous inference and to thereby redefine the Covenant of Redemption and its historical outworking, the Covenant of Grace, is poor hermeneutics at best and unbiblical at worst. It adds content to the definition of a covenant by erroneous inference rather than by stated revelation.

John Owen likewise cautions against making the covenants of promise equivalent to the Covenant of Grace as Louis Berkhof does. Berkhof states:

> This [Abrahamic] covenant is still in force and "essentially identical" with the "new covenant" of the present dispensation.[122]

It is this error that causes paedobaptists to include organic elements of some Old Testament covenants of promise automatically in the Covenant of Grace, as if those covenants of promise were themselves the Covenant of Grace and, by inference, the New Covenant itself.

According to Owen, however, the New Covenant alone *is* the pure Covenant of Grace, revealed in the Old Testament in terms of the promise of grace to come in Christ. Therefore, the Abrahamic covenant itself cannot constitute the Covenant of Grace, or be "essentially identical" to it. The Abrahamic Covenant had primary reference to the coming of Christ as his ultimate physical seed of the New Covenant. As Owen said:

> When we speak of the "new covenant," we do not intend *the covenant of grace absolutely,* as though that were not before in this place. For it was always the same, as to the substance of it, from the beginning. It passed through the whole dispensation of times before the law, and under the law, of the same nature and efficacy, unalterable, "everlasting, ordered in all things, and sure." All who contend

---

[122]Berkhof, *Systematic Theology,* 633.

about these things, the Socinians only excepted, do grant that the covenant of grace, considered absolutely,—that is, the promise of grace in and by Jesus Christ,—was the only way and means of salvation unto the church, from the first entrance of sin. But for two reasons it is not expressly called a covenant, without respect unto any other things, nor was it so under the old testament. *When God renewed the promise of it unto Abraham, he is said to make a covenant with him; and he did so, but it was with respect unto other things, especially the proceeding of the promised Seed from his loins.* But absolutely under the old testament it consisted only in a promise; and as such only is proposed in the Scriptures, Acts ii. 39; Jer. vi. 14–16. The apostle indeed says, that the covenant was confirmed of God in Christ, before the giving of the law, Gal. iii. 17. And so it was, not absolutely in itself, but in the promise and benefits of it. The *nomothesia,* or full legal establishment of it, whence it became formally a covenant unto the whole church, was future only, and a promise under the old testament . . . but now, under the new testament, this covenant, with its own seals and appointments, is the only rule and measure of all acceptable worship. Wherefore the new covenant promised in the Scripture, and here opposed unto the old, is not the promise of grace, mercy, life, and salvation by Christ, absolutely considered, but as it had the formal nature of a covenant given unto it, in its establishment of the death of Christ, the procuring cause of all its benefits, and the declaring of it to be the only rule of worship and obedience unto the church. *So that although by "the covenant of grace," we oftentimes understand no more but the way of life, grace, mercy, and salvation by Christ; yet by "the new covenant," we intend its actual establishment in the death of Christ, with that blessed way of worship which by it is settled in the church* [emphasis mine].[123]

Owen's view of the Covenant of Grace as essentially the promise of salvation in the Old Testament covenants of promise, revealed later as the New Covenant, illustrates why the best definition of a covenant remains that of a bond, promise, or solemn oath further defined in content by the particular revelation concerning each covenant. The promise of the New Covenant, the purer Covenant of Grace, was part of the Abrahamic Covenant. However, the Abrahamic Covenant also contained other elements regarding Abraham's seed that were unique to its administration. A biblical and divine covenant is a solemn promise or oath of God to man. Beyond that, each covenant's content must be determined by specific revelation concerning that covenant, not by an erroneous inference.

---

[123]Owen, *Hebrews,* 6: 74–75.

Content of a Covenant

As I have noted, the content of each covenant arrangement must be determined by the relevant revelation concerning that covenant. Thus, for example, the covenant with Noah was a unilateral promise by God to Noah and to all creation never to destroy the world again by water. There were no conditions attached to man's performance in order to fulfill the covenant promises or to break the covenant. Noah offered sacrifice to God, but there is no evidence that this sacrifice sealed the covenant or that it fulfilled revealed stipulations of the covenant. Even the sign of the covenant was God's work in sending the rainbow, not man's response. The Noahic Covenant was an unbreakable, unconditional covenant (Genesis 9:8–17).

On the other hand, the covenant with Abraham required circumcision as a sign of the covenant and a condition of its fulfillment. Not to circumcise broke the covenant and constituted a rejection of it (Genesis 17:14). In addition, the covenant at Sinai required the performance of the people to fulfill the covenant blessings in Canaan. The latter was a conditional covenant kept by God but broken by Israel (Jeremiah 31:31–34).

These examples of an unconditional and a conditional covenant show why one cannot assume the content of any covenant by mere inference from another. Instituted revelation must determine each covenant's content. It is the covenantal Baptist position alone that allows the biblical student to depend more upon divine revelation expressly set down in Scripture rather than upon non-revealed and faulty inferences when defining a covenant and determining its content. Theological inference must flow from stated revelation, not from logical invention. Grasping this is essential to understanding the distinctiveness of the New Covenant in relation to the previous historical covenants. The next section explores those relationships of unity and diversity between the covenants, again, in a point-counterpoint method.

THE UNITY AND DIVERSITY OF THE BIBLICAL COVENANTS

Every covenantalist, both Baptist and paedobaptist, accepts that there is unity and diversity in the various biblical covenants. Sometimes people say that paedobaptists believe more in the unity of the covenants and Baptists believe more in their diversity. This might be an accurate comparison if one were comparing covenantalists and dispensationalists, but it is not an accurate analysis of the differences between paedobaptist and Baptist covenantalists.

Rather, covenantal Baptists believe that Old and New Testament Scripture defines a real unity between the covenants that is not compromised by accepting the biblically defined diversity between the New Covenant and every other previous historical covenant. This is why it is called new. The diversity between the covenants described through biblical theology must always be the foundation on which systematic theology builds its description of the unity of the covenants. The covenants of promise and the New Covenant have a real unity. That does not mean, however, that they are essentially identical.

Baptists also believe that the paedobaptist, while holding to diversity between the covenants of promise and the New Covenant, exaggerates the unity by erroneous inference that goes beyond revealed truth. This makes meaningless the newness of the New Covenant by ignoring progressive revelation and biblical theology. By this, the New Covenant is robbed of its distinctive glory and proper administration to the church today (i.e., the baptism of disciples alone).

Point 2: Paedobaptist Unity and Diversity

According to paedobaptist theology, the unity of the biblical covenants comes from the fact that they are all the outworking of that one eternal Covenant of Redemption between the Father and the Son (some add the Holy Spirit) to save an elect people before the world began. Though terminology differs among covenant theologians, Berkhof is typical in describing this covenant as the "eternal prototype of the historical covenant of grace."[124] His final definition of the Covenant of Redemption is:

> ... the agreement between the Father, giving the Son as Head and Redeemer of the elect, and the Son voluntarily taking the place of those whom the Father had given Him.[125]

---

[124]Berkhof, *Systematic Theology*, 265–70.
[125]*Ibid.*, 271.

According to Berkhof, this unity of the covenants is shown in the historical covenants, which are an outworking of this plan, though variously administered in history (Noahic, Abrahamic, Mosaic, Davidic, and New Covenant). After the Covenant of Works was broken by Adam in the garden, Berkhof defines the historical Covenant of Grace as:

> ... that gracious agreement *between the offended God and the offending but elect sinner* in which God promises salvation though faith in Christ, and the sinner accepts this believingly, promising a life of faith and obedience [emphasis mine].[126]

This Covenant of Grace was first revealed in history in Genesis 3:15 after the Fall and was progressively worked out in succeeding covenants, thus explaining their unity. From the very beginning salvation has always been by grace through faith in God's promises.

Up to this point, Berkhof defines both the Covenant of Redemption and its historical outworking, the Covenant of Grace, as established only with God's elect; this is the unifying link between the historical covenants. Baptist covenantalists would heartily agree with this. However, Berkhof goes on to explain that this does not mean that the nonelect are outside the Covenant of Grace in every sense of the word. He states that "the covenant of grace is represented in Scripture as an organic idea," namely, "believers and their seed."[127]

Berkhof's unifying addition of believers and their seed to the Covenant of Grace fails to distinguish properly between the historical administration of the Covenant of Grace in the Old Testament covenants of promise and the Covenant of Grace itself with God's elect alone, revealed in the New Covenant (2 Timothy 1:8–10). The administration of the Abrahamic Covenant contained an organic element temporarily in place until the seed to whom the promises were made was born. That does not mean, however, that the Abrahamic Covenant with organic inclusion is identical to the Covenant of Grace. This additional unifying organic principle in the covenants diminishes the biblically stated diversity between them by inference, not revelation.

---
[126]*Ibid.*, 277.
[127]*Ibid.*, 276.

Robertson also picks up this unifying organic idea beyond his basic definition of a covenant as a "bond-in-blood sovereignly administered." He explains that the Covenant of Grace with the elect (the true Israel) also includes a unifying corporate idea:

> By entering into the covenant relationship, God not only makes promise concerning the salvation of the individual believer; he also offers promises with respect to the "seed" of the covenant participant. This genealogical dimension of the corporate concept of the covenant occurs repeatedly with respect to the various covenants in Scripture. It is not lacking in the prophetic development of the new covenant. . . . According to Jeremiah 32:39, the Lord promises that he will give Israel one heart and one way that they may fear him forever, "for the good of them, and of their children after them." The promise of the covenant relates to a community of people. It includes not only the participant himself, but also his children . . . the genealogical principle is an integral aspect of biblical corporateness. It is a gracious promise to be claimed by participants in the new covenant.[128]

It is precisely at this point that we differ. On the one hand, one may say the elect are exclusively "believers and their seed" because all the elect either come as believers out of paganism or from the seed of believers. One may even say that the children of believers are more likely to be saved than children who do not hear the gospel, although none would claim from this text an infallible promise that all seed of believers are elect (Deuteronomy 30:6).

On the other hand, there is no biblical evidence that the eternal Covenant of Redemption (*see* 2 Timothy 1:9; Titus 1:1–3) necessarily included believers and their seed in a nonelect sense as the paedobaptist claims—nor is there evidence that the historical Covenant of Grace, as just defined by Berkhof and others in a salvific way, included believers and their seed in a nonelect sense. Rather, it is in the historical administration of that one Covenant of Grace that we see the concept of believer and their seed in the Old Testament covenants of promise.

It is true that God saved His elect from among the seed of Abraham, though not exclusively. It is also true that God was the God of Israel as a theocracy. However, the genealogical element of the historical Old Testament covenants was necessary only to bring

---
[128] Robertson, *Christ of the Covenants*, 289–90.

forth the final physical seed of Abraham to whom the promises were made, Jesus Christ (Galatians 3:16, 19) and His "seed" (Galatians 3:29) who have clothed themselves with Christ through faith alone.

According to the paedobaptists, the historical covenants are unified by a corporate, organic element. Thus the primary basis for the baptism of infants is found in God's promise of covenant blessing to Abraham and to his seed. In other words, the historical outworking of the Covenant of Grace always includes, by definition, the unifying concept of believers and their seed in each and every covenant administration of the one Covenant of Grace, including, by inference, the New Covenant.

Therefore, according to paedobaptist covenantalists, because Abraham is called "the father of us all" (Romans 4:16), and because believers are referred to as the "seed" of Abraham (Galatians 3:29) and "heirs according to the promise," it seems good and necessary from the unity of the covenants to infer that the sign of New Covenant baptism should be extended to the physical children of Abraham's faith "seed" in baptism as circumcision was extended to the physical children of Abraham's physical "seed" in the Old Testament (see Colossians 2:11, 12). From the paedobaptist perspective, this is one of the most compelling pearls on the string of good and necessary inference for infant baptism.

However, the paedobaptist argument for the unity of the covenants is exaggerated beyond what the biblical data will allow. There is indeed a real unity but also a real diversity between the Old Testament covenants of promise and the New Covenant. The paedobaptist position neglects clear revelation that the New Covenant is "not like" the Sinai Covenant and other Old Testament covenants of promise. It ignores the increased individuality of the New Covenant expressed in texts such as Jeremiah 31:27–34. This difference will be explored further in the Baptistic presentation of the covenants to follow.

In summary, there are several points at which paedobaptist covenantal theology fails to be biblical on the issue of the unity and diversity between the covenants:

1. Its dependence upon erroneous inferences from the Old Testament fails to honor its own hermeneutics that the New Testament must be the final interpreter of how the Old is fulfilled in it.
2. Its exaggerated emphasis upon unity and continuity between the covenants obscures the uniqueness and

diversity of the New Covenant administration as a "new" covenant that fulfills the Old Testament "covenants of promise" in a way that is superior to the Old administration.
3. It fails to recognize biblical evidence that the New Covenant is an effectual covenant that guarantees realized blessings in each and every member.

Counterpoint 2: Baptistic Explanations of Unity and Diversity

Covenantal Baptists agree with their paedobaptist brethren that there is essential unity between the covenants. The Old Testament covenants of promise and the New Covenant fulfillment are all administrations of that historical Covenant of Grace (or way of salvation), which is the historical outworking of the eternal Covenant of Redemption.

However, covenantal Baptists believe also that the automatic inclusion of all organic seed of believers in the New Covenant by good and necessary inference does not do justice to the uniqueness and diversity of the New Covenant as revealed in Scripture. It is Scripture itself that has convinced covenantal Baptists that the paedobaptist view of the New Covenant's present administration and fulfillment of the Abrahamic Covenant is in error. Unified with the Old Testament covenants of promise, the New Covenant fulfillment holds a true diversity in its administration. That diversity is revealed (1) by a change in Abrahamic covenantal relations in the New Covenant and (2) by heightened individual covenantal responsibility.

Abrahamic Covenantal Relations Changed in the New Covenant

Although paedobaptists and Baptists alike agree that the New Covenant of Jesus Christ has a unity with and constitutes the fulfillment of the Abrahamic Covenant, covenantal Baptists further believe that the New Testament describes a fulfillment that shifts the emphasis from family relations to individual responsibility and membership. There is a real change in the New Covenant administration of grace.

The watershed question is this: Does the idea of "covenant" necessarily include organic relations, by definition, that should be superimposed upon all covenants, including the New Covenant? Or is the biblical idea of covenant a more restricted idea that requires specific revelation to determine each covenant's administrative form without assuming all elements of previous covenant administrations? Baptists believe the biblical idea of a covenant is more restricted than the paedobaptist view because of exegetical evidence. Baptists also believe that the New Covenant must be defined by revelation without blind conformity to the administrative forms of prior covenants.

At the root of paedobaptist covenantal theology is the view that God has chosen the organic covenantal family as His primary (though not exclusive) vehicle of salvation in history. Therefore, to paedobaptists, the Abrahamic Covenant becomes the model covenant revealing how God works out His Eternal Covenant in redemptive history, including in the New Covenant. Because Christians are the seed of Abraham, paedobaptists conclude that believers become "little Abrahams," inferring that their children are in the Covenant of Grace and the visible church and are entitled to receive the sign of the New Covenant.

However, several difficult questions remain unanswered by paedobaptists. First, if Christians, both Jew and Gentile, are the "seed" of Abraham and therefore "little Abrahams," should we also not claim physical Canaan as our rightful territory today, an "everlasting" possession that was an essential element of Abraham's covenant? We all agree that New Covenant members will inherit the land in the New Heavens and the New Earth, but the issue is whether New Covenant little Abrahams should claim the land today. Second, if circumcision is a forever sign of the Abrahamic Covenant, then should the New Covenant little Abrahams not continue circumcision as well as infant baptism? And, third, should we Christians baptize not only infants but also all males who are brought or born into our house (Genesis 17:27)?

Paedobaptists frequently respond to these objections by contending that it is not legitimate to identify both children and physical land in the New Covenant era in quite the same terms as they were categorized in the Abrahamic Covenant with regard to the physical covenant promises to Abraham. I quite agree with this. However, what about the 318 male servants who were circumcised by virtue of their being in Abraham's household? They were included in the Abrahamic Covenant. How do they fit into the New Covenant application of the Abrahamic Covenant today?

Meredith Kline attempts to address this knotty concept of the application of covenantal household authority in the New Covenant fulfillment of the Abrahamic Covenant in his book *By Oath Consigned*.[129] However, one comes away after reading him confused as to what he believes. Is household servant baptism a legitimate application in the New Covenant administration or is it not? It appears he rejects this idea on the ground that the New Testament is silent on it and that church discipline would be difficult to administer.[130] However, the very same argument from silence could be mounted against infant baptism; and of course, church discipline is always difficult. Kline does seem to allow for the plausibility of household servant baptism in certain mission situations as a matter of temporary cultural expediency under the New Covenant. Ultimately, he seems willing to leave to the individual covenant head the application of the principles of culture, family, and church to a particular situation. The question is not adequately answered.

Along with most covenant theologians, covenantal Baptists believe that the physical elements of the Abrahamic Covenant, including land and household servants, no longer apply to the present New Testament church because Christ's kingdom at this time is "not of this world," and not a theocratic state. We also are in agreement with Robertson that the New Testament church is the antitypical "Israel of God" (Philippians 3:3; Galatians 6:16).[131] There has been a radical change in the New Covenant fulfillment and the New Covenant Israel. In the future, we shall inherit the New Heavens and the New Earth as the ultimate physical blessings of God, including the Old Testament land. However, for now, we live in a New Covenant of spiritual reality as the heart-circumcised children of Abraham through Jesus Christ, Abraham's final organic seed. We do not baptize household servants as Abraham circumcised them,

---

[129]Meredith G. Kline, *By Oath Consigned* (Grand Rapids, MI: William B. Eerdmans Publishing Co., 1975), 94–102.
[130]*Ibid.*, 98.
[131]Robertson, *Israel of God,* 35–51. Robertson ably explains that the only New Covenant members are the regenerate, Jew and Gentile. To these belong the New Heavens and the New Earth, including the Abrahamic land of promise. Any expectations for a physical return to the land by Jewish descendants is retrogression to Old Covenant forms for New Covenant members.

nor do we circumcise infants by necessity, nor do we join political movements to repossess Canaan.

Paedobaptists assume that the Abrahamic Covenant with its organic elements *is* the Covenant of Grace. This is why Berkhof calls the Abrahamic Covenant "essentially identical" with the New Covenant.[132] Baptists respectfully disagree, believing that the Abrahamic Covenant is simply an administration of the Covenant of Grace later replaced by the greater New Covenant administration with its own distinctive stipulations. Even if one were to assume the organic idea in the New Covenant, does the New Testament teach that it is fulfilled in believers and their seed or in Christ and His elect seed alone? It is clearly the latter. Christ is the covenant Head of a new family (Romans 5:12 ff.).

The Baptist position also holds that God has actually revealed in the New Testament a change in the identity of the children of Abraham entitled to the New Covenant sign of baptism. They are the seed of Jesus Christ, who Himself is the final organic seed to whom the Abrahamic promises were made (Galatians 3:19). The New Testament institutes by revelation an individual emphasis in the New Covenant. A personal relationship to Jesus Christ is required for membership, even though it was not required for membership in the Abrahamic administration (*see* Jeremiah 31:27–34). This preserves a proper unity between the biblical covenants, yet sustains a real diversity by revelation, not by an exaggerated inference.

New Covenant Individual Responsibility Proven

When the New Covenant administration is examined by Baptists, they see ample evidence that the New Covenant does not include the organic idea in covenant membership in the same way the Abrahamic Covenant did. Rather, they see a new individualistic element in the New Covenant administration that was not as patent in the Old Testament "covenants of promise" (Ephesians 2:12).

Yet, even here, it is the Old Testament prophets who first and foremost emphasized this future individualistic element (Jeremiah 31:27–34). When speaking first of the return from captiv-

---

[132]Berkhof, *Systematic Theology,* 633.

ity and then of the establishment of the New Covenant, God declared:

> In those days [that is, *of the New Covenant*] they will not say again, "The fathers have eaten sour grapes, and the children's teeth are set on edge." But every one will die for his own iniquity; each man who eats the sour grapes, his teeth will be set on edge. "Behold, days are coming," declares the Lord, "when I will make a new covenant with the house of Israel and with the house of Judah. . . . I will put My law within them . . . for they shall all know Me . . . for I will forgive their iniquity. . . . " (Jeremiah 31:29–31, 33, 34).

The promise was that, in the days of the New Covenant, God would cease bringing generational covenantal curses upon men for the sins of their fathers as He did upon members of Old Testament organic Israel. The link would be changed. Each would die for his own sins, not the sins of his father. According to O. Palmer Robertson, every heart in the New Covenant Israel will be individually changed and directly responsible to God (Galatians 6:15–16):

> The treasured phrase that has distinguished the people of God from all others is now applied to the combination of Jews and Gentiles who are justified by faith in Jesus Christ. As John Calvin says, "In a word, he gives the appellation of *the Israel of God* to those whom he formally denominated the children of Abraham by faith (Gal. 3:29), and thus includes all believers, whether Jews of Gentiles, who were united into one church." This new body of people constitutes "the Israel of God."[133]

In other words, although the Israel of God in the Old Testament included all naturally born children under the blessings and curses, the New Covenant "Israel of God" only includes regenerate individuals in the covenant, not the organic seed. There is a heightened individualism in the New Covenant.

Matthew Henry affirms the change that God brought in the New Covenant arrangement:

---

[133]Robertson, *Israel of God,* 44–45. I will say again, it is a mystery to me why Dr. Robertson did not address the issue of covenant children in the New Israel, because such an idea is essential to the argument for infant baptism.

> That they shall be reckoned with no further for the sins of their fathers (v. 29, 30): *They shall say no more* (they shall have no more occasion to say) that *God visits the iniquity of the parents upon the children,* which God had done in the captivity, for the sins of their ancestors came into the account against them, particularly those of Manasseh: this they complained of as a hardship. Other scriptures justify God in this method of proceeding, and our Saviour tells the wicked Jews in his days that they should smart for their fathers' sins, because they persisted in them, Matt. xxiii. 35, 36. But it is here promised that this severe dispensation with them should be brought to an end, that God would proceed no farther in his controversy with them for their fathers' sins, but remember for them his covenant with their fathers and do them good according to that covenant: *They shall no more* complain, as they have done, that *the fathers have eaten sour grapes and the children's teeth are set on edge* (which speaks something of an absurdity, and is an invidious reflection upon God's proceedings), but *every one shall die for his own iniquity* still; *though God will cease to punish them in their national capacity, yet he will reckon with particular persons that provoke him* [emphasis mine].[134]

Matthew Henry recognized that Jeremiah 31 contains a promise for New Covenant days when God deals with men as individuals rather than through a national covenant or in an organic sense. When he commented on the same proverb in Ezekiel 18:1–9, he criticized Israel's continued use of this proverb during the Babylonian captivity as their complaint against God's justice. God takes Israel to task for disobeying His command in Jeremiah 31:27–30 not to use this proverb anymore.[135] Some have mistakenly taken Israel's derogatory use of this proverb against God in the Ezekiel passage to explain away God's increased individuality in the Jeremiah passage. However, in both places, Henry explains that it is a just proverb because God specifically punishes Israel for Manasseh's sins (2 Kings 21:11–15; 23:26–27). However, in the New Covenant days, God will deal with His people primarily as individuals, not primarily as a national, organic people.

This heightened individualistic element is revealed also in the doctrine of the remnant (Jeremiah 6:9; 23:1–6, 31:7–8, 32:37;

---

[134]Matthew Henry, *Matthew Henry's Commentary on the Whole Bible,* vol. 4, *Isaiah to Malachi* (McLean, VA: Macdonald Publishing Company, 1712), 605–606.
[135]*Ibid.,* 852.

Isaiah 11:1–12; Malachi 2:15). In New Covenant days, there will be a new heart in every New Covenant member:

> For I will take you from the nations, gather you from all the lands, and bring you into your own land. Then I will sprinkle clean water on you, and you will be clean; I will cleanse you from all your filthiness and from all your idols. Moreover, I will give you a new heart and put a new spirit within you; and I will remove the heart of stone from your flesh and give you a heart of flesh. And I will put My Spirit within you and cause you to walk in My statutes, and you will be careful to observe My ordinances (Ezekiel 36:24–27).

The Old Testament remnant of Israel in the New Covenant day is the regenerate Israel of God.

Herman Ridderbos, a paedobaptist, affirms this view and argues that Jesus' kingdom teachings are nothing more than New Covenant content. According to him, Jesus used the kingdom motif because it was less offensive to his hearers than a "new" covenant. Therefore, he says, the members of the kingdom are the same as the members of the New Covenant: "Unless one is born of water and the Spirit, he cannot enter the kingdom of God" (John 3:5). Like Robertson, Ridderbos identifies repentant and regenerate individuals as those who make up the New Covenant Israel and kingdom of God:

> The term "the children of the kingdom" indicating Israel "according to the flesh" (Matt. 8:12), is now used in the new sense of the "good seed" (Matt. 13:38). *The special relation to God that was first applied to the totality of Israel, is now restricted (and extended) to those who respond to the preaching of the kingdom with faith and repentance and have been elected by God to this end. This change, noticeable in the gospel, finds its basis already in the Old Testament (Jer. 31).* . . . In the light of the whole gospel they are the people who have accepted the preaching of the gospel in faith and conversion. It is they, and no one else, who receive the salvation of the kingdom. They are "Israel," "God's people," and it is to them that all the promises of the covenant apply . . . the circle in which it is granted and *where God's people are found, is no longer that of the empirical Israel, but it is that of those who are given remission of sins in Christ's death, and whose hearts have been renewed by the Holy Spirit* [emphasis mine].[136]

---

[136]Ridderbos, *Coming of the Kingdom,* 200, 202. *See* Ridderbos' excellent discussion of the New Covenant, 192–202.

If Robertson and Ridderbos are correct, and covenantal Baptists believe that they are, then not only are all New Covenant members individually regenerate, but Jesus' teachings about baptism constitutes New Covenant instruction; that is, the baptism of disciples alone (John 4:1–2; Matthew 28:19–20). Based on this reasoning, John Murray's attempt to separate Jesus' baptism from New Covenant baptism cannot stand. Jesus' teachings about credobaptism are instituted New Covenant content.

As we have seen, there is a real unity and a real diversity between the biblical covenants. Diversity is seen in God's changed dealings with Israel in New Covenant days, from unregenerate covenantal families in the covenants of promise to heart-changed covenantal individuals. Every individual in the New Covenant Israel will be regenerate, but this diversity is missed by covenantal paedobaptists. A refusal to let God's revelation concerning the New Covenant, even in Old Testament texts, determine its form, content, and membership constitutes a hermeneutical error that elevates the misuse of good and necessary inference over biblical revelation. This error is refuted by the priority of New Testament revelation concerning the individuality of the New Covenant membership and the regenerate identity of the New Covenant Israel as supported even by Old Testament prophecy. Surely, we must depend upon revelation over possibly erroneous inference on such an important matter.

SUMMARY

This chapter has laid the foundation for the next chapter, an explanation of how the New Covenant has been fulfilled in the New Testament and how this refutes infant baptism, thus establishing credobaptism, the baptism of disciples alone. The Baptist model of defining a covenant, determining its content and explaining the unity and diversity between the covenants of Scripture, does greater justice to actual texts concerning the covenants than does the model of supposed "good and necessary inference" of the paedobaptist. The Baptist model of covenant theology preserves the uniqueness of the New Covenant administration while also preserving its full unity with the covenants of promise that preceded its historical establishment. This is why a Baptistic covenant theology alone can identify the proper recipients of New Covenant baptism as disciples alone. This, of course, corresponds exactly to the New Testament record (Acts 2:41).

The next chapter defines the New Covenant in more detail, amplifying the point that its very definition and presentation in Scripture refutes infant baptism in favor of the baptism of disciples alone.

Chapter 4

The Covenant Theology of the Bible (Part II): New Covenant Fulfillment and Infant Baptism

It is my contention that the Scriptures that describe, define, and explain the New Covenant actually eliminate the automatic, organic inclusion of believers' children in the New Covenant as the basis for their infant baptism. Although the Scriptures contain promises concerning the future salvation of New Covenant believers' children (Deuteronomy 30:6), that is not the same as including them in the New Covenant by organic connection.

The following discussion clarifies the differences between Baptist and paedobaptist understandings of the content of the New Covenant as it relates to the practice of infant baptism versus the baptism of disciples alone.

THE NEW COVENANT DEFINED AND APPLIED TO INFANT BAPTISM

The New Covenant Defined

What is the New Covenant? What blessings are found in the New Covenant? Who participates in the New Covenant? What does the New Covenant say about infant baptism?

All these questions must be answered to discern whether infant baptism is a biblical practice in these days of the New Covenant. The following is a covenantal Baptist definition of the New Covenant. It is a prophecy, a divine covenant, and a "new" covenantal administration.

A Prophecy

The New Covenant is a prophecy fulfilled in the New Testament. According to Matthew 26:28 (and its parallel Luke 22:20), our Lord Jesus Christ established the New Covenant by the mediating sacrifice of His life and death. This is the first place where the term *New Covenant* is used in the New Testament. This simply means that our Lord came to establish the covenant prophesied in Jeremiah 31:31–34, which is the longest Old Testament passage quoted in the New Testament (Hebrews 8:8–12; 10:16–17) and the only Old Testament passage to use the term *New Covenant* by name. Jeremiah 31:31–34 states:

> "Behold, days are coming," declares the LORD, "when I will make a new covenant with the house of Israel and with the house of Judah, not like the covenant which I made with their fathers in the day I took them by the hand to bring them out of the land of Egypt, My covenant which they broke, although I was a husband to them," declares the LORD. "But this is the covenant which I will make with the house of Israel after those days," declares the LORD, "I will put My law within them, and on their heart I will write it; and I will be their God, and they shall be My people. And they shall not teach again, each man his neighbor and each man his brother, saying, 'Know the LORD,' for they shall all know Me, from the least of them to the greatest of them," declares the LORD, "for I will forgive their iniquity, and their sin I will remember no more."

Following the hermeneutical principles just established, the New Covenant is a solemn bond, promise, or oath of God that must be defined by the revelation concerning its content. Furthermore, the New Testament must have final authority when interpreting the fulfillment of the Old Testament prophecies concerning the New Covenant.

According to 2 Timothy 1:9–10, the New Covenant of our Lord Jesus Christ is the final and purest earthly fulfillment of the eternal plan and purpose of God's grace. Theologically, the historical New Covenant *is* the fulfillment of the eternal Covenant of Redemption:

> . . . who has saved us, and called us with a holy calling, not according to our works, but according to His own purpose and grace which was granted us in Christ Jesus *from all eternity, but has now*

been revealed by the appearing of our Savior Christ Jesus [emphasis mine].

Further, the New Covenant is the prophetic fulfillment of the historical Old Testament "covenants of promise." It fulfills the promise of Genesis 3:15 to bring forth a seed of the woman who would destroy the seed of the serpent. It fulfills the promises to Abraham and David that a seed to come would establish a New Covenant as a new covenant head (Galatians 3:19). It fulfills the promises to Abraham that a seed would come, in which all included in it would have the faith of Abraham their father, whether Jew or Gentile (Romans 4:16; Galatians 3:7, 9, 14, 26, 29). It is a fulfillment of the Sinai Covenant, which was added temporarily to the Abrahamic Covenant "because of transgressions *until* the seed should come to whom the promise has been made" (Galatians 3:19). It is established by the headship of the Mediator who took on the conditions of the failed Covenant of Works and provided the atoning sacrifice needed to establish His New Covenant with His prophesied seed (Romans 5:12–19). "For you shall call His name Jesus, for it is He who will save His people from their sins" (Matthew 1:21).

Just as Adam represented the whole human race in his covenant (Hosea 6:7; Romans 5:12), just as Abraham represented his posterity in the covenant God made with him, just as the high priest represented all of Israel at the mercy seat under the Mosaic Covenant, so our Lord Jesus represents all His people for whom He died in the establishment of His New Covenant with them.[137] Christ loved the church and gave Himself up for her. He laid down His life for the sheep. He is an effectual Mediator for all His covenant people (Hebrews 9:15). For this reason, no one can be *in* the Covenant of Works under Adam and *in* the New Covenant of Jesus Christ at the same time (Romans 5:12–19). By contrast, a person in the Old Testament could have been in the Covenant of Works and in the Abrahamic Covenant at the same time. However, to say that children of believers are automatically in the New Covenant of Jesus Christ is to declare them released from the Covenant of Works, an impossibility unless they are truly *in* the New Covenant.

---

[137]Berkhof, *Systematic Theology,* 268.

In summary, the New Covenant is a prophecy fulfilled and instituted by our Lord Jesus Christ at His coming to raise up a new people of God.[138] It is a better covenant, replacing the previous historical covenants of promise. It is the fulfillment of all that was promised in the Old Testament covenants of promise.

A Divine Covenant

Further, the New Covenant is a divine covenant sovereignly instituted by God. It is a unilateral covenant that contains no conditions required by man to ratify or to break it, nor are there curses upon those in the covenant who refuse to keep any conditions. Rather, the Lord Jesus Christ is the Head of the New Covenant, who fulfilled the conditions of obedience in the Covenant of Works by His righteous life and endured the curse of that Covenant of Works by His atoning death on behalf of all members of the New Covenant. This is so that God the Father may be just and the justifier of all who come to Christ in order to enter that covenant (Romans 3:26).[139] Once in the New Covenant, one is no longer subject to the Covenant of Works (Romans 5:12–19).

According to Berkhof, the conditions of repentance and faith required of those who enter the New Covenant are in fact sup-

---

[138]Carl B. Hoch, Jr., *All Things New* (Grand Rapids, MI: Baker Book House, 1995), 285. The issue of who is Israel and Judah in the Jeremiah 31:31–34 passage, quoted as fulfilled in Hebrews 8:8–12, has been adequately answered in numerous books and articles, including the author's dissertation. Older dispensationalists reserved the New Covenant for the Jews alone. However, most modern interpreters recognize that Israel and Judah were types of the New Testament church. The New Covenant was established with the New Testament people of God, the true Jews (Romans 2:29), the true circumcision (Philippians 3:3), and the true Israel of God (Galatians 6:16). Certain progressive dispensationalists, like Carl B. Hoch, Jr., admit that Gentiles are "children of Abraham" and "the circumcision" along with Jewish believers now, but refuse to identify the church as the typologically fulfilled new Israel of Jeremiah 31:31–34. Hoch reasons, "The reason seed of Abraham is used of Gentiles, then, is not to teach that Gentiles become spiritual Israelites, but that believing Gentiles by exercising the same kind of faith Abraham exercised are blessed *with* Abraham" (285). However, contra Hoch, to be similarly blessed *with* Abraham is not the same as to be designated the true "seed of Abraham," a sufficient title to qualify any believing Jew and Gentile as members of the new Israel (Galatians 3:28–29; 6:16–17).

[139]Berkhof, *Systematic Theology,* 280.

plied by God the Father and God the Son by the effectual work of the Holy Spirit in the hearts of those predestined by God to be members of the New Covenant.[140] Thus, the question of whether the New Covenant is conditional or unconditional is swallowed up in the grace of God, Who establishes the New Covenant and guarantees its success through the work of an effectual Mediator, a particular redemption for all in the covenant by His substitutionary sacrifice, and an effectual calling of all members of that covenant.

Perhaps a better way to view the New Covenant is not in terms of the conditional/unconditional issue but in terms of whether it is breakable or unbreakable. The Sinai Covenant was breakable by covenant members because of their weakness (not God's), and because that covenant contained a blessing-cursing formula within it. This blessing and cursing formula for the physical nation of Israel included the possibility of failure of the people to circumcise their hearts (Deuteronomy 10:16). However, the New Covenant is not like the Sinai Covenant in this respect. It is unbreakable simply because God supplies the circumcised heart in every member by which they will keep it (Deuteronomy 30:6; Ezekiel 36:26; Jeremiah 32:40; Joel 2:28).[141] The New Covenant is a divine unilateral covenant.

Further, as the Ten Commandments written upon stone tablets were called the Sinai Covenant itself (Deuteronomy 4:13), so the writing of the law upon the heart is called the New Covenant itself:

> *"For this is the covenant* I will make with the house of Israel after those days," says the Lord, *"I will put my laws into their minds and write them on their hearts; and I will be their God, and they shall be My people"* [Hebrews 8:10; emphasis mine].

It is this sovereign writing of the law upon the heart in every elect covenant member that is the essence and "newness" of the New Covenant. By definition, every heart in the New Covenant is circumcised by God (Jeremiah 32:40; Romans 2:29; Philippians 3:3; Colossians 2:11–12). That is why repentance and faith are

---

[140]*Ibid.*, 280–81.
[141]Ridderbos, *Coming of the Kingdom,* 200–202. Ridderbos agrees that the New Covenant is unbreakable simply because it is guaranteed effectual by God.

required as evidence of New Covenant membership and heart circumcision before every baptism (Acts 2:38–41).

The New Covenant is a divine covenant, so unilateral, so effectual in its form, that there is no possibility of failure in any member. Difficult texts dealing with apostasy, which only appears to be covenant breaking, will be dealt with later in this chapter.

A "New" Covenant

Also, the New Covenant is a "new" covenant (Greek *kainae*). It is new because it is not like the Old Covenant at Sinai. Those who try to establish an exaggerated unity and continuity between the covenants as a basis for infant baptism do not emphasize this stated newness enough.

It is generally agreed that the Sinai Covenant was a conditional covenant requiring obedience from the people in order for them to receive blessings in the land to which they were going (Deuteronomy 5:33).[142] It is also clear that an obedient heart in each and every member was not a necessary part of establishing that covenant arrangement and membership. To define the New Covenant as a conditional arrangement of blessings and cursings for obedience or disobedience imposes a Sinaitic arrangement upon the New Covenant. Likewise, to ignore the giving of a new heart to each and every member causes the New to remain like the Old. Both errors ignore the New Covenant's self-definition as new in contrast to the Sinai Covenant. These errors impose Old Testament conditional covenant forms, which were breakable, upon the New Covenant by erroneous inference rather than by revelation. To repeat John Owen, " . . . there is no precept or promise of God except that which may be so called."[143]

Robert Booth, a paedobaptist, shows how far paedobaptists are driven to ignore simple statements of Scripture regarding the newness of the New Covenant in order to defend an exaggerated continuity, unity, and conditionality:

> The Hebrew word for "new," *hadash,* used in reference to the new covenant in Jeremiah 31:31, is not the word meaning "brand

---

[142]Bolton, *True Bounds,* 99. *See* Bolton for a discussion of this view by a classic covenantalist.
[143]Ferguson, *John Owen,* 21.

new"; rather, it means "renewed" or "fresh." The new covenant, like previous covenantal administrations, added to and expanded the redemptive revelation of God. *It renewed the previous covenants, rather than replacing them* [emphasis mine].[144]

This is simply wrong. For Booth to say that the Hebrew word *hadash* does not mean *brand new,* but only *renewed* or *fresh,* is inaccurate and extremely misleading to the untrained reader. O. Palmer Robertson, a paedobaptist and Hebrew scholar, disagrees with Booth. He says, "A 'new' covenant shall *replace* [emphasis mine] all of God's previous covenantal dealings."[145] The fact is that *hadash* is used in the Old Testament of a brand-new king (Exodus 1:8), house (Deuteronomy 22:8), wife (Deuteronomy 24:5), cart (1 Samuel 6:7), song (Psalm 33:3), heavens (Isaiah 66:22), earth (Isaiah 66:22), and heart (Ezekiel 36:26), as well as a brand-new covenant (Jeremiah 31:31–34). Also, the New Testament word for "new," *kainae,* is used similarly of a brand-new wineskin (Matthew 9:17), tomb (Matthew 27:60), commandment (John 13:34), doctrine (Acts 17:19), creature (2 Corinthians 5:17), and a new covenant (Hebrews 8:8). Such etymological gymnastics by Booth cannot overrule clear biblical usage.

Further, it is a misrepresentation of Scripture, and even classic paedobaptist covenantalism, to call the New Covenant a "renewal" of the previous covenants, especially when the New Covenant passages themselves reject the idea of a continuance of the broken Sinai Covenant. The New Covenant is more than a renewal or a refreshing of previous covenants; it is a new fulfillment and, as Robertson agrees, a replacement. There is something really "new" about the New Covenant. Even paedobaptists such as Samuel Bolton and John Brown agree that the Sinai Covenant is no longer a covenant in force or renewed.[146]

As an aside, Booth's reasoning leaves the door open to theonomy and its views that the Mosaic case laws apply in the New

---

[144]Booth, *Children of Promise,* 51.
[145]Robertson, *Christ of the Covenants,* 281.
[146]Bolton, *True Bounds,* 99; and John Brown, *An Exposition of the Epistle of Paul the Apostle to the Galatians* (1853; reprint, Minneapolis: James Family Christian Publishers, 1979), 153, 175. Both of these resources recognize the temporary nature of the Sinai Covenant "until" the coming of Christ and His New Covenant (Galatians 3:16–19).

Covenant era, not only to the church but also to the civil magistrate. Calvin rightly rejected what is today called theonomy.[147]

In summary, one of the essential elements of the New Covenant is that it is an effectual and successful covenant in each and every one of its members. This is one of the major differences between the New Covenant and the previous covenants of promise. It really is a *new* covenant.

The New Covenant Blessings "Realized"

According to Jeremiah 31:31–34, there are three major blessings or elements of the New Covenant with the new Israel and Judah:

1. God will put His laws into their minds and write them upon their hearts.
2. They will all know the Lord from the least to the greatest of them.
3. Their sins and their lawless deeds He will remember no more.

If one takes the mention of Israel and Judah with strict literalism from Old Testament priority over New Testament revelation, then one is driven to believe that the New Covenant is meant only for the Jewish nation in the New Testament. This is exactly the position of the older dispensationalists.[148] They concede to Gentiles the forgiveness of sins from the New Covenant but rarely mention, if at all, the law written on the heart for them. This has led to the carnal Christian doctrine and the non-Lordship salvation of classic dispensationalists. The New Testament church is regarded as a parenthesis in God's plan and His Law written upon the heart is just not applicable to New Testament believers.

---

[147]Calvin, *Institutes,* 4:20:14–16 (1502–5). Booth's redefinition of a covenant is matched by his redefinition of *new.* Both redefinitions serve theonomic views held by Booth. A major principle of theology is that systematic theology must be based upon exegetical and biblical theology, a principle violated by Booth's position at the very beginning.

[148]John Darby, *Synopsis of the Books of the Bible,* vol. 5, *Colossians-Revelation* (New York: Loizeaux Brothers, n.d.), 286; and *The Scofield Reference Bible,* ed. C.I. Scofield (New York: Oxford University Press, 1917), 1297–98.

However, more covenantal commentators agree that the church universal of Jew and Gentile elect is the typological fulfillment of Israel and Judah in this passage (Hebrews 8:8–12). Bernard Ramm actually uses Hebrews 8:8–12 and 10:16–17, the New Covenant passages, to illustrate proper typological interpretation of the prophetic Scriptures, "Interpret prophecy literally unless the implicit or explicit teaching of the New Testament suggests typological interpretation." Following this rule, he affirms that the church of Jewish and Gentile believers is the typological Israel and Judah of the New Covenant passages.[149]

Progressive dispensationalists, such as Blaising and Bock, agree that Jew and Gentile believers are included in the New Covenant, though they hesitate to call the church "the new Israel." They maintain a distinction between Gentile Christians and Jewish Christians in the future millenium.[150] The main difference between progressive dispensationalists and covenantal Baptists is that the covenantal Baptist believes New Covenant typology in the New Covenant passages themselves describes "realized blessings" for every New Covenant member, Jew and Gentile, as the antitype of Israel and Judah; it does not describe just "potential blessings" for the church in general.

Also in contrast to covenantal Baptists, paedobaptists hold to a view that some people, namely, unregenerate covenant children, may be members of the New Covenant yet not actually have an effectual mediator nor have the reality of the blessings of the covenant. Therefore, instead of describing the blessings of the New Covenant as effectual and realized in each and every member, as do the prophecies, they often describe them as being potential blessings in salvation history, or as awaiting an eschatological fulfillment in each and every member. Booth explains:

> First, the new covenant *brings with it,* through the work of the Holy Spirit, and as a fulfilled promise of the Abrahamic covenant (Gal. 3:14), the enabling power of obedience (Jer. 31:33). . . . Second, the new Covenant *promises an extension of* the knowledge of the Lord to all nations (Heb. 8:11; Jer. 31:34; Matt. 28:19). All the world

---

[149]Ramm, *Protestant Biblical Interpretation,* 261–267.
[150]Craig A. Blaising and Darrell L. Bock, *Progressive Dispensationalism* (Wheaton, IL: Victor Books, 1993), 202.

is to be taught about God's gracious covenant. More people are to know more about the Lord. Third, the new covenant *brings with it* the promise of redemption accomplished. . . . [emphasis mine].[151]

In this statement Booth describes the New Covenant institution as simply the beginning, potential, and availability of New Covenant blessings in salvation history, rather than explaining that every covenant member "realizes" the law written upon the heart, knows the Lord, and possesses the forgiveness of sins. According to Booth, the New Covenant "brings with it" the promise of redemption. This attempt to objectify the blessings of the New Covenant as inaugurated in salvation history enables the paedobaptist to define a New Covenant in broad terms so that one may enter into it externally through infant baptism yet not possess internally the blessings that are described as the very essence of New Covenant membership.

Baptist covenantalists understand the New Covenant to be, *in its essence,* the possession of these blessings by every covenant member. Those professors in the visible church who prove to be apostate or false converts perhaps made an insincere covenant with God, but they were never a part of the New Covenant any more than they were ever a part of the universal church.

Again, the Jeremiah 31:31–34 prophecy says that God *actually* will write His law upon the minds and hearts of Israel and Judah, the recipients of the New Covenant, which is the church universal, the antitypical Israel of God (Romans 2:29; Philippians 3:3; Galatians 6:16). He *actually* will remember their sins no more—and all *actually* will know the Lord by experience so that there will be no need to teach each man his neighbor and brother to know the Lord. They will all know Him by virtue of being in the New Covenant established with antitypical Israel and Judah. As John Owen says:

> For *all those with whom this covenant is made shall as really have* the law of God written in their hearts, and their sins pardoned, according unto the promise of it, as the people of old were brought into the land of Canaan by virtue of the covenant made with Abra-

---

[151]Booth, *Children of Promise,* 64.

ham. These are the true Israel and Judah, prevailing with God, and confessing unto his name [emphasis mine].[152]

The attempt of paedobaptists to make the New Covenant blessings simply the beginning of a new covenant arrangement, with better blessings to follow, does violence to the text of Scripture which defines the New Covenant as *realized blessings* in the heart of each New Covenant member, "from the least to the greatest of them."

The New Covenant Members

Who then is a member of the present New Covenant administration? New Covenant members are those disciples of Jesus Christ who have the law written on their heart by the Holy Spirit of God, who know God experientially by faith, and who possess in reality the forgiveness of sins (Hebrews 8:8–12). These are the circumcised of heart, the true Jew, the faith seed of Abraham, the seed of Christ, the people for whom He died, the sheep whom He will keep from falling and bring safely to the eternal kingdom. They individually possess all New Covenant blessings, have Christ as an effectual Mediator, and are the true fulfilled seed of Abraham, the new Israel of God (Galatians 6:16). These alone are entitled to the New Covenant sign of baptism, evidenced by their confession of Christ as Lord.

New Covenant Individual Blessings

As introduced briefly in the previous chapter, the New Covenant passage in Jeremiah 31:27–34 defines a heightened individual membership in the covenant relationship, with each member experiencing its blessings:

> But this is the covenant which I will make with the house of Israel after those days," declares the LORD, "I will put My law within them, and on their heart I will write it; and I will be their

---

[152]Owen, *Hebrews,* 6:118.

God, and they shall be My people. And they shall not teach again, each man his neighbor and each man his brother, saying 'Know the LORD,' for they shall all know Me, from the least of them to the greatest of them," declares the LORD, "for I will forgive their iniquity, and their sin I will remember no more."

This text teaches that New Covenant members are only those individuals who have the law of God written upon the mind and heart, have the forgiveness of sins, and know God. All members, "from the least to the greatest," experience all of the blessings of the covenant. In the New Covenant, no longer is there a tier of those circumcised in the flesh but not of the heart (Deuteronomy 10:16; Jeremiah 4:4; Romans 2:29; Philippians 3:3). No longer are there some who know God and some who do not. No longer are there some who know the law of God written on tablets of stone but do not have those laws written upon the heart. The New Covenant is a covenant wherein every individual participant experiences all of its blessings simply because that is the distinctive nature of this new covenant.

As a result, the New Covenant salvation is a Lordship salvation that always bears the fruit of its covenantal confession. Not to bear covenantal fruit is to put into question one's own salvation and professed New Covenant membership (Hebrews 6:4–6; 10:26–31), simply because to be a New Covenant member is, by definition, to possess the fruit of all three covenantal blessings. All three New Covenant blessings are quoted in the New Testament as fulfilled in Jesus Christ's salvation for every individual New Covenant member.

The Law Written on the Heart

Jeremiah 31:31–34 and Ezekiel 36:26–27 describe the work of the Holy Spirit in the New Covenant as being the writing of God's law upon the heart (Hebrews 8:8–12; 10:16), something the Israelites could not do for themselves. This is the essence of regeneration by the Spirit, the creation of a new heart that delights after God and His law (Romans 7:14–8:4).

In context, the only law that God wrote in the Old Testament by His own hand was the Ten Commandments. Therefore, it is my belief that the law written on the heart in the New Covenant is the very same moral law that is *summarized* in the Ten Commandments and was first written on Adam's heart as the law of nature. This is why even ignorant Gentiles show the remaining evidence of the "work of the law" (Romans 2:14–15) in their hearts, their conscience bearing them witness. Which law? That natural moral law that was later revealed more clearly in the Sinai Covenant as the Ten Commandments written by God's own finger. It is only fitting that God should write these laws now on human hearts instead of tablets of stone. These Ten Commandments are summarized by Christ as the two great commandments to love God and man (Matthew 22:37–39), although of course He taught all of them.

Christ said: "If you love me, you will keep My commandments" (John 14:15). He taught all Ten Commandments, including the Sabbath (Matthew 12), and commanded His disciples to teach other disciples whatever He commanded them (Matthew 28:18–20).

Paul said, "Do we then nullify the Law through faith? May it never be! Rather we establish the Law" (Romans 3:31) " . . . for I delight after the law of God in the inner man" (7:22) " . . . Love does no wrong to a neighbor; love therefore is the fulfillment of the law" (13:10). If one asks to which law Paul is referring in these texts, it is not the Sinai Covenant as a whole, but rather the Ten Commandments as God's law for the Christian (Romans 2:20–23; 6:17; 7:7, 12, 22, 25; 13:8–10).

All agree that the Christian lives by faith, but he lives by faith so that he may have the power to keep God's law (John 14:15; Romans 3:31). The failure to live a faith-life of obedience to God's law as a professing Christian reveals an unregenerate heart: "I never knew you; depart from Me, you who practice lawlessness" (Matthew 7:23; cf. Galatians 5:19).

We cannot explore all the issues surrounding the doctrines concerning the Law and the Gospel in this book. However, suffice it to say that every New Covenant member has a love for Christ and endeavors to keep His commandments. Lordship salvation is not just evidenced by a profession of faith alone in Christ alone, but it also is revealed in a new heart that "delights after the law of God in the inner man" (Romans 7:22) and loves Christ, seeking to keep His commandments (John 14:15). Faith alone in Christ alone saves, but faith without works is dead faith (James 2:26).

The Personal Knowledge of God

Every New Covenant member knows God by faith in Christ. Jesus said, "no one knows the Father, except the Son, and anyone to whom the Son wills to reveal Him" (Matthew 11:27). "And this is eternal life, that they might know Thee, the only true God, and Jesus Christ whom Thou hast sent" (John 17:3). In these passages, the personal knowledge of God is what is meant by eternal life. It is the fulfillment of all the hopes of the covenants of promise that "I will be your God, and you shall be My people." Everyone in the New Covenant knows God and has eternal life in Him.

Possibly referring to Jeremiah 31:34, Jesus said, "It is written in the prophets, 'And they shall all be taught of God.' Every one who has heard and learned from the Father, comes to Me" (John 6:45). There will be no need for each man to teach his neighbor to know the Lord, because all will know God in the New Covenant, having been taught by Him. Jesus said, "I know My own; and *My own know Me*" [John 10:14; emphasis mine].

Some have opposed this heightened individualism in the New Covenant by proposing that Jeremiah 31:31–34 is an eschatological reference describing the lack of a need to teach one's neighbor in the Church triumphant and glorified. "Do we not need to teach each other in the New Covenant," they ask? Of course we do! But in addressing Israel, God is referring to neighbors and brothers in the New Covenant Israel! There is no need to evangelize the participants in the New Covenant Israel because they all individually know the Lord! Certainly members of the New Covenant teach each other to observe all that Christ commanded us (Matthew 28:18–20), but there is no need to teach them to know the Lord because they already know Him, having been individually taught by God Himself (John 6:44, 45; 1 John 2:27; 1 Thessalonians 4:9).

Through Jesus Christ, the Mediator of the New Covenant, every individual member knows the Lord.

The Forgiveness of Sins

Finally, every individual New Covenant member shall have the forgiveness of sins, received in the realm of time through repentance and faith in Jesus Christ. The author of Hebrews, perhaps Paul, quotes Jeremiah 31:33–34 in Hebrews 10:16–17 to show that every New Covenant member actually receives the forgiveness of sins. "This," together with the law written on the heart and knowing God personally, "*is* the [New] covenant that I will make with them" (Hebrews 10:16). The dependence upon God's promise of forgiveness in the New Covenant is the very basis for the believer's bold approach to God (Hebrews 10:11–22). Those who depend upon Christ's once for all sacrifice, which established the New Covenant (Hebrews 10:10, 12, 14), can be sure that their sins are forgiven. Every New Covenant member possesses the forgiveness of sins.

For this reason, every individual, from the least to the greatest, who is in the New Covenant and the kingdom of God, is greater than John the Baptist, who was regenerated in the womb (Matthew 11:11). Therefore, we cannot concede that a believer's child is conclusively *in* the New Covenant, thereby being greater than John the Baptist, until that child shows individual evidence of regeneration and New Covenant membership by repentance and faith. While recognizing that our Sovereign God may regenerate children of believers in the womb, they should not be considered *in* the New Covenant until they show the evidence of regeneration by repentance and faith. This is, in fact, the required New Testament evidence for baptism to be administered to any individual. Christian baptism is a credobaptism; a baptism for disciples alone (Acts 2:38–41).

New Covenant Sacrifice for Members Only

Another problem with the paedobaptist position that all physical infants of believers are in the New Covenant is that it does violation to the doctrine of particular redemption. Every New Covenant member has Jesus Christ as his effectual Mediator (Matthew 1:21). As Ridderbos says:

> God's people are those for whom Christ sheds his blood of the covenant. They share in the remission of sins brought about by him and in the unbreakable communion with God in the new covenant that he has made possible.[153]

To call unregenerate infants "God's people" and members of the New Covenant for "whom Christ sheds his blood of the

---

[153] Ridderbos, *Coming of the Kingdom,* 202.

covenant" violates particular redemption simply because no one can be in the New Covenant without the effectual mediatorial sacrifice that establishes the covenant with every member.

Hebrews 9 reminds us that God's New Covenant requires mediation through blood:

> And for this reason He is the mediator of a new covenant, in order that since a death has taken place for the redemption of the transgressions that were committed under the first covenant, *those who have been called* may receive the promise of an eternal inheritance [Hebrews 9:15; emphasis mine].

The Passover Lamb brought deliverance for all Israel in the Sinai Covenant because all ate of it. The Annual Atonement (Leviticus 16) was offered on behalf of the whole assembly, all Israel in the Sinai Covenant. Of course, these sacrifices could not cleanse the conscience, but their design was for the particular covenant people of God in the Old Testament. In the same manner, the Reformed faith believes that our Lord's New Covenant sacrifice was only for the true people of God: "Christ loved the church and gave Himself up for her (Ephesians 5:25)." He is the effectual covenant Head of "those who have been [effectually] called," justified and glorified (Romans 8:29–30).

If Christ's effectual sacrifice is offered up only for His people as the "blood of the [New] Covenant" (Luke 22:20; Mark 14:24), then how can the unregenerate children of believers be said to be in the New Covenant without an effectual Mediator? They cannot. Neither can they be in the Covenant of Works and in the New Covenant at the same time: "For sin shall not be master over you, for you are not under law, but under grace" (Romans 6:14). Everyone is either in the Covenant of Works or in the Covenant of Grace, but never in both or neither—nor can infants be removed from the Covenant of Works and engrafted into the New Covenant, and then returned to the Covenant of Works later: "There is therefore now no condemnation for those who are in Christ Jesus" (Romans 8:1). Indeed, Hebrews 9:15 defines Jesus as an *effectual* Mediator of the New Covenant to ensure that "all those who have been called may receive the promise of the eternal inheritance."

Can one be said to be in the New Covenant without an effectual Mediator? Can one be under the Covenant of Works and the Covenant of Grace at the same time? I think not, especially when one considers the clear New Testament teaching that the visible church consists of professing disciples (Acts 2:38–41). Though all would agree that false professors were charitably addressed as members of the universal church for which Christ's effectual blood was shed, yet they were so addressed on the basis of their profession as members of the church visible, not their parent's faith (Hebrews 3:1). Even then, they were to be put out of the visible church if their profession proved spurious by their life, demonstrating they were not members of "the church of the firstborn who are enrolled in heaven" (Hebrews 12:23).

Therefore, there is no clear basis for saying infants of believers are in the church, universal or visible, unless we are also willing to say that they are in the "church of God which He purchased with His own blood" (Acts 20:28). Indeed, in Acts 20, the elders are exhorted by Paul to shepherd the visible Ephesian church, charitably concluding that they are in the "church of God which He purchased with His own blood" because they were designated "the disciples" (Acts 20:30), not the seed of disciples. The church was considered an assembly of professing disciples as the charitable evidence that they had an effectual Mediator.

No, if an infant is said to be in the New Covenant administration of the one Covenant of Grace, and in the church without effectual mediation, violence is done to the biblical truth that "Christ loved the church and gave Himself up for her." Can an unregenerate infant be called *in* the New Covenant by Christ's effectual mediation and not receive salvation? Not according to Scripture. Therefore, those who include unregenerate infants in the New Covenant do violence to the doctrine of Particular Redemption. One is either in the Covenant of Works or the Covenant of Grace (New Covenant), but one cannot be in both at the same time.

Only those who are redeemed are participants in the New Covenant. Therefore, baptism must be applied only to *the disciples* who repent and confess faith as evidence that they are trusting in Jesus Christ's effectual atonement.

Christ and His New Covenant Members as Abraham's Seed

I have now defined the New Covenant, its blessings, and its members. The question remaining is: How does the New Testament define the application of the Old Covenant promises to Abraham and his seed to the New Covenant fulfillment in the church? How does the New Testament, as the clearest and final authority, explain how the Old is fulfilled in it? And what does this have to say about infant baptism as the necessary inference from Abrahamic circumcision? Let us define from Scripture who exactly constitutes the New Covenant seed of Abraham who should receive the New Covenant sign and blessings as his seed.

In Galatians 3, Paul indicates that physical descent and circumcision have no necessary relation to the fulfillment of the Abrahamic Covenant in the New Covenant. He declares that the promises of the Abrahamic Covenant were made to Abraham and to his one seed, namely Jesus Christ (Galatians 3:16). He is the ultimate seed of Abraham to whom the promises of the Abrahamic Covenant were made.

Jesus Christ is the physical fulfillment of the promise of Genesis 3:15, carried out through the physical seed of Abraham, Israel as a physical people. He also is the fulfillment of the promise to David that his son would sit on an eternal throne and rule an eternal kingdom. Therefore, the New Covenant fulfillment of the promise to make Abraham the father of many nations is through Jesus Christ, his physical seed.

In the covenants of promise in the Old Testament, it was necessary to include believers and their seed as an organic element of each administration of the Covenant of Grace in order to bring into existence the final physical seed of the woman, Abraham, and David—our Lord Jesus Christ. Now, if there is any organic or genealogical promise of the Covenant of Grace remaining in the final New Covenant administration, it is to Christ and His seed, whoever they may be. It is a grave mistake of hermeneutics to transfer the physical elements of the Old Testament covenants of promise back into the eternal Covenant of Redemption or forward into the New Covenant administration. As we have already seen, each covenant must be defined by its own revelatory content, not by an inference from other covenant administrations. Only Jesus Christ and His seed of faith are the children of Abraham in the New Covenant fulfillment (Galatians 3:28–29).[154]

Further, Abraham is called the father of us all in Romans 4. There we find that God has fulfilled His promise to him to become

---

[154]Robertson, *Israel of God,* 44–49. Robertson quotes Calvin on Galatians as approving the truth that only Christ's seed of faith are the Israel of God, the descendants of Abraham.

the father of many nations by defining his New Covenant seed as those who are "of the faith of Abraham" (4:16). This definition states that Abraham's seed is made up of those who possess "the righteousness of the faith he had while uncircumcised"—whether they are uncircumcised or circumcised (4:11–12). There is no mention here of the physical descendants of believers as being included in the New Covenant fulfillment of the Abrahamic Covenant. Rather, it is only those who actually have obtained "the righteousness of faith" (4:12–13). The actual definition of the Abrahamic seed, then, is: "those who are of faith" (Galatians 3:7, 9). If you belong to Christ, then you are Abraham's seed, "heirs according to the promise" (Galatians 3:29). For this reason, the organic seed of Abraham's New Covenant "faith-seed" cannot be considered Abraham's "grand-seed" and entitled to the covenant sign of baptism. Under the New Covenant, Abraham has no organic grandchildren, only children—of his same faith.

According to these passages, the only definition of the fulfilled seed of Abraham in the New Covenant is Christ Himself and His seed who have experienced the reality of saving faith (Galatians 3:14, 29). Who are the New Covenant seed of Christ to whom belong the promises and heirship of the Abrahamic Covenant? Those who "belong to Christ" (Galatians 3:29). The only ones who have a claim to be the inheritance of God are the children of God by the Spirit's regeneration (Romans 8:9, 14–17). Therefore, no one is considered an inheritor of the Abrahamic promises until he comes into the line of the seed of Abraham through Abraham's literal seed, Christ—and we "belong to Christ" only through the faith that evidences regeneration (Galatians 3:22, 29).

In addition, paedobaptists who hold that baptism is the counterpart of circumcision are faced with the problem of Galatians 3:27, where all who were baptized into Christ have clothed themselves with Christ. Only prejudice defines this in no relation to their water baptism.[155] It is alluding to their experience of union with Christ by faith, symbolized by their confirming experience of water baptism.

Certainly, no one would claim that all the participants in the Old Covenant circumcision experienced the spiritual reality of

---

[155]George W. Marston, *Are You a Biblical Baptist?* (Philadelphia, PA: Great Commission Publications, 1977), 21–22. Marston sees only spiritual baptism into Christ in this passage, a theological necessity to maintain his view.

saving faith, nor would anyone claim that all who receive New Covenant baptism are truly Abraham's faith-seed. However, the New Covenant fulfilled the Abrahamic promise of a "seed" by making members only those who are of faith and receive heart circumcision, which is confessed in baptism as the outward sign. This is the Baptist understanding of the seed of Abraham. Only Abraham's New Covenant seed, evidenced by repentance and faith, should receive the New Covenant sign of baptism, whether it is the direct fulfillment of circumcision or not.

All New Covenant members possess all of the blessings, have Jesus Christ as an effectual Mediator, and are Abraham's new seed. This is why baptism is reserved for disciples alone, the confessors of the faith of their father Abraham. Christian baptism is a credobaptism.

PAEDOBAPTIST OBJECTIONS TO EFFECTUAL NEW COVENANT MEMBERSHIP REFUTED

Paedobaptists often object that many who seemed to be in the New Covenant by profession finally fall away, seeming to break the New Covenant itself. This proves, they say, that one can be *in* the New Covenant as possibly unregenerate infants and yet finally be put *out* of it as covenant breakers. Some point to Hebrews 6:4–8, John 15:1–8, Romans 11:11–24, and Hebrews 10:29 as examples sustaining their view that it is possible to break the New Covenant. This view is based upon faulty hermeneutics and erroneous exegesis of those passages.

Baptists agree that there are those who profess faith in Christ and seem to be members of the New Covenant and the church universal, recipients of all of its blessings, but who ultimately fall away as false professors. Most Reformed Baptists, however, would say that individuals who fall away were never members of the New Covenant, with its realized blessings, to begin with; they only appeared to be part of the New Covenant (Hebrews 6:4–8). They were given baptism, made visible church members, and admitted to the Lord's Supper on the basis of their profession of faith in charitable hopes that they were true members of the New Covenant and church universal, not because the New Covenant of its nature includes those who prove to be covenant breakers. These individuals may have made a verbal covenant confession out of some motive other than true repentance and faith in Christ, but God never made a new covenant with them according to the New Covenant passage. Rather, as our Lord said, "I *never* knew you" (Matthew 7:23).

Paedobaptists erroneously appeal to several passages of Scripture that they argue "prove" that one can be a true member of the New Covenant yet break it. They claim these passages support the inclusion of possibly unregenerate infants in the New Covenant who are entitled to its sign of baptism.

Hebrews 6:4–8

Hebrews 6:4–8 is one of several "warning passages" in Scripture. There is a charity in the New Testament toward professing believers who appear to be falling away. New Testament writers seem to assume they are New Covenant members and true Christians until proven otherwise. However, these individuals are warned against apostasy in light of their profession of faith, not in light of their infant membership in the New Covenant. These warning passages are difficult for both Baptists and paedobaptists to explain.

Hebrews 6:4–8 describes the case, hypothetical or real, of a person who appears to be a Christian and New Covenant member yet who falls away:

> For in the case of those who have once been enlightened and have tasted of the heavenly gift and have been made partakers of the Holy Spirit, and have tasted the good word of God and the powers of the age to come, and then have fallen away, *it is impossible to renew them again to repentance, since they again crucify to themselves the Son of God, and put Him to open shame* [Hebrews 6:4–6; emphasis mine].

It appears from this passage that some people were considered in the New Covenant by outward profession of faith and repentance, yet had fallen away from that repentance. However, in verse 9 the author of Hebrews gives this evaluation:

> But, beloved, we are convinced of better things concerning you, and things that accompany salvation, though we are speaking this way.

This warning passage certainly calls professing believers to persevere to the end. However, it never defines apostates as members of the effectual New Covenant. The basis for addressing them as Christians is their outward repentance and faith, not their New Covenant membership: "... let us hold fast our *confession*" (4:14; *see also* 3:1; 10:23). Even if it were true that they were considered in the New Covenant by their profession, they were not infants. They had outwardly repented as professing disciples (6:4).

This passage simply provides no support for infant New Covenant membership.

John 15

John 15 often is used to describe people who once were members of the New Covenant but who have been cast out as covenant breakers.[156] Jesus said:

> Every branch in Me that does not bear fruit, He takes away; and every *branch* that bears fruit, He prunes it, that it may bear more fruit.... If anyone does not abide in Me, he is thrown away as a branch, and dries up; and they gather them, and cast them into the fire, and they are burned (John 15:2, 6).

The claim is that if this passage describes actual former members of the New Covenant as "covenant breakers," then it is permissible to allow infants of believers to be in the New Covenant and visible church so that they are entitled to baptism (and for some the Lord's Supper) even though later they may become covenant breakers.

However, John 15 makes clear that those *disciples* who do not "abide in Christ" were never "in" the New Covenant to begin with. The footnotes to the paedobaptist *New Geneva Study Bible* describe John 15:1–17 as "the union of Christ the Mediator with

---

[156]Booth, *Children of Abraham,* 56, 85–88; and Wilson, *Standing on the Promises,* 51–66. Booth and Wilson both appeal to these passages to establish that one may be truly in the New Covenant yet be cast out for breaking it, just as one who was in the Old Covenant Israel could be cast out for breaking it. Again, both overlook the distinctive difference between the Old and New Covenants as stated in Jeremiah 31:27–34.

His *redeemed* people" [emphasis mine].[157] They continue to state that professing *disciples* who do not abide in Christ, and prove it by bearing no fruit, were not *disciples* at all (15:8), for "no branch that is Christ's can be wholly fruitless."[158] The issue in John 15, therefore, does not concern whether someone can be in the New Covenant yet fruitless, but instead deals with who is a *disciple* at all and who is *really* in the effectual New Covenant.

Jesus clarified, "By this is My Father glorified, that you bear much fruit; *so you will be My disciples*" (15:8). Jesus' statement that "every branch *in Me* that does not bear fruit He takes away" (15:2) is dealing with those who are professing *disciples*, "in Christ" by profession, but who end up being false professors. They were never New Covenant members because it is "my *disciples*," according to Jesus, who actually bear fruit, possess the forgiveness of sins, and show evidence of a new heart.

Thus, John 15 is dealing with the proof of true conversion in professing *disciples*, not the definition of the New Covenant and whether it includes covenant breakers, especially infants. To use this passage to define the New Covenant would be as wrong as using Matthew 13:38, as paedobaptists often do, to justify including unregenerate persons as members of the kingdom of God:

> And the field is the *world* [not the "church" as paedobaptists often interpret it]; and as for the good seed, these are sons of the kingdom; and the tares are the sons of the evil one.

To include the unregenerate in the kingdom of God is in direct contradiction to Christ's clear statement that you must be born again to see or to enter the kingdom of God (John 3:1–7). To use John 15, a metaphor, in like manner to justify the existence of the unregenerate in the visible church is both poor contextual exegesis and poor hermeneutics. The clearer didactic texts that describe realized blessings in all New Covenant members (Jeremiah 31:27–34; Hebrews 8:8–12) take precedence over figurative texts that do not deal with the same subject anyway.

---

[157]*The New Geneva Study Bible,* ed. R. C. Sproul (Nashville, TN: Thomas Nelson Publishers, 1995), 1,693. *See* notes on 15:1–17. There is no mention of who is in or not in the covenant in this study Bible edited by Reformed theologians. The emphasis is upon true discipleship, not formal definitions of covenant membership.

[158]*Ibid.,* 1,694. *See* note on 15:2, 6.

Romans 11

In Romans 9–11, Paul tells the largely Gentile Roman church that God's plan of election still includes both Jew and Gentile, even though it appears on the surface that God has forsaken the Jews and turned to the Gentiles alone. God still has a remnant from the Jews that He is now saving, says Paul (11:1–11). For this reason, the Roman church needs to give to the suffering Jewish Christians in Jerusalem and give generously (15:27). They must not be haughty toward Jews as a people, whether believing or unbelieving, because they are indebted to them in spiritual things. God may yet decide to turn away from saving Gentiles primarily and once again engraft a large number of Jewish believers:

> But if some of the branches were broken off, and you, being a wild olive, were grafted in among them and became partaker with them of the rich root of the olive tree, do not be arrogant toward the branches; but if you are arrogant, *remember that* it is not you who supports the root, but the root *supports* you. You will say then, "Branches were broken off so that I might be grafted in." Quite right, they were broken off for their unbelief, and you stand *only* by your faith. Do not be conceited, but fear, for if God did not spare the natural branches, neither will he spare you. Behold then the kindness and severity of God; to those who fell, severity, but to you, God's kindness, if you continue in His kindness; otherwise you also will be cut off (Romans 11:17–22).

Romans 11:11–24 specifically deals with the issue of the unbelieving Jews being broken off from the root *because of their unbelief* about Christ and Gentiles being grafted in *because of their faith* (Acts 13:47–48). The warning to Gentiles is that if they do not continue in faith, and have a better attitude toward Jews, then God may once again turn generally from them and engraft Jews into the root by their faith.

The issue in Romans 11 is not that of an individual being a New Covenant member who has been broken off as a covenant breaker. Rather, Paul speaks of faith, not ethnic origin, as the prerequisite of being engrafted into the root in the New Covenant era, whether Jew or Gentile. According to Robertson's discussion of Romans 11:26:

"All Israel," then, consists of the entire body of God's elect from among both Jews and Gentiles. This is the group whom Paul calls "the Israel of God" in Galatians 6:16, where he insists that Christians must walk according to the rule that no distinction is to be made between circumcised and uncircumcised people (v. 15). Here Paul clearly uses the term *Israel* to refer to the elect Jews and elect Gentiles as constituting the true Israel of God.[159]

This text, therefore, does not deal at all with whether an individual can be placed in the New Covenant and then removed as a covenant breaker. Rather, it is a promise that God's election of grace does not fail and includes both Jew and Gentile according to His sovereign choice. No group should be haughty toward another, simply because God is the One who sovereignly chooses whom He will save in the flow of redemptive history.

Significantly, neither John Murray nor Keith Mathison consider this passage to define unregenerate New Covenant members or covenant breakers.[160] Murray particularly restrains himself from using this passage to define who is in the New Covenant and who is not; and with good reason, because that is not Paul's purpose in discussing the root and branch metaphor. Murray is careful to explain this passage in terms of Israel's future fullness and restoration by faith.[161] God's election has turned away primarily from Israel as branches were broken off for unbelief, yet some still are being saved (Romans 11:5). God has engrafted the believing Gentiles more fully than Israel but may break off branches again to re-engraft Israelites. Mathison also describes the root as natural Israel, the branches broken off as unbelieving Israelites, the branches not broken off as believing Israelites, and the engrafted branches as believing Gentiles.

---

[159]Robertson, *Israel of God,* 188–189. *See* Robertson's whole chapter on Romans 11. He makes no mention of New Covenant members, then breakers. The whole issue is who is now the Israel of God; to which he responds, the elect alone. It is also interesting that in his entire book, he never mentions the children of believers as in the New Covenant in any sense, although such an idea is essential to paedobaptist covenantal theology.
[160]John Murray, *The Epistle to the Romans,* in The New International Commentary on the New Testament, ed. F. F. Bruce (Grand Rapids, MI: William B. Eerdmans Publishing Company, 1968), 75–103; and Keith A. Mathison, *Dispensationalism: Rightly Dividing the People of God?* (Phillipsburg, NJ: Presbyterian and Reformed Publishing Co., 1995), 33–34.
[161]Murray, *The Epistle to the Romans,* 85.

Only believers are now God's people, heirs of Old Testament Israel. They alone are in the root. According to Mathison, the only heirs of the covenants of promise are New Covenant believers.

Using the metaphors of John 15 and Romans 11 to redefine clearer New Covenant prophecies and definitions and thereby to create a New Covenant that has curses and real members who do not possess all of the realized blessings of the New Covenant is erroneous hermeneutics and poor exegesis. As Dan McCartney has said, "Literal passages are more determinative than symbolic ones."[162] It is this overlooking of clearer didactic passages, which clearly define the New Covenant, by giving preference to symbolic ones or passages dealing with false profession and haughty spirits that is the hermeneutical error of some paedobaptists.

These passages do no more than demonstrate that false professors were never really in the unbreakable New Covenant by faith and, therefore, were not true disciples of Jesus Christ to begin with.

Hebrews 10:29

One more verse is frequently used by paedobaptists to advocate the view that one can be a New Covenant member, then rejected as a covenant breaker:

> How much severer punishment do you think he will deserve who has trampled under foot the Son of God, and has regarded as unclean *the blood of the covenant by which he was sanctified,* and has insulted the Spirit of grace? [Hebrews 10:29, emphasis mine].

Some have called the italicized phrase in this quotation the *locus classicus* (classic proof text) supporting the view that one who is in the New Covenant, sanctified by the blood of the covenant, may fall away and break the New Covenant as an apostate. If this view holds, paedobaptists say, then infants of believers may be considered in the New Covenant, and entitled to the covenant sign of baptism, even if they later fall away as covenant breakers. However, this position ignores that the author is dealing with the Hebrews as confessors of faith (Hebrews 3:1; 4:14; 10:23).

---

[162] McCartney and Clayton, *Let the Reader Understand,* 197.

There are several problems with this faulty interpretation of Hebrews 10:29. First and foremost, it ignores several fundamental principles of hermeneutics. It fails to take into account the context; the passage is not designed to define who is in the New Covenant, as are Hebrews 8:8–12 and 10:16–17. It is not wise to take a secondary or passing reference to overrule a clearer didactic passage that clearly defines covenant members.

Another hermeneutical principle violated is that of building a doctrine on a disputed or unclear text. It is never wise to do this. Berkhof warns against this practice:

> A doctrine that is clearly supported by the analogy of faith cannot be contradicted by a contrary and obscure passage. . . . When a doctrine is supported by an obscure passage of Scripture only, and finds no support in the analogy of faith, it can only be accepted with great reserve.[163]

In other words, the many passages describing effectual New Covenant membership cannot be overturned by appeal to an obscure and contrary passage.

There is no real question that this is an obscure and disputed text. John Owen and others understand "by which *he* was sanctified" to refer to Christ Himself, "sanctified" or set apart forever as a high priest through His blood of the covenant (John 17:19; Hebrews 2:10, 5:7–9, 9:11–12).[164] Yet Simon Kistemaker, a paedobaptist, takes another position of how sanctification is involved:

> That is, at one time he professed his faith in Christ, listened to the preaching of the Word of God, and partook of the holy elements when he celebrated the Lord's Supper. But his faith was not an internal fulfillment. In word and deed he now repudiates his relationship to Christ's work. He breaks with the past.[165]

It is interesting that Kistemaker, as do Baptists, understands this passage as a false profession, not a definition of broken New

---

[163]Berkhof, *Principles,* 166.
[164]Owen, *Hebrews,* 6:545–46.
[165]Simon Kistemaker, *Exposition of the Epistle to the Hebrews,* New Testament Commentary (Grand Rapids, MI: Baker Book House, 1984), 295.

Covenant membership. Further still, John Brown disagrees with both Owen and Kistemaker:

> I cannot say that I am satisfied with either of these modes of interpretation. I do not think that Scripture warrants us to say that any man who finally apostatizes is sanctified by the blood of Christ in any sense, except that the legal obstacles in the way of human salvation generally were removed by the atonement He made. . . . I apprehend the word is used impersonally, and that its true meaning is, "by which there is sanctification." It is just equivalent to—"the sanctifying blood of the covenant."[166]

It is interesting that any of these three paedobaptist interpretations of Hebrews 10:29 all are acceptable to covenantal Baptists. None of the interpreters just quoted see a definition of New Covenant membership in the text that would permit unconverted apostates admittance in the New Covenant. The text is unclear, disputed, and obscure at best as a defining text for either New Covenant membership or infant baptism. No one should appeal to it to form a doctrine of unconverted New Covenant membership when clearer texts deny such a possibility.

This is particularly true when the paedobaptist interpretation renders the passage absurd. If one were to accept that these texts teach unconverted New Covenant membership, then one must also allow apostates and false teachers to be bought by Christ's particular atonement by the same hermeneutics:

> But false prophets also arose among the people, just as there will also be false teachers among you, who will secretly introduce destructive heresies, even denying *the Master who bought them,* bringing swift destruction upon themselves [2 Peter 2:1; emphasis mine].

Is Peter including apostates in particular redemption? Those who deny particular redemption sometimes use this passage as a *proof text* for general redemption. Peter, however, is not defining apostates and false teachers as participants in the redemption; he is simply dealing with the false confession of those who

---

[166]John Brown, *Hebrews* (1862, reprint, Edinburgh: The Banner of Truth Trust, 1976), 473–74.

claimed to have been bought by Christ and considered Him a *despotes* (tyrant) in the text, not a loving *kurios* (Lord).

The only members of the New Covenant entitled to baptism are those who have the law written on the heart, who know God by experience, and who possess the forgiveness of sins, evidenced by their repentance and faith. All others are interlopers by their own fault and will bear judgment as false members, not covenant breakers, having never been in covenant with God according to the biblically defined New Covenant. The sign of the New Covenant is baptism. It is to be given only to members of the New Covenant, namely, believers.

THE NEW COVENANT AND INFANT BAPTISM

In conclusion, then, let us summarize how the lengthy discussion in this chapter about how the New Covenant relates to infant baptism. It is simply this: The New Covenant does not contain a blessing and curse formula like the Sinai Covenant, nor does it include organic relations (i.e., Covenant members' children) as members by default as did the Old Testament covenants of promise.

Rather, the curse has been taken away for all New Covenant members by the effectual and particular sacrifice that established this covenant, in contrast with the ineffectual sacrifices that established the Sinai Covenant of cursing and blessing. That is the new "good news" about the New Covenant. All members have been transferred from the Covenant of Works to the New Covenant of Jesus Christ (Romans 5:1–6:14). There is no such thing as a New Covenant member who has not received the effectual mediatory sacrifice of Jesus Christ as the "bond-in-blood" that "cuts" or establishes the covenant with God on behalf of each covenant member. One may break his own falsely professed covenant with God, but no true New Covenant member can or will break God's New Covenant (Jeremiah 32:40; Jude 24–25).

The New Covenant is an effectual covenant for every member. This is why none should be considered in the New Covenant unless they publicly repent of sins and profess trust in the substitutionary sacrifice of Jesus Christ on their behalf. By definition, this excludes infants. This is exactly why the New Testament uniformly presents "disciples alone" as candidates for baptism. Even though there may be false professors who receive the New Covenant signs of baptism and the Lord's Supper, the New Testament uniformly institutes such a professed repentance and faith as the basis for receiving the signs. This is simply because the New Covenant itself places emphasis upon realized blessings, not potential blessings. Infant baptism does not give proper respect to the New Testament revelation as the final, clearer interpreter of how the Old is fulfilled in it. It is an unbiblical and extra-biblical practice, never one of the "sacraments instituted by Christ."

Further, the New Covenant removes the inclusion of organic relations in the covenant by definition simply because it fulfills the organic promises of the Old Testament covenants of promise in the final, organic seed of Abraham, Jesus Christ. Thus, the only seed of Abraham in the New Covenant fulfillment are those who become his seed through faith in Jesus Christ, the One to whom the Abrahamic promises were made. True Christians alone are His seed. This is exactly how the New Covenant defines itself; it places the realized blessings of the covenant in each and every member. This is exactly why the New Testament requires an outward profession of repentance and faith before baptism and the Lord's Supper. To do otherwise would violate the effectual nature of the New Covenant in its members. Thus, infants are excluded from baptism and the Lord's Supper until they show some evidence that they have received the New Covenant realized blessings. They must first become professing disciples, then they should be baptized.

Having examined the beautiful pearl of covenant theology, we find that it cannot fit upon the string of good and necessary inference for infant baptism. The final, clearer revelation of the New Covenant positively institutes the signs of the covenant, baptism, and the Lord's Supper, to be applied only to those who give evidence of repentance and faith as evidence of having received the "seal" of the New Covenant, the Holy Spirit (2 Corinthians 1:22; Ephesians 1:13, 4:30). These and these alone are entitled to baptism and the Lord's Supper because of their outward profession as evidence that they are New Covenant members. *Solis discipulis!*

Chapter 5

The Relationship Between Circumcision and Baptism

Circumcision is the second pearl placed upon the string of good and necessary inference that supposedly supports the doctrine of infant baptism. According to paedobaptists, circumcision and baptism are parallel signs and seals of their respective covenants.[167] Therefore, by a supposed good and necessary inference, the subjects of baptism must be the same as the subjects of circumcision (i.e., believers and their infant seed).

This chapter explores the relationship between the Abrahamic Covenant sign of circumcision and the New Covenant sign of baptism. Is New Covenant water baptism the fulfillment and counterpart of Abrahamic Covenant circumcision? Is baptism further a sign and seal of the New Covenant to be applied to believers and their seed in the same way as circumcision was to Abraham and his seed? Again, let us go to the Scriptures to explore these issues.

THE PLACE OF CIRCUMCISION IN THE OLD TESTAMENT

In Genesis 17, God introduced circumcision into the Abrahamic Covenant after Abraham was justified by faith, having believed in God and the certainty of His promises:

> "And I will establish My covenant between Me and you and your seed after you throughout their generations for an everlasting

---

[167]Murray, *Christian Baptism,* 50–61; and Robertson, *Christ of the Covenants,* 147–66.

covenant, to be God to you and to your seed after you. And I will give to you and to your seed after you, the land of your sojournings, all the land of Canaan, for an everlasting possession; and I will be their God." God said further to Abraham, "Now as for you, you shall keep My covenant, you and your seed after you throughout their generations. *This is My covenant,* which you shall keep, between Me and you and your seed after you; *every male among you shall be circumcised.* And you shall be circumcised in the flesh of your foreskin; and it shall be *the sign of the covenant* between Me and you. And every male among you who is eight days old shall be circumcised throughout their generations, a servant who is born in your house or who is bought with money from any foreigner, who is not of your seed. A servant who is born in your house or who is bought with your money shall surely be circumcised; thus shall My covenant be in your flesh for an everlasting covenant. *But an uncircumcised male who is not circumcisged in the flesh of his foreskin, that person shall be cut off from his people; he has broken My covenant* (Genesis 17:7–14).

This covenant sign of circumcision, itself called "the covenant," was continued among the descendants of Abraham as the defining characteristic of Jewishness. It was continued under the Sinai Covenant because that covenant was "added to" the Abrahamic Covenant (Galatians 3:19). Not to be circumcised as a member of Abraham's household was to break the covenant. It was considered to be a refusal to enter God's covenant administration. Yet, circumcision was not, for some unclear reason, practiced by Moses in the "church in the wilderness" (Acts 7:38, Joshua 5:2–7).[168]

---

[168] The fact that circumcision was not practiced in what Stephen called "the church in the wilderness" has fascinated me. Paedobaptists argue that the church in the wilderness is one with the New Testament church. This one-to-one comparison is sometimes used as an argument *for* infant baptism; that is, the wilderness church was made of covenant members and their seed, so the New Testament church must be made up of covenant members and their seed. Yet, the seed of the wilderness church were not circumcised. If one wishes to push the identity between the wilderness church and the New Testament church, then it would appear that the New Testament church should *not* apply the covenant sign to infants as the "church in the wilderness" *did not.* This argues *against* infant baptism. Attempts to make the Old Testament and the New Testament people of God identical in every detail fail in the light of such inconsistencies.

Further, under the Sinai addition to the Abrahamic Covenant, the people were told to circumcise their hearts as well as their bodies by loving God and keeping His commandments (Deuteronomy 10:16). They were in the Abrahamic and Sinaitic Covenants even though their hearts were yet uncircumcised. Later, God prophesied that after captivity and future restoration, in the New Covenant days, He "will circumcise your heart *and the heart of your seed,* to love the Lord your God with all your heart and with all your soul, in order that you may live" [Deuteronomy 30:6; emphasis mine]. It is this passage that paedobaptists sometimes use to justify the infant baptism of believers' children in the New Covenant.

However, what is overlooked by these paedobaptists is that Deuteronomy 30:6 says more. God promises to circumcise every heart of every New Covenant member. It is exactly this point of the prophecy that Baptists believe. God will cause every covenant member's heart to be circumcised—by definition. The further promise of Deuteronomy 30:6 is that God will circumcise "the heart of your descendants" as well. This cannot mean that every descendant of every circumcised heart also will be heart-circumcised; even paedobaptist interpreters deny that. Therefore, it must mean that God promises to continue His heart work from generation to generation, with the seed of believers being those to whom the gospel will be preached (though, of course, not exclusively) and among whom God will give heart circumcision. Baptists find hope for their children in that promise to believers. This is what God further prophesied through Jeremiah with respect to the days of the everlasting New Covenant:

> "Behold, I will gather them out of all the lands to which I have driven them in My anger, in My wrath, and in great indignation; and I will bring them back to this place and make them dwell in safety. And they shall be My people, and I will be their God; and I will give them one heart and one way, that they may fear Me always, for their own good, and *for the good of their children* after them. And I will make an everlasting covenant with them that I will not turn away from them, to do them good; and *I will put the fear of Me in their hearts so that they will not turn away from Me* [Jeremiah 32:37–41; emphasis mine].

Here again, every heart in the everlasting covenant is changed and will not break the covenant. They will not turn away. This everlasting covenant is just another name of the New Covenant that cannot be broken because God promises to give a new heart to keep it. Jeremiah 32:39 does not say that every seed of the heart-changed will be heart-changed as well, but only that it will be for "the good of their children after them." This simply means that it will be good for the children to be raised in a heart-changed home, to hear about the everlasting covenant themselves, and to know the promise to parents that God will save from among their children.

Under Abraham, every physically circumcised male was introduced into membership in his covenant. Not to be circumcised as a member of Abraham's household was to be considered a covenant breaker, even though the person refusing technically was never in the covenant to begin with (Genesis 17:14). If paedobaptists want to look to the Abrahamic Covenant and find a basis for covenant breaking in the New Covenant, this is the only correspondence possible—the refusal to enter the New Covenant by repentance and faith of one who was never in the covenant. The New Covenant cannot be broken by one who is a member of the covenant, regenerated by the Spirit of God. In the New Covenant, no one can be considered in the covenant unless he shows evidence of this New Covenant circumcised heart by his confession. Should he apostatize, it only shows that he was never in it.

CIRCUMCISION IN THE NEW TESTAMENT

Circumcision is widely discussed in the New Testament. The Jerusalem Council decided that Gentile Christians did not have to be circumcised in order to be saved (Acts 15:1ff.). Paul vigorously agreed in his letter to the Galatians (Galatians 6:12–14). Yet, Paul had Timothy circumcised immediately after the Jerusalem Council (Acts 16:3); he had Timothy become a Jew in order to win Jews (1 Corinthians 9:19–23).

The New Testament attitude toward circumcision is one of strong opposition to its practice as a work for justification (Galatians 5:2). However, it still was practiced by many Jewish Christians out of respect for biblical tradition (Acts 21:20–21), or out of accommodation to Jewish customs for evangelism (1 Corinthians 10:32; Acts 16:3). Paul strongly opposed the Judaizers of

Galatia (Galatians 1:9) and Colosse (Colossians 2:8–11) because they made circumcision a means of justification. Paul knew that "neither is circumcision anything, nor uncircumcision, but a new creation" (Galatians 6:15). Galatians 6:15 provides an exegetical connection between circumcision as the Old Testament type and regeneration as the superior antitype, which will be explained in the next heading. The fulfilled circumcision of the New Covenant is regeneration (Philippians 3:3; Colossians 2:11–12; Romans 2:28–29).

Although Paul opposed circumcision as a work required for justification, he affirmed in Acts 21:18–25 that he did not discourage Jewish Christians from voluntarily practicing Mosaic laws. Some paedobaptists have misunderstood Paul's permission of circumcision for those with a Jewish background to be the approval of circumcision as a Christian entrance sign to the New Covenant, thus paving the way for infant baptism as well. Douglas Wilson, for example, believes that Christian circumcision was practiced in the early church, giving Jewish infant sons admission to the New Covenant and the Christian church:

> Circumcision remained an ordinance of God, marking the initiation of the one who received it as a member of the visible covenant community. Circumcision continued to mean that the one who had received it was under an obligation to be a true son of Abraham— i.e., a *Christian*. There is no hint in the New Testament that circumcision ceased having a religious signification; there is a tremendous amount of teaching concerning the true *Christian* signification of it. For just one example, circumcision (as practiced by Christian Jews) pictured the removal of the body of sins of the flesh (Colossians 2:11).[169]

Apparently Wilson believes that circumcision "remained an instituted ordinance of God" for Jewish Christians until A.D. 70, even though the New Covenant was the only salvific covenant administration in force. He affirms that God still "required both (circumcision and baptism) of all the Jews."[170]

---

[169] Douglas Wilson, "Circumcision in the New Covenant," *Christianity and Society*, 4, no. 4 (October 1994), 23.
[170] *Ibid.*, 27.

Yet, Paul said:

> For though I am free from all men, I have made myself a slave to all, that I might win the more. And to the Jews I became as a Jew, that I might win Jews; to those who are under the Law, as under the Law, *though not being myself under the Law,* that I might win those who are under the Law; to those who are without law, as without law, though not being without the law of God but under the law of Christ, that I might win those who are without law. To the weak I became weak, that I might win the weak; I have become all things to all men, that I may by all means save some [1 Corinthians 9:19–22; emphasis mine].

Paul was still a Jew, yet he did not see himself as under the law of Moses as a covenant in force any longer, including food laws and circumcision. Neither Peter nor Paul kept the whole law of Moses out of necessity, but only parts of it, out of accommodation to the ignorance of believing and unbelieving Jews. The official apostolic position is that the Mosaic Covenant, including circumcision, was in force only "until the seed should come to whom the promise had been made" (Galatians 3:19). Wilson's idea that "God required both circumcision and baptism of all the Jews" at the same time from 30 to 70 A.D. is profoundly unbiblical.

In addition, Wilson's example of Colossians 2:11 as approval of a physical circumcision "practiced by Christian Jews" is exegetically untenable and extreme. Paul makes clear in Colossians 2:11 that theirs was "a circumcision made *without hands.*" It is a spiritual circumcision, not a literal, physical circumcision practiced by Christian Jews. Furthermore, Wilson's statement that "there is no hint in the New Testament that circumcision ceased having a religious signification" is extremely overstated. It always had a religious signification, but that does not mean that it should be practiced any more than religiously significant blood sacrifices. Romans 2:25–29, Ephesians 2:15 and Galatians 6:15 state that circumcision and uncircumcision no longer matter; what matters is becoming a new creation, which is the real counterpart and fulfillment of circumcision.

In fact, Colossians 2:8–11 defines why physical circumcision is unnecessary:

> See to it that no one takes you captive through philosophy and empty deception, according to the tradition of men, according to the

elementary principles of the world, rather than according to Christ. For in Him all the fulness of deity dwells in bodily form, and in Him you have been made complete, and He is the head over all rule and authority; and *in Him you were also circumcised* with a circumcision made *without hands,* in the removal of the body of flesh by the circumcision of Christ [emphasis mine].

The reality of physical circumcision is replaced by heart circumcision, making physical circumcision unnecessary. Wilson seems to think that New Testament statements explaining the fulfillment of Old Testament circumcision in New Covenant blessings, thus eliminating its necessity, actually are teaching Jewish Christians how they should continue to practice circumcision. This is a novel view without foundation. Most commentators consider this passage to be an explanation of Christ's superior spiritual circumcision, not an explanation of the meaning of Christian physical circumcision.

Wilson also believes that the use of the term *synagogue* in James 2:2–4 means that Christian Jews practiced infant admission to the Christian church through circumcision in a similar manner as their non-Christian Jewish counterparts did regarding admission to the synagogue. According to Wilson:

> . . . if there was Christian circumcision (and there was), and if there were Christian synagogues (and there were), and if the Christians who went to these synagogues were the same believers who circumcised their sons (and they were), the necessary conclusion is that *we know with certainty* that some first-century churches had infant members.[171]

Wilson artificially boxes the reader into three possible explanations of the relationship between circumcision and membership in the Christian synagogue and church: (1) either the apostles were wrong to permit circumcision, or (2) they wrongly changed its meaning, or (3) circumcision made an infant a member of the Christian synagogue and church. From this artificial construction, he concludes that when Gentile parents brought their uncircumcised infants to the elders of the Christian synagogue for admission along with the circumcised Jewish children,

---

[171]*Ibid.,* 25.

the elders would certainly have practiced infant baptism to include Gentile children in the church.[172] Wilson considers this to be an example of grammatical-historical exegesis that establishes a "we know with certainty" biblical case for infant church membership by baptism.

Yet Wilson provides no exegetical evidence, biblically or historically, that Jewish circumcised infants were automatically admitted to the Jewish synagogue or church as members. Nor does he provide a shred of evidence that Jewish circumcised infants were automatically considered baptized and admitted to the Christian church, much less any evidence that the Gentile parents requested infant baptism so that their children would not be left out. This is pure speculation, not exegesis. It is a prime example of the fanciful interpretation wrought by the use of an erroneously applied good and necessary inference.

There is a fourth possibility, ignored by Wilson, which actually fits the New Testament evidence much better than Wilson's three alternatives. It is simply this: A disciple's baptism was required of both Jew and Gentile for admission to the church, although Jewish Christians still practiced their Jewish custom of circumcision for tradition's sake. The fact that circumcision was still practiced by Jewish Christians by no means proves that their infants were accepted as members of the Christian synagogue-church apart from a profession of faith and disciple's baptism. It only means that they desired to retain their Abrahamic and Mosaic heritage. In reality, those professing Jewish Christians who continued to practice circumcision were continually tempted to depend upon this fleshly practice to make them real covenant children of Abraham, instead of depending on faith alone in Christ alone (Galatians 3–6). This temptation was the very reason why Paul wrote Galatians.

The biblical record is that Christian Jews had a distinct awareness that the Christian church was founded upon principles other than the Jewish synagogue. This is seen in the fact that only those 3,000 Jews who "received his (Peter's) word were baptized" (Acts 2:41). This is why Peter and Paul, faithful Jews themselves, learned from God to reject the Mosaic food laws, as well as the necessity of circumcision, for salvation. Were they not

---

[172]*Ibid.*, 27.

faithful Jews? It is perfectly harmonious with the New Testament data that one could still practice Jewish customs and the Mosaic laws, including circumcision, yet not be considered a member of the Christian church without disciple's baptism (John 4:1–2; Matthew 28:18–20; Acts 2:38–41; 11:29).

SIGN AND SEAL

In Romans 4:9–25, Paul cites Abraham as an example of how God justifies the believer by faith alone, apart from his works, including circumcision as a work of the law. In this passage, circumcision is called "a seal of the righteousness of the faith which [Abraham] had while uncircumcised" (4:11). Paedobaptists take this language to mean that baptism is the exact parallel to circumcision, the corresponding New Covenant sign. They use it to call baptism the sign and seal of the New Covenant, just as circumcision was the sign of the Abrahamic Covenant and the seal of Abraham's faith which he had while uncircumcised.

It is certainly true that circumcision was called a *sign* of the Abrahamic Covenant (Genesis 17:11), but it was never called a *seal* of that covenant. Rather, in only one place in Scripture is it called a *seal* and that was of the righteousness of the faith which [Abraham] had while uncircumcised (Romans 4:11). In other words, circumcision was a seal, not of every member of the Abrahamic Covenant, but of the salvation experience, or personal faith, of Abraham alone. Neither is baptism ever called the seal of the New Covenant. The New Testament never calls baptism a seal of the Covenant of Grace.

Instead, something else is the seal of the New Covenant. Holy Spirit regeneration is the fulfillment of what circumcision signified under the Abrahamic Covenant, a circumcised heart:

> Now He who establishes us with you in Christ and anointed us is God, who also *sealed* us and gave us the Spirit in our hearts as a pledge (2 Corinthians 1:21–22). . . . In Him, you also, after listening to the message of truth, the gospel of your salvation—having also believed, you were *sealed* in Him with the Holy Spirit of promise, who is given as a pledge of our inheritance (Ephesians 1:13–14). . . . And do not grieve the Holy Spirit of God, by whom you were *sealed* for the day of redemption [Ephesians 4:30, emphasis mine].

The seal of the New Covenant is the Holy Spirit regeneration that seals the heart of faith in direct fulfillment of Abrahamic circumcision.

CIRCUMCISION AND BAPTISM

Romans 2:25–29

In Romans 2:25–29, we find that circumcision was always meant to represent the inward work of the Spirit on the heart. This was the definition of a true Jew:

> For indeed circumcision is of value, if you practice the Law; but if you are a transgressor of the Law, your circumcision has become uncircumcision. If therefore the uncircumcised man keeps the requirements of the Law, will not his uncircumcision be regarded as circumcision? And will not he who is physically uncircumcised, if he keeps the Law, will he not judge you who though having the letter of the Law and circumcision are a transgressor of the Law? For he is not a Jew who is one outwardly; neither is circumcision that which is outward in the flesh. *But he is a Jew who is one inwardly; and circumcision is that which is of the heart by the Spirit, not by the letter;* and his praise is not from men, but from God [emphasis mine].

Paul says here that the outward sign of circumcision was to symbolize that which God desired inwardly of the heart. However more than that, the circumcised heart, the reality behind the symbol, also had to be present for a person (including uncircumcised Gentiles) to be a true Jew and thereby a receiver of all of God's New Covenant blessings (Philippians 3:3).

This same truth is taught in Romans 9:6–8, where Paul says, "They are not all Israel who are from Israel;" rather, the children of the promise are the elect. This is again the faithful remnant idea that began in the physical nation of Abraham's descendants and took fruition in the New Covenant people of God. This is further explained in Romans 4:12–13 where the promised seed of Abraham are not those of physical descent but only those who are of the faith of their father Abraham, whether circumcised or not. These, and these only, are his fulfilled seed (Romans 4:23). It is those who are of faith, Jew and Gentile, who are the heart-circumcised seed of Abraham. In all these Scriptures the true Jew, or Abraham's seed, in fulfillment of God's promise to him, are those Jews and Gentiles who have been circumcised in the heart by the Spirit, as revealed by their faith (Galatians 3:14, 28–29).

Colossians 2:9–12

Now let me attempt to bring this discussion to bear on the question of circumcision and baptism in the New Covenant. The most quoted text to link circumcision with water baptism is Colossians 2:9–12:

> For in Him all the fullness of Deity dwells in bodily form, and in Him you have been made complete, and He is the head over all rule and authority; and in Him you were also circumcised with a circumcision made without hands, in the removal of the body of the flesh by the circumcision of Christ; having been buried with Him in baptism, in which you were also raised up with Him through faith in the working of God, who raised Him from the dead.

However, this text has been misinterpreted by many covenant paedobaptists. Speaking to Gentile Christians, Paul says that they have "been made complete" and have received the "circumcision of Christ" which is "without hands" (2:10–11). They did not need to be circumcised physically because of that fact.

What is the circumcision of Christ that they already had received (whether physically circumcised or not)? Grammatically, the genitive, of Christ, may be interpreted to identify either the death of Christ objectively as a circumcision or the experiential circumcising of the believer's heart by Christ. Either way, Paul is speaking of the manner in which the believer has been "circumcised also" through the benefits of Christ's death and resurrection. Because of Christ's death, we have received a better circumcision than the Judaizers received "in the removal of the body of the flesh by the circumcision of Christ, having been buried with Him in baptism, in which you were also raised up with Him through faith in the working of God, who raised Him from the dead" (Colossians 2:11,12).

Here is a definite link between circumcision and baptism. Christians have been circumcised *also* by being buried with Christ in baptism—but is Paul referring only to the actual water baptism as the counterpart of circumcision? To quote Paul from elsewhere, "May it never be!" This circumcision is "made without hands." There is no human hand involved in its administration, whether by knife or by water. Further, Paul's full definition of this circumcision is:

> the removal of the body of the flesh by the circumcision of Christ; having been buried with Him *in baptism, in which you were also raised up with Him through faith in the working of God,* who raised Him from the dead [Colossians 2:11–12, emphasis mine].

To summarize, the Christian's circumcision, then, is that union with Christ's death and resurrection, symbolized by baptism, and evidenced by their personal faith in the working of God and made visible (or public) at the time of their baptism. Infants cannot participate in this baptism until they express personal faith. Verses 13 and 14 of Colossians 2 also confirm this view by defining those who have received the circumcision of Christ as those who have actually experienced the new birth and blotting out of sins:

> And when you were dead in your transgressions and the uncircumcision of your flesh, He made you alive together with Him, having forgiven us all our transgressions, having cancelled out the certificate of debt consisting of decrees against us *and* which was hostile to us; and He has taken it out of the way, having nailed it to the cross.

This new life of faith by the Holy Spirit's regeneration is the New Covenant heart-circumcision antitype that fulfills the type of Old Testament circumcision. Only people of faith were buried with Christ in baptism in this passage—and that because their hearts already had been circumcised. Their water baptism symbolized and made public their prior spiritual baptism or union with Christ by faith (Romans 6:3–4). This baptism was applied only to those who exhibited a prior faith, which is exactly what the New Testament institutes, describes, and prescribes.

In the following lengthy but valuable quotation, O. Palmer Robertson comes very close to the Baptist position when describing the fulfillment of Old Testament circumcision, not in baptism, but in Holy Spirit regeneration:

Philippians 3:3 draws the closest possible parallel between the essence of the new covenant and the circumcision symbol of the old. "We *are* the circumcision," affirms the apostle. The one who worships in the Spirit of God personifies the reality of the cleansing rite of the old covenant.

This series of passages relates the circumcision-symbol of the old covenant to the reality of the new. The verses aid the new covenant believer in appreciating the significance for himself of the old covenant seal.

Secondly, the application of the same vocabulary of "sealing" (sphragizesthai) to the rite of circumcision and to the possession of the Holy Spirit provides a bridge to connect the two concepts. In Romans 4:11, circumcision is described as "a seal (sphragis) of the righteousness of faith." Elsewhere, Paul applies the same term in its verbal form (sphragizesthai) to the possession of the Holy Spirit by the New Testament believer (he quotes 2 Cor. 1:22; Eph. 1:13, 4:30). . . . *The application of the same terminology to circumcision and Spirit-possession binds the two concepts together. The covenant ritual of sealing finds its fulfillment in the new covenant reality of sealing.*

Thirdly, the interconnection between the seal of circumcision and the seal of the Holy Spirit provides the formal basis by which the corresponding purification rites of the old and new covenants relate to one another. *Circumcision under the old covenant is replaced by baptism under the new covenant* (emphasis mine). The cleansing rite of the one covenant is replaced by the cleansing rite of the other. This relationship between circumcision and baptism finds specific development in Colossians 2:11–12 [emphasis mine].[173]

Baptists agree with Robertson that "the covenant ritual of sealing finds its fulfillment in the new covenant *reality* of sealing" (i.e., Holy Spirit regeneration). By standard hermeneutics of typology, the type of circumcision (entrance into the Abrahamic Covenant) is fulfilled in its antitype, regeneration (entrance into the effectual New Covenant). Unfortunately, Robertson is not typologically consistent in his conclusion that "circumcision under the old covenant is replaced by baptism under the new covenant." To say that circumcision under the old covenant is replaced by regeneration or heart circumcision would be more consistent with the biblical data and with Robertson's own analysis.

---

[173]Robertson, *Christ of the Covenants,* 161–62.

This is exactly what Baptist covenantalists believe. The seal of regeneration, exhibited outwardly by a confession of faith, is the true New Testament fulfillment, antitype, and replacement of Old Testament circumcision. Baptism then is the sign, not seal, of regeneration. Regeneration itself, the circumcision of the heart, is the seal of the New Covenant. This is why water baptism should be applied only to those who confess faith in Christ as an outward evidence of that New Covenant regeneration, as the New Testament institutes and prescribes.

A great inconsistency of some covenant paedobaptists is that they will correctly consider union with Christ in baptism in Romans 6:3, 4 as a secondary reference to water baptism and count it primarily as a reference to the new birth.[174] However, they will also use the same concept of union with Christ in baptism in Colossians 2:11, 12 as a primary reference to water baptism's relation to circumcision instead of its clear intended purpose of relating circumcision to regeneration.[175] My conclusion is that Paul defined the circumcision of Christians in Colossians 2:9–12 as primarily heart union with Christ by faith, secondarily symbolized in their water baptism as a confession of that faith which they received in regeneration (as in Romans 6:3, 4; 1 Corinthians 12:13; and Galatians 3:29).

SUMMARY

What then is the counterpart and antitype of the Old Testament sign and seal of circumcision in the New Covenant? The Scriptures define it to be the inward circumcision of the heart by the Spirit, which is exhibited outwardly in the disciple's faith. This is why Paul prohibited physical circumcision in Galatia and Colosse. They had received its reality already in the new heart given by the Holy Spirit (Galatians 3:3; Colossians 2:9–14). Paul forcefully told the Galatians that they did not need physical circumcision to enter into the covenant relationship with God because they had already entered that covenant relationship by

---

[174]Murray, *Romans,* 214–15; *see* n. 3, 215; and Murray, *Christian Baptism,* 29–33; and George Marston, *Are You A Biblical Baptist?* (Philadelphia: Great Commission Publications, 1977), 8.
[175]Murray, *Christian Baptism,* 50–51; and Marston, *Biblical Baptist,* 19–23.

the circumcision of Christ, by the receipt of a new heart, by union with His death and resurrection. Therefore, as circumcision (the shadow or type) was the sign of entrance into the Abrahamic Covenant, and the seal of Abraham's personal faith, so regeneration (the form or antitype) is the seal of entrance into the New Covenant (Ephesians 1:13–14; John 3:5–6), signified in the sign of disciple's baptism.

Baptism is then the indirect counterpart of physical circumcision only through its association with the direct counterpart, or typological fulfillment, spiritual circumcision. This is why we only see disciple's baptism in the New Testament record. It was easy to know who entered the Abrahamic Covenant; they were born into the household and were outwardly circumcised. But how can you tell if one has entered the New Covenant and has experienced spiritual circumcision, entitling them to the sign of baptism? Only by their repentance and faith, publicly signified by the outward sign of water baptism. Acts 2:37–42 is clear exegetical proof that the only children baptized were those who received Peter's word of repentance and faith in Christ (Acts 2:38, 39, 41). They outwardly showed inward circumcision and then were baptized. This was how Christ ordained to build His church (Matthew 16:16–18; 28:19). *Therefore circumcision was a prospective sign of the need of heart-circumcision, while baptism is a retrospective sign of that heart-circumcision already received and confessed.* This is the biblical connection between the two signs.

The argument for infant baptism as a direct New Covenant parallel, antitype, or fulfillment of Abrahamic circumcision simply cannot be sustained by New Testament evidence. Infant baptism is not a sacrament instituted by Christ or prescribed by Holy Scripture. It is an invention of a well-meaning men using erroneous inferences, who allow the Old Testament to determine how it is fulfilled in the New, rather than depending upon the New to determine how the Old is fulfilled in it.

For this reason, the sign of baptism may be applied only to disciples who show evidence of the Holy Spirit's seal, regeneration, revealed in their outward repentance toward God and faith in our Lord Jesus Christ. It is a baptism of disciples alone.

Chapter 6

Household Baptisms, The "Oikos Formula," and Infant Baptism

The question of household baptisms has long been used as a support for paedobaptism. These are the baptisms of the households of Cornelius, Lydia, the Philippian jailer, Stephanas, and Crispus. These household baptisms supposedly provide examples of the "*oikos* formula" (*oikos* is Greek for household), a justification for infant baptism systematized by Joachim Jeremias.[176]

However, paedobaptists still dispute among themselves about whether household baptisms actually provide any support for infant baptism. Thomas E. Watson marshals paedobaptist quotes from Neander, Pierre Marcel and James Bannerman, concluding that none of the household baptisms hold any evidence for infant baptism. He then quotes John Murray, Thomas Boston, Richard Baxter, and Louis Berkhof who all admit that there is no example or direct evidence of infant baptism in the New Testament.[177] This divided opinion between paedobaptists concerning the validity of the household baptism argument offers no sure evidence for the practice of infant baptism in the household baptisms.

First, we will examine the *oikos* formula theory, then the instances of household baptisms in the New Testament, followed by conclusions concerning infant baptism.

---

[176]Joachim Jeremias, *Infant Baptism in the First Four Centuries,* trans. David Cairns (Philadelphia, PA: The Westminster Press, 1962), 19.
[177]Watson, *Babies Be Baptized?,* 38–41.

THE *OIKOS* FORMULA THEORY

Joachim Jeremias has systematized the argument concerning the "*oikos* formula." Jeremias begins with the fact that "the New Testament was written in a missionary situation," and from this he rightly concludes that all New Testament references to baptism deal with adult, missionary baptism to believing Jews and Gentiles. However, he then goes on to contend that evidence for household children's baptism is hidden behind the adults' missionary baptism.[178]

Jeremias argues that the household baptisms in the New Testament continued from Old Testament household unity (citing 1 Corinthians 1:16; Acts 11:14; 16:15; 16:33; 18:8), thus affirming the baptism of any infants in those households. The *oikos* idea assumes that all who were in the households were baptized, from infants to slaves, as was done for circumcision in the Abrahamic Covenant. Yet without any greater substantiating evidence than he has for the presence of infants, Jeremias inconsistently counts it "extremely unlikely" that slaves were present in these households.[179] This inconsistency reflects the arbitrary speculation of those who employ the *oikos* formula as an inference from the Old Testament.

Following E. Stauffer, Jeremias also appeals to Old Testament evidence to support his *oikos* formula. He concludes that the Old Testament formula "he and his house" in cultic situations carries over to the New Testament household situations as formal cultic language regarding baptism and the Lord's Supper. The innocent reader may not realize that this conclusion is based upon Jeremias' liberal, form-critical, and redaction-critical speculations. In Jeremias' view, it is not necessary to prove or disprove the existence of infants or slaves in the household baptisms, simply because the *oikos* formula indicates "the solidarity of the family in baptism."[180]

Jeremias then dates Jewish proselyte baptism to pre-Christian times as the immediate historical background for Christian house-

---

[178]Jeremias, *Infant Baptism,* 19. I do not use the term "adult baptism" because Peter offered baptism to children who repented and believed (Acts 2:41). Paedobaptists sometimes erroneously charge Reformed Baptists with believing in adult baptism only.
[179]*Ibid.,* 19–20.
[180]*Ibid.,* 21–23.

hold and infant baptism. He claims that the baptism of the Jewish proselyte's children with him is sufficient evidence that Christian parents would also baptize their children upon their conversion. He appeals to the *Testament of Levi* 14:6 for support, even though the words *bapto* or *baptizo* are never used to apply to Jewish proselyte baptism.[181] Jeremias also appeals to various early funeral inscriptions, as well as the works of Tertullian, to postulate infant baptism in the early church.

However, Kurt Aland, a paedobaptist using the same resources, refutes Jeremias and concludes there is no historical evidence for infant baptism until the third century A.D.[182] He examines the missionary baptism argument and the household baptisms of the New Testament, concluding that neither offers any evidence for infant baptism. Against Jeremias, he affirms the real possibility that slaves were present in households of that day.[183]

There is no question that the *oikos* formula was at work in the Old Testament covenants of promise, as demonstrated by Abraham's household circumcisions of infants and slaves, but that proves too much, even for Jeremias. He has to resort to pure speculation that no slaves were in the households of the New Testament to avoid the complicating implications of adult slave baptism without personal repentance and faith. Even if Jewish proselyte baptism existed in the first century A.D., a disputed point, it also proves too much because infants in the womb during the mother's baptism were not baptized after birth, nor were any later-born infants. In the final analysis, the *oikos* formula presents no solid evidence to justify infant baptism as a logical or common practice of the New Testament church.

In fact, the real problem with the *oikos* formula theory is that it appeals to a cultural and sociological concept not clearly specified in Scripture in order to justify infant baptism, while ignoring the immediate New Testament context that clearly rejects infant baptism: the baptism of disciples alone by John and Jesus. If the *oikos* formula was so inevitably linked to baptism that household infants were included, why then did John and Jesus reject such a connection when they baptized only the repentant?

---

[181]*Ibid.*, 26–28.
[182]Kurt Aland, *Did the Early Church Baptize Infants?*, trans. G. R. Beasley-Murray (Philadelphia, PA: The Westminster Press, 1963), 10.
[183]*Ibid.*, 90–91.

Are we really supposed to conclude that the apostles would ignore the previous baptism of disciples alone as the immediate cultural and sociological context to baptism in the Great Commission and at Pentecost, turning instead to Old Testament household circumcision and questionable Jewish proselyte baptism to overrule such a clearly established historical precedent and context? And if the *oikos* formula was so obvious, why then did Jesus not practice it? Was He ignorant of the idea? Was He disobedient to the required Abrahamic *oikos* formula? No, it is much more plausible and hermeneutically consistent to accept the previous baptism of disciples alone by John and Jesus as the immediate historical, cultural, and sociological background to post-Pentecost Christian baptism. The literal-grammatical-historical method of interpretation and contextual exegesis demand such a conclusion.

THE HOUSEHOLD BAPTISMS

It will be seen in the following discussion of household baptisms that there is no certain evidence that anyone was baptized who did not first repent and believe the gospel, exactly the same requirement stated by Peter at Pentecost for the hearers, their children, and those afar off:

> And Peter said to them, "Repent, and let each of you be baptized in the name of Jesus Christ for the forgiveness of your sins; and you shall receive the gift of the Holy Spirit. For the promise is for you and your children, and for all who are far off, as many as the Lord our God shall call to Himself." And with many other words he solemnly testified and kept on exhorting them, saying, "Be saved from this perverse generation!" So then, *those who had received his word were baptized;* and there were added that day about three thousand souls [Acts 2:38–41; emphasis mine].

This passage teaches that, at Pentecost, only "those who had received his word" were baptized, whether children or adults. According to standard principles of interpretation, this baptism only of repentant believers establishes the most immediate precedent and context by which the following household baptisms must be evaluated (i.e., the baptism of disciples alone).

Cornelius' Household

The account of Peter's preaching the gospel to Cornelius' household (Acts 10:22; 11:12, 14) does not support infant baptism:

> While Peter was still speaking these words, the Holy Spirit fell upon all who were listening to the message. And all the circumcised believers who had come with Peter were amazed, because the gift of the Holy Spirit had been poured out upon the Gentiles also. For they were hearing them speak with tongues and exalting God. Then Peter answered, "Surely no one can refuse the water for these to be baptized who have received the Holy Spirit just as we did, can he?" And he ordered them to be baptized. . . . (Acts 10:44–48).

Peter did preach the gospel to the whole household, plus many guests, and "all who were listening to the message," and who repented, were saved. How do we know that? It is expressly stated in Acts 10:44 and Acts 11:15. The Holy Spirit fell upon them "all" and led them all to repentance and faith (11:17, 18). In fact, Peter explicitly stated in 10:47 that he baptized only those who "received the Holy Spirit as we did." Here Peter actually refers to Pentecost as the immediate precedent to what happened to Cornelius and his household. Only those who "received his word" were baptized (Acts 2:41).

This extension of Pentecost to the Gentiles clearly defines who was baptized. There is no mention of infants in the household but only those who were "listening to the message" (10:44). Infants are capable of being regenerated by God and may have been present, but they are not capable of listening to the gospel and "speaking with tongues and exalting God" (Acts 10:46). I do not believe in paedoglossalalia (infants receiving the gift of tongues). Only those people who were listening to the message received baptism as a sign of the Abrahamic promise of the Spirit upon Gentiles (Galatians 3:14).

J. A. Alexander, a paedobaptist, concludes that there is no evidence for infant baptism in the text.[184] I also conclude that the episode in Cornelius' household does not support infant baptism and indeed is a strong indicator for disciple's baptism alone.

---

[184] Joseph Addison Alexander, *The Acts of the Apostles* (1857; reprint, London: The Banner of Truth Trust, 1963), 2:126–27.

Lydia's Household

The case of Lydia is inconclusive at best: "And when she and her household had been baptized . . ." (Acts 16:15). Where was Lydia's husband? Was he baptized upon her faith? She may not have been married at all. Only women are mentioned at the riverbank. It appears that she and her household were baptized at the river before she took Paul back to her house. This opens the probability that only women were in her household (and all members of her household were at the riverbank with her) because she was an unmarried or widowed businesswoman. Even if she were married and had children with her on the riverbank, there is no mention of infants or older children in her household. Even many paedobaptists believe that this instance of household baptism does not help their case.

The Philippian Jailer's Household

The Philippian jailer's baptism (Acts 16:30–34) is probably the best possibility for including infants in the household baptism:

> And they said, "Believe in the Lord Jesus, and you will be saved, you and all your household." And they spoke the word of the Lord to him together with all who were in his house. And he took them that *very* hour of the night and washed their wounds, and immediately he was baptized, he and all his household. And he brought them into his house and set food before them, and rejoiced greatly, having believed in God with all his household (Acts 16:31–34).

There is no question that all in the jailor's household were baptized. However, paedobaptists relying on this passage to prove their case illicitly apply the promise of verse 31 to the covenantal baptism of the household based upon the jailer's faith. Luke records that Paul and Silas preached the gospel to "all who were in his house" (v. 32) and that his "whole household" (v. 34) believed in God with him.

It should be pointed out that there is a translation problem with this text that needs to be examined. J. A. Alexander agrees that verse 31 is simply a promise of salvation by faith to the jailer and to his household upon belief by both. Verse 34 is more complicated. The NASB, NIV, KJV, Williams and Beck translations indicate that faith evidenced in his whole household was the basis for their rejoicing: " . . . having believed in God with his whole household." However, the participle "having believed" is masculine singular and seems to describe the faith of the jailer only: "He greatly rejoiced with his whole household, having believed [the jailer] in God." The emphasis seems to be that the household rejoiced with him because he had found faith (RSV, NEB).

If this is true, we still have the problem of infants rejoicing upon their father's faith. It is true that infants in a household can detect joy and participate in it, but I do not believe that infants can rejoice because they realize their father has found faith in God. This seems to be the basis for the whole household's rejoicing. However, because of the context of preaching the word to all in the house, and because all were ultimately baptized, I believe their rejoicing was the same as the jailer's rejoicing—the evidence of a newfound faith and redemption expressed in the joy of the Holy Spirit's regeneration.

Because they all heard the gospel, were baptized, and rejoiced, it is a legitimate conclusion that they all repented and believed. Or were older children and household servants baptized upon his faith as well? He and his "whole household" were baptized because they all believed. Can infants hear the word and respond in repentance and faith? I think not. If infants were present, for which there is no proof, the context denies that they were baptized. In fact, the context seems to define no infants present. This case of household baptism could actually support confessor's baptism.

Crispus' Household

The example of the baptism of the household of Crispus supports disciples-only baptism: "And Crispus, the leader of the synagogue, believed in the Lord with all his household, and many of the Corinthians when they heard were believing and being baptized" (Acts 18:8). Here it is plain that the whole household believed in the Lord as well as Crispus, its head. This is why they were baptized. In addition, the same verse indicates that many Corinthians outside Crispus' household were baptized because they had first believed. It seems clear that the whole household first believed and then were baptized as did the others. This case also supports disciple's baptism within households.

Stephanas' Household

The last household baptism mentioned is that of Stephanas by Paul: "Now I did baptize also the household of Stephanas . . . you know the household of Stephanas, that they were the first fruits of Achaia, and that they have devoted themselves for ministry to the saints . . ." (1 Corinthians 1:16; 16:15). This text arises out of the context of controversy among the Corinthian believers over factionalism. In responding to this controversy, Paul states that he is thankful he did not baptize many of them, except for Crispus and Gaius and the household of Stephanas.

Paul's statements here do not support infant baptism. First, it seems they were capable of knowing who baptized them, thus excluding infants. Further, 1 Corinthians 16:15 describes the "household of Stephanas" as persons who have devoted themselves for ministry to the saints. Infants, of course, cannot self-consciously devote themselves in such a way. The most that can be said is that we do not know if infants were present. Again, to adopt a practice from silence is to follow the normative principle of worship. The approach more faithful to the regulative principle is to reject a practice never mentioned (here, infant baptism). This account also fails to support infant baptism and actually supports the baptism of disciples alone.

SUMMARY

In summary, the accounts of Lydia's and Stephanas' households are inconclusive and therefore provide no support for the practice of infant baptism, while the accounts of households of Cornelius, Crispus, and the jailer favor conscious belief as evidence of regeneration before baptism. Therefore, I conclude that the weight of the household baptisms supports the baptism of disciples alone.

Neither can the *oikos* formula be used to justify infant baptism in the household baptisms of the New Testament. Such a construction depends upon speculative theories about the date and practice of Jewish proselyte baptism, yet ignores the clear and inspired evidence that the disciples-only baptisms of John, Jesus, and Pentecost were the immediate historical background to Christian baptism.

Proper historical exegesis of the Scriptures must accept the practice of John, Jesus, and Peter as having a greater authority and a more immediate influence upon Great Commission baptism than questionable Jewish proselyte baptism, even if it did exist at that time. There is no evidence that Jewish proselyte baptism or the Old Testament concept of households influenced either Jesus, John, or Peter to baptize the households of their baptized disciples just because they lived in the same house.

How then can either of these *oikos* influences be said to establish a good and necessary inference for infant baptism in the church at Pentecost and after? Did Jesus and John miss the point? Was the *oikos* formula suspended for Jesus and John? Or have those who argue for it ignored the immediate context of John's and Jesus' baptisms of disciples alone, not to mention Pentecost?

I conclude that neither the *oikos* formula nor the household baptisms recorded in Scripture offer any example of or authority supporting infant baptism. Rather, upon closer inspection, the baptism of disciples alone is fully maintained.

Chapter 7

Answering the Infant Baptism Proof-Texts

Thus far we have concluded that Abraham's New Covenant "seed" are only those "of faith" and of the Spirit (Galatians 3:14–15), and that the circumcision of the New Covenant is not Abraham's but Christ's circumcision in regeneration. This is outwardly symbolized by the baptism of disciples alone. I will now deal with the pearl of specific proof-texts that paedobaptists have used to support the baptism of so-called "covenant children."

Once again, the interesting thing about these proof-texts, as demonstrated so clearly by Thomas E. Watson, is that paedobaptists disagree among themselves concerning whether or not each text supports or teaches infant baptism.[185]

ACTS 2:38–39

Acts 2:38–39 is a pivotal text used in the argument for infant baptism:

> And Peter said to them, "Repent and let each of you be baptized in the name of Jesus Christ for the forgiveness of your sins; and you shall receive the gift of the Holy Spirit. For the promise is for you and your children, and all who are far off, as many as the Lord our God shall call to Himself."

Paedobaptists like Berkhof, Murray, and Marston sometimes cut the text off at "the promise is to you and to your children . . ." and declare that these Jews immediately assumed that the covenant

---

[185]Watson, *Babies Be Baptized?*, 35–42.

sign of baptism was to be administered to their children.[186] However, the text also states equally that the promise is "to those afar off, as many as the Lord our God shall call to Himself." There are two things that must be defined in this text: What is the "promise" and who is to receive it?

The word *promise* (*epaggelia*) in verse 39 refers to the promise of the Holy Spirit. Luke 24:49, Acts 1:4 and Acts 2:33 identify the promise as the pouring out of the Spirit through Christ's mediation. One might point out that this was a Jewish audience and that hearers would immediately think of the promise to Abraham and to his seed. That would be correct. For in Galatians 3:14, we find that the promise to Abraham is fulfilled in the pouring out of the Spirit on his seed, Jew and Gentile, as prophesied throughout the Old Testament (Joel 2:28–29; Ezekiel 36:26–27). However, this promise is given only to those "of faith" (Galatians 3:22). The promise of Acts 2:39, therefore, is not the promise to Abraham that his children should be circumcised in his covenant. It is the promise that the Holy Spirit would be poured out to raise up regenerate children of Abraham.

Going further, one is an heir according to the promise, and Abraham's seed, if and only if one belongs to Christ (Galatians 3:14, 29). Romans 4:16 states that the promise to Abraham is made certain to each and every seed of Abraham, Jew and Gentile, *by faith* that it may be in accordance with grace, not of the flesh. Romans 9:6–8 states that only the children of the promise

---

[186]Louis Berkhof, *Systematic Theology,* 633; Murray, *Christian Baptism,* 70–71; and Marston, *Biblical Baptist,* 15–16. Typically, Murray's comments on Acts 2:38–39 do not even mention "and those who are far off, as many as the Lord our God shall call to Himself" (Acts 2:39). The Scripture text teaches that the same promise of the Spirit is offered to three groups (hearers, their children and all who are far off), upon the condition of each one's repentance and faith. Murray, however, by a subtle comment, shifts the emphasis to children being included with their parents by covenantal relations. He also ignores the effectual call of God as the ultimate condition for the repentance and faith of all three groups. Murray thus erroneously concludes: "Simply stated, this means that the promise is to the children as well as their parents and that, in respect of this property, *the children are included with their parents*" [emphasis mine], 70. This ignores the grammar of the verse as well as its context. The grammatical structure actually separates the children from the parents and places them in the same class as "all those afar off" subject to God's effectual call. Only if the children repent as do the parents and "all afar off" may they receive the New Covenant sign.

(i.e., the elect, regenerated by the Holy Spirit) are regarded as Abraham's seed and the true Israel. And this is in the context of sovereign election, which determines who receives the promise, even within the covenant family of Isaac. The rest of Romans 9 clearly identifies the children of promise through Isaac as the regenerate remnant of Jew and Gentile.

To briefly summarize, the promise to Abraham to be heir of the world (Romans 4:13) is fulfilled in the New Covenant by the pouring out of the promised Spirit upon his seed who come to God through the perfect mediation of Jesus Christ, Abraham's final physical seed. Only those who receive the promise of the Spirit through repentance and faith in Christ are actually Abraham's seed and heirs. Only those who exhibit such repentance and faith (disciples alone) are entitled to the sign of the New Covenant as the children of Abraham. This is exactly what happened in Acts 2:38–41. Only those "who received [Peter's] word were baptized" (2:41).

Again, who is offered the promise of the Spirit through repentance and faith in Christ in Acts 2:38? All those mentioned in verse 39: "you and your children and all those afar off." But is this an indiscriminate assurance that each of those mentioned will definitely receive the promise? No. Only "*as many as* the Lord our God may call to Himself [emphasis mine]." Here is the ultimate condition of the reception of the promise: the effectual calling of God, not parental connection.

The real question is to whom does *osous an* [as many as] refer? Does *osous an* refer only to "those afar off" (fairly well agreed to refer to future converts, Jew or Gentile), or does it refer to the whole phrase including "you and your children"? According to Arndt and Gingrich, *osous an* introduces a conditional relative clause that denotes action of the verb as dependent upon some circumstance or condition.[187] This condition is, namely, the sovereign will of God in effectual calling expressed in the subjunctive of *proskaleo* [may call]. *Osous an* is the direct object (masculine accusative plural) of the verb *proskaleo*, identifying whom the Lord may call—and since *teknois, humin,* and *pasi* [children, you, and all] are collectively offered the promise by use of the conjunction *kai* [and], we may refer to these three dative

---

[187]William F. Ardnt and Wilbur F. Gingrich, *A Greek-English Lexicon of the New Testament,* (Chicago, IL: The University of Chicago Press, 1957), 48.

plurals as the compound indirect object. Further, because *teknois* and *pasi* are masculine, *osous an* may legitimately modify both of them. Therefore, all three classes are offered the promise of the Spirit through their own repentance and faith. Yet, in *osous an,* the condition of reception by all three must depend on the sovereign effectual calling of God. There is not a greater promise to the children of those addressed than is given to those Jewish parents and the future called ones. This is further correlated in the context in that not all those addressed received the promise, but only those who "received" Peter's word of repentance and faith by God's effectual calling, including the children (Acts 2:41).

One objection to this exegesis is that there would be no need to mention "and your children" if they were given the same promise as their parents—they would have been included in the "you" that addresses the multitude. Therefore, according to paedobaptist theology, the mention of "and your children" is evidence for the continuation of the covenant family concept and the application of the covenant sign upon one's children by the *oikos* formula.

However, as we have already seen, the *oikos* formula is invalid for baptism. In addition, the mention of the children here is better explained by considering that the apostle wanted to ensure that there was no misunderstanding; that they were not to receive baptism unless they also repented and believed as did their parents, as verse 38 clearly requires. Only those who received Peter's word were baptized (Acts 2:41). This is why the children were mentioned in the invitation to repent, to prevent misunderstanding by Jewish parents who might assume from the Abrahamic Covenant that it was permitted to baptize their infants without their personal repentance. A second answer to this objection is that all those baptized devoted themselves to the apostles' teaching, the Lord's Supper, and such (v. 42). If infants were baptized, did they also do these things? The paedobaptist position does not stand close examination.

Paedobaptists contend that Acts 2:39 must be read through the eyes of the Abrahamic Covenant. However, biblical hermeneutics require that the fuller revelation of the New Testament must define how the Abrahamic Covenant is fulfilled in it, rather than relying upon the Abrahamic Covenant to overrule the New Testament revelation of its fulfillment. Acts 2:38–41 supports the principle that New Testament revelation should define the participants of the New Covenant fulfillment of the Abrahamic Covenant rather than vice-versa; only the children in the crowd who received Peter's word were baptized. There is no other exegetical possibility in the text.

The only possible conclusion, by ordinary hermeneutics, is that those who received Peter's word and claimed God's promise were baptized. There is no mention of infants being baptized in this passage along with their parents. Were there no children present? Because Peter referred to children in the promise, and it is likely that there were infants and small children among the many thousands in Jerusalem listening to Peter, the text is even stronger against infant baptism; only those who received the word, and who repented and believed, were baptized.

Watson uses Albert Barnes as an example of a paedobaptist who disagrees with typical paedobaptist interpretations of Acts 2:39. Watson quotes Barnes:

> *To your children.* In Joel, to their sons and daughters, who should, nevertheless, be old enough to prophesy. Similar promises occur in Is. 44:3, "I will pour out my Spirit on thy seed, and my blessing on thine offspring" and Is. 59.21. In these and similar places their descendants and posterity are denoted. It does not refer to children as children, and *should not be adduced to establish the propriety of infant baptism* [emphasis mine].[188]

Watson also quotes Dr. Hammond, a nominee to the Westminster Assembly who never sat in session, as one who disallowed Acts 2:38–39 as having any reference to infant baptism, even though the passage is referenced in the Larger Catechism (Question 166) as supporting the concept. According to Dr. Hammond, it was meant to denote the Jews' posterity.

I conclude that Acts 2:39 actually supports the idea of disciples' baptism. Those who were baptized were those effectually called by God; that is, those who received the gospel as evidenced by their repentance and faith. It was a disciple's baptism alone.

1 CORINTHIANS 7:12–16

1 Corinthians 7:12–16 is a passage that describes the children of a mixed marriage as "holy" instead of "unclean":

> But to the rest I say, not the Lord, that if any brother has a wife who is an unbeliever, and she consents to live with him, let him not send her away. And a woman who has an unbelieving husband, and

---

[188]Watson, *Babies Be Baptized?*, 37.

he consents to live with her, let her not send her husband away. For the unbelieving husband *is sanctified* through his wife, and the unbelieving wife *is sanctified* through her believing husband; for *otherwise your children are unclean, but now they are holy.* Yet if the unbelieving one leaves, let him leave; the brother or the sister is not under bondage in such cases, but God has called us to peace. For how do you know, O wife, whether you will save your husband? Or how do you know, O husband, whether you will save your wife [emphasis mine]?

This passage often has been used by paedobaptists to illustrate the special position of believer's children "in" the visible church and Covenant of Grace, thus giving them the right by physical line to baptism. G. I. Williamson goes so far as to say:

> As might be expected, then, the evidence that children were baptized in the early New Testament Church is circumstantial. We will here give a mere sample of this kind of evidence. In 1 Corinthians 7:14 Paul says that children born to marriages in which at least one parent is a Christian are *holy. The word translated holy is the standard word in the New Testament for professing adult Christians (often translated saints). Paul calls these infants saints* [emphasis mine].[189]

Does Williamson actually mean that these children (no matter how old) are to be considered saints by their connection to a believing parent before they profess faith in Christ? What if the child was twelve and not a professing Christian? Should he still be called a saint? Imagine what confusion this would cause parents concerning the spiritual condition of their children and whether or not they should evangelize them.

There are at least five problems with Williamson's misinterpretation of 1 Corinthians 7:14:

First, typical of paedobaptist comments on this text, Williamson ignores the immediate context that Christians should stay in the condition of life they were in when saved, thus showing God's approval of mixed marriages and the approved *status* of the children. When Israel put away unbelieving wives in mixed marriages, they also put away their children. It is more than possible that Paul is dealing with similar issues in the Christian assembly.

---

[189] G. I. Williamson, *The Shorter Catechism*, 2: Q. 39–107 (Nutley, NJ: Presbyterian and Reformed Publishing Company, 1975), 103.

Could not Paul simply be telling Christians that, contrary to Old Testament practice, Christians should stay in a mixed marriage and that children of such a marriage are also acceptable to God? God had complained against Israel that some of the Israelites had married pagan wives so that the "holy seed" had been mixed with the peoples of the land (Ezra 9). Ezra 10:2–3 reads:

> And Shecaniah the son of Jehiel, one of the sons of Elam, answered and said to Ezra, "We have been unfaithful to our God, and have married foreign women from the peoples of the land; yet now there is hope for Israel in spite of this. So now let us make a covenant with our God to *put away all the wives and their children,* according to the counsel of my lord and of those who tremble at the commandment of our God; and let it be done according to the law" [emphasis mine].

If paedobaptists believe that Acts 2:38–39 must be read through the eyes of the Abrahamic Covenant, then surely 1 Corinthians 7:14 must be read through the eyes of Ezra 10:2–3. The better reading is simply that Paul is saying that, under the New Covenant, believers should stay with unbelieving spouses and the children of the marriage are accepted by God as holy. The covenant family concept has changed since Ezra 10:2–3.

Second, Williamson also ignores that "the word translated holy" is not a noun for "saints" but actually a predicate adjective meaning *set apart,* describing something as set apart for or approved by God (Holy Spirit, holy city, holy angels, holy prophets, holy covenant, holy ground, holy scriptures, holy law, holy temple, holy body, holy kiss, etc.). The same Greek word is also used sometimes as a noun in substantive form for "saints" or "holy ones," as Williamson claims, but when it is in noun form, it is usually prefaced by the article *the,* as in "the saints." The fact is, no reputable English Bible translates "holy" as the substantive noun form "saints," but all translate it as a predicate adjective in some way contrasted to "unclean" (see 1 Corinthians 7:34).

Williamson also ignores the fact that Paul says here that the unbelieving husband "is sanctified." Sanctification, of course, usually refers to Christians, as well as to things set apart or approved (Hebrews 10:14; 1 Timothy 4:5). Williamson is inconsistent in his hermeneutic because he will not call the unbelieving spouse a Christian as he does the children. Yet Grosheide, another paedobaptist, goes so far as to say that the unbelieving husband here "is sanctified" in the sense that he "is called a brother, namely of the other believers, the church."[190] Should we call unbelieving spouses "brothers" to Christians in the church? Not according to the common use of *brethren* in the New Testament. The confused and inconsistent explanations of this text by paedobaptists to justify the practice of infant baptism demonstrate the incredible weakness of the argument.

Thomas E. Watson lists several paedobaptist commentators who agree that there is no support for infant baptism in this text. Albert Barnes, for example, argues that 1 Corinthians 7:14 merely explains the legitimacy of a mixed marriage and the resulting legitimacy of the children.[191]

Third, as stated earlier, the theme of the entire chapter is Paul's admonition that Christians remain in the state in which they were called (7:20, 24, 26–27, 40). Paul declares that a mixed couple should remain married because the unbelieving partner *is sanctified* by God in the marriage through the believer. It is important to note that the child is *holy* not because of the believer alone, but because of the unbeliever's sanctification as well. The rest of Scripture denies that this unbelieving adult is sanctified in a salvific way by the relation to the Christian partner (Acts 26:18). Rather, the unbeliever is sanctified only in the sense of receiving God's recognition of a legitimate marriage, contrary to Ezra 10:2–3. This is the main point!

Paul's further point is that therefore (*gar* [for] in the causative sense) the children are not *akatharta* [unclean] but *hagia* [holy] in light of the unbelieving spouse's sanctification. Many have seen this as support for a special position that believer's children have with God. However, the context and usage of *akatharta* [unclean] must help define the sense of *hagia* [holy] here. Although the main thought seems to be the recognition of the Christian's and the non-Christian's marriage by God, Paul may be dealing with the parallel situation of a Jew married to a Gentile, producing unclean children as in the case of Timothy (Acts 16:1). If the marriage was not accepted by God, then it would be illegitimate and

---

[190] F. W. Grosheide, *Commentary on the First Epistle to the Corinthians* in *The New International Commentary on the New Testament* (Grand Rapids, MI: William B. Eerdmans Publishing Company, 1964), 165.
[191] Watson, *Babies Be Baptized?*, 39–41.

unclean, and so would the children. Paul takes pains to point out that this is not true.

A significant use of *akatharta* in the New Testament, when referring to a person, is in Acts 10:28. There, Peter tells Cornelius, not yet a believer in Christ, that God has instructed him to consider no man *akatharta* [unclean] anymore. Although Cornelius was a God-fearer and worshipped the God of Israel, he was still a Gentile and considered unclean by the Jews. He had to stay outside the assembly of God's people. God, however, had changed the status of Gentiles in the New Covenant administration. In the same way, the unbelieving spouse and therefore the children of this mixed marriage are not unclean; they are holy. Williamson appears to have forgotten that children of an illegitimate union could not enter the assembly of God's people under the Sinai Covenant (Deuteronomy 23:2)—but they can under the New Covenant.

The appendix on baptism to the *1689 London Confession* summarizes why the children were declared holy in light of the unbelieving spouse's sanctification, and why their resulting holiness could extend no further than that of the unbelieving spouse's:

> And we do think that although the Apostle's asserting of the unbelieving yokefellow to be sanctified by the believer, should carry in it somewhat more than is in the bare marriage of two infidels, because although the marriage covenant has a divine sanction so as to make the wedlock of two unbelievers a lawful action, and their conjunction and cohabitation in that respect undefiled, yet there might be no ground to suppose from thence, that both or either of their persons are thereby sanctified; and the Apostle urges the cohabitation of a believer with an infidel in the state of wedlock from this ground that the unbelieving husband is sanctified by the believing wife; nevertheless here you have the influence of a believer's faith *ascending from an inferior to a superior relation;* from the wife to the husband who is her head, *before it can descend to their offspring.* And therefore we say, whatever be the nature or extent of the holiness here intended, we conceive it cannot convey to the children an immediate right to baptism, because it would then be of another nature, and of a larger extent, than the root, and original from whence it is derived. For it is clear by the Apostle's argument that holiness cannot be derived to the child from the sanctity of one parent only, if either father or mother be (in the sense intended by the Apostle) unholy or unclean, so will the child be also, therefore for the production of an holy seed it is necessary

that both the parents be sanctified; and this the Apostle positively asserts in the first place to be done by the believing parent, although the other be an unbeliever; and then consequentially from thence argues, the holiness of their children. Hence it follows, that as the children have no other holiness than what they derive from both their parents, so neither can they have any right by this holiness to any spiritual privilege but such as both their parents did also partake of: and therefore if the unbelieving parent (though sanctified by the believing parent) has not thereby a right to baptism, neither can we conceive that there is any such privilege derived to the children by their birth-holiness.[192]

A fourth problem with Williamson's view is that the children may be called holy because they have a gospel heritage as opposed to children without Christian parents.

The real question here is how can an unbelieving spouse be sanctified and how can the child of a believer be called holy under the New Covenant administration of grace? If the basic meaning in both these words is *set apart* unto God, the question arises as to how each of the parties are set apart unto God and what is the relationship of each to the New Covenant?

Most agree that the unbelieving spouse is not in the New Covenant until regeneration (Acts 26:18). However, Meredith Kline is arbitrary in attempting to argue that the believing husband's marital covenantal authority has changed from including his wife in the Old Covenant while not including her in the New Covenant.[193] Yet, inconsistently, he maintains that the believing husband's parental covenantal authority is still valid in the New Covenant as the basis for his children being in the covenant and receiving baptism; he also includes the possibility of baptizing household slaves. Kline's logic is intricate but ultimately unavailing. The better view is that, by the unbeliever's union with the believer, God recognizes the marriage as holy in that He promises to accept and set apart that marriage to fulfill His purposes.

With respect to the children in this mixed marriage, the way in which they are set apart is more difficult to determine. Two passages often used to support the children's participation in the

---

[192]*See* Appendix D.
[193]Kline, *By Oath Consigned,* 94–102.

New Covenant fulfillment of the Abrahamic Covenant are Romans 11 and Ephesians 6:1–4. First, Paul states in Romans 11:16 that his kinsmen in the flesh, the branches presently cut off from participation in the olive tree of the New Covenant, are still holy because their root is holy. However, these "beloved for the sake of the fathers" (v. 28) shall be grafted in again if they do not continue in unbelief (v. 23).

Here is the case of physical descendants of Abraham and the covenant promises (Romans 9:1–5) who are holy yet not in the New Covenant and kingdom, nor entitled to baptism, until they believe. They are holy because of their heritage. Also, the firstborn may be called holy to the Lord (Luke 2:25), without being in the New Covenant. These verses confirm the view that the children of 1 Corinthians 7:14 can be considered holy for the sake of their parents and their heritage in the gospel blessings yet not in the New Covenant administration until they believe. Therefore, they may be considered holy as were the physical seed of Abraham (Romans 11:16), yet be refused the covenant sign till repentance and faith.

Further, if we strictly say that the children of Ephesians 6:1–4 are addressed and accepted as saints (1:1), we also have to strictly say they have believed and were sealed with the Holy Spirit of promise (1:13). However, there is no sound argument concerning the inclusion of children in the church without regeneration and conversion. The fact that the children would be able to understand Paul's exhortation and are called saints, sealed by the Spirit, makes it more plausible that he is talking to regenerate children who were full members of the New Covenant Church.

It is possible that Paul is addressing the children in the congregational gathering who sit under the preached word of God without woodenly insisting that they are in the New Covenant Church. The fifth commandment (honor your father and mother) is required of all children, those whose parents are believers and unbelievers alike. It is not uncommon for pastors to address churches as the "saints" when there is an unchurched child of unchurched parents in the assembly. Is Paul's exhortation applicable to them? Of course! Nonetheless, it still is clutching at straws to make unbelieving children members of the New Covenant. If we are going to make the children of Ephesians 6 members of the church, it is only because there is better evidence that they are regenerate and, have undergone disciple's baptism

(Ephesians 1:13; 4:1–6). The inadequate appeal to Ephesians only further supports the possibility that the children may be considered set apart as privileged by their gospel heritage and exposure, yet not actually in the New Covenant Church and entitled to baptism.

Therefore, both context and word study seem to point to *hagia* [holy] as referring to the legitimacy or sanctifying of the marriage and of the children rather than necessarily referring to the covenant promises of salvation and sanctification—and if the latter view were taken, how old are the children of this legitimized marriage? Are they infants, toddlers, pre-teens, teenagers, or adults? Pierre Marcel considers twelve-years-old to be the age of discretion. If the latter view opens the way to covenant baptism, should all children still living at home be considered *hagia* and therefore baptized into the covenant relationship, even if preteen, teenaged, or adult? No, Scripture prescribes the baptism of disciples alone, no matter the age.

Finally, Jeremias argues from Jewish proselyte baptism that 1 Corinthians 7:14c "bears no reference to baptism." In fact, he argued that children born after a new Christian mother was baptized were considered holy. If such were the case, it is more than possible that Paul was affirming to Christian parents of mixed marriages that their children were holy and did not need either circumcision or baptism.

Later, Jeremias no longer excluded the baptism of children on the eighth day, but he stated that the Corinthian reference still does not enjoin infant baptism.[194] Those who appeal to Jeremias for the *oikos* formula argument yet neglect his view of 1 Corinthians 7:14 are woefully inconsistent and arbitrary in their arguments.

E. Stauffer, to whom Jeremias himself appealed as an authority, also teaches that 1 Corinthians 7:14 has nothing to say about infant baptism because the concept was something Paul did not know much about. Kurt Aland also systematically rejects each of Jeremias' arguments and evidences for infant baptism.[195]

Using the *oikos* formula to establish infant baptism in households yet neglecting its implications in 1 Corinthians 7:14 reveals once again the uncertainty of silence as the basis for infant baptism. To establish a practice never mentioned (the normative

---

[194] Jeremias, *Infant Baptism,* 47–48.
[195] Aland, *Baptize Infants?,* 30.

principle) is not the same kind of argument from silence as rejecting a practice never mentioned (the regulative principle).

To summarize, it is my conclusion that 1 Corinthians 7:14 refers either to the children's legitimacy in a legitimate marriage in the eyes of God or to their set-apart position for the sake of their parents' gospel heritage. The verse does not support a covenant position for the children. In addition, there is no mention of household covenant baptism, a subject Paul would have explained to these Gentile Corinthians if it had existed. Whatever holy means, then, it is certain that Paul did not appeal to infant baptism, but rather to the child's relationship to a believing and unbelieving parent. The use of this text to support covenantal infant baptism cannot stand.

1 CORINTHIANS 10:1–14

A few paedobaptists have claimed that 1 Corinthians 10:1–14 proves the validity of infant baptism:

> For I do not want you to be unaware, brethren, that our fathers were all under the cloud, and all passed through the sea; and all were baptized into Moses in the cloud and in the sea; and all ate the same spiritual food; and all drank from the same spiritual rock which followed them; and the rock was Christ; nevertheless, with most of them God was not well pleased; for they were laid low in the wilderness. Now these things happened as examples for us, that we should not crave evil things, as they also craved. And do not be idolators. . . . Now these things happened to them as an example, and they were written for our instruction, upon whom the ends of the ages have come. Therefore let him who thinks he stands take heed lest he fall (1 Corinthians 10:1–7, 11–12).

The paedobaptist argument is that all were "baptized into Moses" when they passed through the sea on dry ground, including the infants. Thus, by good and necessary inference, here is an example of infant baptism from the Old Testament.

There are several hermeneutical reasons, however, for rejecting the claim that this passage grants permission for paedobaptism. Once again, the inferences from this passage to establish an example of infant baptism are neither good nor necessary. First, Paul is obviously speaking figuratively here, and one must be careful not to press in every detail a figurative passage. Second, the obvious and overriding purpose of the passage in context is to warn "those who have been sanctified in Christ Jesus, saints by calling, with all who in every place call upon the name of our Lord Jesus Christ . . ." (1 Corinthians 1:2). These *professing Christians* "who call upon the name" (thus excluding infants) are not to fall into sin as those who "were laid low in the wilderness" did. Third, he identifies "our fathers" as the subject of the figure. He is dealing with those who consciously craved evil things and were punished by God, not their infants (Hebrews 3–4). Fourth, he is addressing disciples, warning them to flee from idolatry, and, fifth, he does not identify the subjects of baptism as he would in a didactic passage designed for that purpose. Such figurative passages cannot overthrow clear New Testament instructions for a sacrament instituted by Christ.

The same passage is used figuratively by some to justify sprinkling or pouring from the cloud as the true form of baptism, a very questionable exegesis, overruling the clear meaning of *baptizo* as *to dip or to immerse* in the Gospels. This position is refuted in Appendix B on the mode of baptism.

If one wishes to use 1 Corinthians 10:1–14 as an example of Old Testament infant baptism in the church in the wilderness, then one must also use the lack of circumcision of those born in the wilderness church as a rejection of the parallel between circumcision and infant baptism in the church today.

Appealing to metaphorical and disputed passages to establish a sacrament and its practice is not hermeneutically sound. As Berkhof warns, figurative and disputed passages cannot overrule the analogy of faith in passages more clearly taught.[196]

SUMMARY

Having examined the important pearl of proof-texts for infant baptism, I come away more doubtful than convinced. It remains my conviction that the paedobaptists' own proof-texts support disciple's baptism over infant baptism.

---

[196]Berkhof, *Principles,* 82ff., 166

Chapter 8

Jesus' Attitude Toward Children

Paedobaptists often use one particular set of proof-texts to argue that Jesus taught the inclusion of believers' children in the Covenant of Grace. This is the group of passages that show Jesus interacting with children.

The paedobaptist understanding of these texts is that they admit infants into the kingdom of God, thus entitling them to baptism. Baptists, however, and even many paedobaptists, disagree.

MATTHEW 18:1–10

The first set of parallel passages is Matthew 18:1–10; Mark 9:33–37; and Luke 9:46–48:

> And He *called a child to Himself* and stood him in their midst, and said, "Truly I say to you, unless you are converted and become like children, you shall not enter the kingdom of heaven. Whoever then *humbles himself as this child,* he is the greatest in the kingdom of heaven . . . but whoever causes one of *these little ones who believe in Me* to stumble . . . [Matthew 18:2–4, 6; emphasis mine].

In this passage (and its parallels), Jesus set a little child before His disciples to teach them a lesson. The disciples had come to Jesus with the question, "Who is the greatest in the kingdom of heaven?" Christ used the example of a child to confront their pride. In Matthew 18, we find that the *paidion* [little child] responded to Jesus' call in the participle *proskalesamenos* [having called to himself]. This is the same verb used in Acts 2:39 that conditions the reception of God's promise through repentance and faith by God's effectual calling. This means that the child was not an infant and was capable of responding to Jesus' call to Himself.

In the context of this passage, Jesus taught His disciples three things. First of all, they must be converted and become "as little children" to enter the kingdom of heaven. I do not quarrel with the Scriptural truth that Jeremiah, John the Baptist, and others were regenerated in the womb, but the necessity of conversion and humility, as illustrated by the example of the child, to enter the kingdom of heaven is clear. This passive use of *converted* or *otrepho* (meaning *to turn or change*) as an entrance requirement into the kingdom of heaven is similar to the New Birth discussed in John 3. The disciples' vain claims at greatness possibly testified to unregenerate hearts, no small warning. Jesus here defines what He meant in verse 3 by the inferential *oun* [therefore] of verse 4. A person must be converted and humble himself "as *this* little child" to enter into and to be great in the kingdom of heaven. This little child came humbly to Jesus at His call without regard to anything within himself.

The second thing Jesus taught the disciples was that they must receive even insignificant children who come to Him. They must honor the least, as Christ Himself did, instead of thinking themselves to be greater (*see* Jeremiah 31:33, 34; Matthew 11:11).

The third thing He taught them was that to cause one of "these little ones who believe in Me" to stumble was an offense against God Himself and would bring upon them the stumbling block of God's wrath. The verse indicates that this child was a believer.

I conclude that these passages have nothing to do with whether infants are in the covenant because this *paidion* [little child] responded to Jesus' call, *proskaleo,* and believed in Him. This humble submission of a child to Christ as Lord was what He was trying to teach His disciples about entrance into and greatness in the kingdom. It does not support infant baptism.

MATTHEW 19:13–15

Paedobaptists have more often referenced another passage for support of infant covenant privileges in baptism, Matthew 19:13–15 (and parallels Mark 10:13–16 and Luke 18:15–17):

> Then some children were brought to Him so that He might lay His hands on them and pray; and the disciples rebuked them. But Jesus said, "Let the children alone, and do not hinder them from coming to Me; for the kingdom of heaven belongs to such as these." And after laying His hands on them, He departed from there (Matthew 19:13–15).

Here, the disciples rebuked some people for bringing little children to Jesus. Luke records that Jesus called the children to Himself (once again, *proskalesamenos,* or having called to himself). Then He commanded the disciples to stop restraining the children from coming to Him.

Although some paedobaptists have pointed out that Luke called the children mentioned in this passage *brephe* [infants], the reflexive pronoun *auta* [them] defines those who were restrained from coming to Jesus as the *brephe* themselves, not the parents who brought them. It seems that the context defines these infants as being old enough to be capable of responding to Jesus' call. Also, it may be pointed out that Paul reminded Timothy that he had known the Scriptures from a *brephous* [a babe]; that is, infancy. So, it seems that *brephe* may be used to describe a child of such age as one who could learn the Scripture.

The picture seems to be that the parents brought children to be blessed by Jesus; then Jesus called the children to come to Him. The children who came to Him were picked up and blessed. Jesus teaches here that one must *receive* the kingdom of God as a little child receives it to enter the kingdom. There is no promise to these children unless they come to Jesus and receive the kingdom as well.

In fact, if any passage in Scripture teaches the fallacy of paedobaptism this one does. Neither Jesus nor His disciples baptized these children even though they had a perfect opportunity to do so. Instead, Jesus and the disciples only blessed them. Still the question remains: If Jesus believed in the *oikos* formula, why did He not baptize these small children whether they came to Him or not? And if Jesus did not feel the weight of the *oikos* formula when the children were brought to Him, why should we?

In summary, Jesus did bless children as they were presented to Him by their parents, but no promise of entrance into the kingdom is made to these children unless they also come to Jesus and receive the kingdom as examples of the way adults should receive it. The most that can be seen in these passages is infant blessing, but not infant baptism. Those paedobaptists who sometimes explain to Baptist visitors that infant baptism is simply the infant blessing or infant dedication of Jesus are misleading them. Paedobaptism implies much more than infant dedication and actually withholds from the children their own responsibility to obey the Lord's commandment to all men: repent and be baptized.

SUMMARY

Several paedobaptist authors such as Matthew Poole, B. B. Warfield, and John Murray have agreed that there is no warrant for or an example of infant baptism in these passages on Jesus' dealings with children.[197] For example, John Murray says:

> To conclude: these two assertions—(1) that little children belong to the kingdom of God; (2) that they are to be received in Christ's name—do not provide stringent proof of infant baptism and they do not provide us with an express command to baptise infants. They do, however, supply us with certain principles which lie close to the argument for infant baptism and without which the ordinance of infant baptism would be meaningless.[198]

Although Murray admits that these passages we have been examining present no evidence for infant baptism, he also asserts that they contain principles that "lie close to the argument for infant baptism." This latter argument is meaningless, however, if the ordinance of infant baptism is not instituted by Scripture. Arguments that "lie close" are often expanded by a misuse of good and necessary inference into unsupported evidence for what is supposed to be an instituted ordinance. Once again, though, such flimsy evidence cannot establish a sacrament supposedly instituted by Christ. To adopt a practice from

---

[197] *See* Watson, *Babies Be Baptized?*, 24–25, for quotes from these three authors. Warfield said: "Nobody supposes that Jesus and His disciples were in the habit of baptizing children" (*Studies in Theology*, 399).
[198] Murray, *Christian Baptism,* 65.

silence (the normative principle) is not the same as rejecting a practice never mentioned (the regulative principle).

Finally, if the *oikos* formula is the historical background for Christian baptism at Pentecost, as paedobaptists claim, thus permitting infant baptism, then one must ask why Jesus did not apply this principle and just baptize these children as well. Why did He not baptize whole households upon the parents' faith? Simply put, the answer is that He did not follow the supposed *oikos* formula for His baptism because He did not believe that it applied to baptism. He baptized disciples alone (John 4:1–2). In Jesus' mind, the supposed *oikos* formula did not apply to the instituted sacrament of baptism, before or after Pentecost.

Chapter 9

The Disjunction of John's and Jesus' Baptisms with Christian Baptism

Paedobaptists have attempted to separate the intent and subjects of John's and Jesus' baptisms from the intent and subjects of Christian baptism. John Murray, in particular, identifies Christian baptism as the baptism of the Great Commission. He then attempts to distinguish his "Christian" baptism from John's and Jesus' baptisms. Of course, to be consistent, he must do this, because if Jesus' baptism was Christian baptism, then Christian baptism would be of disciples alone, not infants (John 4:1–2).[199] I believe this to be an unbiblical separation.

In Chapter 1, I showed the fallacy of Murray's basic argument. On the one hand, he argues for infant baptism by good and necessary inference from Old Testament circumcision, stating that the positive institution of disciple's baptism is not sufficient to abrogate the Abrahamic inclusion of infants into the covenant sign. On the other hand, he denies the relation of John's and Jesus' baptisms to Christian baptism by good and necessary inference because the positive institution of Great Commission "Christian Baptism" is regarded by him as sufficient to abrogate all previous ones. He cannot have it both ways.

JOHN'S AND JESUS' BAPTISMS

There can be no separation of the subjects of baptism between John's and Jesus' baptisms. It is fairly well admitted by Baptists and paedobaptists alike that John baptized professing subjects alone, not infants, upon condition of repentance (Matthew 3:6;

---
[199]*Ibid.*, 4–8.

Mark 1:4) unto the forgiveness of sins. It is also clear that the disciples of Jesus baptized only those who were made disciples first, not infants:

> When therefore the Lord knew that the Pharisees heard that Jesus was making and baptizing more disciples than John, although Jesus Himself was not baptizing, but His disciples were (John 4:1–2).

There is no mention of, or evidence for, infant baptism of the children of those who were made disciples in either John's or Jesus' baptisms.

Another question is this: Who baptized Jesus' disciples into Christian baptism? It could not have been Jesus (John 4:1–2). Apparently it was John and/or other disciples. John baptized at least Andrew and another disciple (John 1:35, 40), yet there is no record of their rebaptism by other disciples at Pentecost. Because Jesus Himself did not baptize (John 4:2), it is highly probable that, contrary to Murray's position, the baptism of Jesus' disciples by John or by each other before Pentecost was accepted as their Christian baptism.

In Apollos we see at least one example of a disciple of John for whom there is no record of rebaptism after Pentecost. He understood the gospel already as a baptized follower of John (Acts 18:24–28). Further, at Pentecost, only those unbaptized Jews conversing with Peter received his word and were baptized (Acts 2:37–42). Were the 120 men and women praying in the upper room rebaptized into Murray's Great Commission baptism? As far as we know, they were not; rather, they were baptized by John and/or the twelve, and were not rebaptized into Christian baptism. It may even be that these 120 people helped baptize the 3,000 who were converted. If Great Commission baptism is the only legitimate Christian baptism, as Murray claims, it seems odd that the twelve and the 120 were not rebaptized into Murray's Christian baptism.

The only place we have a possible rebaptism of John's disciples is in Acts 19:1–7, and Calvin disagrees with the typical paedobaptist interpretation that this passage refers to water baptism. It seems that these disciples of John's baptism did not have the complete message of John about Jesus and the Holy Spirit when they were first baptized. In other words, they had an insufficient profession before their baptism. Therefore, Paul rebaptized them into

Christ after their proper profession of faith. Calvin comments that this rebaptism was not necessarily by water but was rather Christ's baptism with the Holy Spirit. He points out that Paul's laying on of hands is mentioned but there is no mention of water in the passage.[200] Others disagree, and obviously, there is much disagreement on this text. Nonetheless, it certainly cannot be used to separate John's baptism from Christian baptism.

JESUS' BAPTISM AND CHRISTIAN BAPTISM

There does not seem to be a definite line of demarcation between John's, Jesus', and Christian baptism. This observation is bolstered by Mark 1:1, which describes "the beginning of the gospel of Jesus Christ" as occurring with the coming of John in verse 2. Because the subjects of John's and Jesus' baptisms were of disciples alone, Christian baptism as well must apply to disciples alone. Jesus affirmed this in the Great Commission where He gives the command to make disciples of all the nations, baptizing and teaching them. The "them" who are baptized and taught refers to those who are made disciples. Jesus also commanded the eleven to teach those baptized disciples all that He had commanded them. The things He commanded them includes His instructions to baptize only repentant disciples. Thus, to separate Jesus' baptism from Great Commission baptism literally is to violate the Great Commission itself!

Every use of the word *disciple* in the New Testament refers to a self-aware, willful follower of a teacher. Therefore, in the Great Commission, Christ defined the subjects of baptism and Christian teaching as self-aware disciples. It might be added that Jesus clearly defined the basis for building His church in Matthew 16:16–19, 24–26 as the example of Peter's apostolic confession of faith. This supports the contention that the intended subjects of baptism for His church were professing disciples alone.

If we call baptism a sacrament *instituted by Christ* for the outward sign of admission into His confessional church, then

---

[200]John Calvin, *Commentary on the Acts of the Apostles*, trans. Christopher Fetherstone (1585; reprint, Grand Rapids, MI: Baker Book House, 1981), 2:205–11.

why do paedobaptists not trust His positive instructions concerning the subjects of baptism? Are we not obligated to teach whatever He commanded and taught (Matt. 28:18–20), including the baptism of disciples alone? His instituted instructions for founding His New Covenant church must hold priority over a possibly erroneous inference regarding the application of the Abrahamic Covenant, rather than vice-versa.

Some paedobaptists continue to claim that the Great Commission constituted the initial institution of Christian baptism. They say it would not have been unusual to see a missionary-minded Christ giving instructions for disciple's baptism alone, naturally assuming the baptism of their infants to follow. This ignores the fact, however, that Christ instituted baptism and practiced it Himself (through His disciples) long before the Great Commission (John 4:1). In His earlier baptism, He clearly baptized only those made disciples, not including their infant children. If we are going to assume the Great Commission to be the official institution of Christian baptism, and if we are to teach what He commanded, we logically must assume that Christ's baptism of disciples alone was Christian baptism!

The practice and command of both Jesus' and John's baptisms names professing believers or disciples alone as the only authorized subjects of baptism. It is a credobaptism. I am not prepared to contradict either Christ's teaching or example on the basis of erroneous inference.

SUMMARY

The teaching and example of Jesus needs to be applied to the baptisms in Acts. In the Great Commission, we are called to teach baptized disciples to do whatsoever Jesus commanded His disciples. This includes His instructions concerning the baptism of disciples alone. It is often overlooked that a common designation for the church visible in Acts is *the disciples* (Acts 1:15; 6:1f.; 9:19, 26, 28; 11:29; 13:52; 14:20, 22, 28; 15:10; 18:23, 27; 19:9, 30; 20:1, 7, 30; 21:4, 16). In Acts 11:26, we are told: "And it came about that for an entire year [Saul and Barnabas] met with *the church,* and taught considerable numbers; and *the disciples* were first called Christians in Antioch" [Acts 11:26, emphasis mine]. The church is called the disciples because it was made up of those who followed Christ as baptized disciples. These disciples were first called Christians in Antioch—and only disciples were called Christians in Antioch. There is no room in these designations for the children of believers to be called visible church members or Christians simply by organic relation. The church visible is an assembly of baptized disciples, not disciples and their children.

For all these reasons, I conclude that John's, Jesus', and Christian baptisms are not to be artificially separated as some paedobaptists have done. There is an exegetical connection among them. Thus, Scripture provides no sure evidence for this discolored "pearl" and, therefore, no sure evidence that the subjects of baptism after Pentecost were any different than the subjects before—confessing disciples alone.

Chapter 10

The Weight of Precept, the Argument of Silence, and the Regulative Principle of Worship

Amazingly, one of the most widely used arguments by paedobaptists to support the practice of infant baptism is the fact that the New Testament does *not* prescribe or mention it. The principal line of argument is that giving covenant children the covenant sign was so obviously a part of the Covenant of Grace that there was no reason to mention it, much less to defend it.

However, an argument from silence to establish an instituted sacrament is logically faulty and can quickly lead to error. It is my contention that the argument for paedobaptism from silence does not bear up under examination for three reasons:

1. The weight of precept
2. The more consistent argument of silence itself
3. The regulative principle of worship

THE WEIGHT OF PRECEPT

Let us first consider the weight of precept. If we were to list the positive commands (or precepts) in the New Testament supporting paedobaptism, we would find exactly zero. Each of the positive New Testament precepts concerning baptism apply only to disciples because repentance and faith are necessary requirements for New Covenant baptism (Acts 2:38–41).

Many paedobaptists agree with this so far. However, they attempt to extract themselves from a dilemma by arguing that these precepts are not controlling because they arise in the context of a missionary church. Therefore, they say, the precepts requiring repentance and faith before baptism do not apply to infants of believers in an established church. Further, they say that for them to be convinced of the error of their position, it would take an express precept specifically prohibiting infant baptism to override the prior Abrahamic Covenant stipulations regarding circumcision and the supposed "good and necessary inferences" arising from it.

This is an absurd position for three reasons: (1) It would require stated New Testament prohibitions against other things such as household servant's baptism or adult relatives' baptisms to preclude them from being acceptable practices by good and necessary inference from the Abrahamic practice of circumcising both; (2) it demands of God a specific prohibition for a practice never mentioned against His stated precept of credobaptism; and (3) it is inconsistent with the position of many paedobaptists against paedocommunion. The same paedobaptists who would require a stated prohibition of infant baptism to abandon it (i.e., Berkhof and Murray) quote the command to examine oneself as sufficient precept to prohibit the paedocommunion of unregenerate children of the Abrahamic Covenant, even though paedocommunion is also not explicitly prohibited in the New Testament.

The weakness of this unreasonable requirement—that there be an express command prohibiting a practice—is exposed in the light of Acts 2:41–42, where all those baptized were permitted entrance to the breaking of bread, the Lord's Supper. If infant baptism is admitted in Acts 2, then so also must infant and small children's communion be permitted. It was many years later when Paul, by inspiration, wrote to the Corinthians the precept of self-examination because of irreverent partaking (1 Corinthians 11).

So, in the paedobaptist position, there is a confusion concerning the ground of entrance to the Lord's Supper—is it baptism or self-examination? And how shall the elders know to whom the Lord's Supper should be served if the primary ground is self-examination? In the light of these considerations, the one precept of self-examination before partaking of the Lord's Supper (though I believe it to be legitimate) does not compare in strength to the many attested precepts of repentance and faith before baptism. There is great inconsistency here and great danger in being so selective in the application of these hermeneutical principles.

Because of the more numerous instances calling for repentance before baptism, there is much more conclusive precept in barring believer's infant children from baptism than from the Lord's Supper. It is my belief that the instituted precepts of disciple's baptism do expressly and sufficiently prohibit infants from the covenant sign by their positive prescription (Matthew 28:18–20). To let silence concerning infant baptism overpower the clear positive precepts of disciple's baptism is a dangerous method of biblical interpretation.

THE MORE CONSISTENT ARGUMENT OF SILENCE

Ironically, if the argument of silence is applied consistently, there is even greater support for disciple's baptism against infant baptism. The council of Jerusalem in Acts 15 was called to deal with the Judaizers who required circumcision for new Christians. The answer of the council concerning circumcision was that Christians are saved by grace alone without circumcision (v. 11) and that it is good to "abstain from things sacrificed to idols and from blood and from things strangled and from fornication" (v. 29). If baptism is the direct counterpart of circumcision, then why did the council not simply say, "You and your children have been circumcised in the baptism of Christ and do not need physical circumcision"? Here the argument of silence speaks against baptism as the direct counterpart of circumcision and in favor of salvation by grace or regeneration as its direct counterpart and ground for its sufficient abrogation (v. 11).

Furthermore, Paul wrote the entire letter of Galatians to deal with the Judaizers who were requiring Gentile Galatian believers to be circumcised as well (Galatians 5:2, 3). Why did not Paul simply say, "After believing, you and your children were baptized; thus, you have already received the New Covenant counterpart of circumcision and no longer need it?" Here, again, the argument from silence speaks against baptism as being the direct counterpart of circumcision and speaks in favor of the receiving of the Spirit by hearing "with faith" as its counterpart and basis for abrogation (Galatians 3:2, 3).

An objection to this line of argument is that Paul would not allude to baptism as the reason for not receiving circumcision because that would put baptism in the class of works salvation like the Judaizers claimed for circumcision. I do not agree. Paul could easily have explained that neither circumcision nor baptism contribute to salvation in any way, yet water baptism is the fulfillment of circumcision and it is no longer applicable in the New Covenant administration—but Paul did not do that. After clearly stating that circumcision has nothing to do with salvation, he explains that the new creation is the answer to the Judaizers for Gentile entrance into the true circumcision, the Israel of God (Galatians 6:15, 16; Philippians 3:3). The whole teaching of Galatians is that it is not the children of the flesh and circumcision but the children of faith and regeneration, who are the true children of Abraham and the Israel of God (Galatians 3:14, 29; 6:14–16). Thus, the argument of silence as based upon the responses of the council and Paul does not favor the equating of circumcision and baptism in the New Covenant and, therefore, the equating of infant circumcision and infant baptism.

Some paedobaptists have tried to bolster the argument of silence concerning infant baptism by referring to New Testament silence concerning, for example, the Christian Sabbath and the admission of women to the Lord's Supper. Yet, while the fourth commandment is not repeated in the New Testament epistles, it was certainly taught by our Lord (Matthew 12; Mark 2) and there are explicit references to the Lord's Day as being practiced by Christians on the first day of the week (Acts 20:7; Rev. 1:10). There are also further correlating principles concerning the law written on the heart, the Ten Commandments, for Christian practice (Romans 8:4; Jeremiah 31:31–34). Thus, there is no correlation between the Sabbath issue and infant baptism because the New Testament is not silent regarding the keeping of the Sabbath.

Concerning the admission of women to the Lord's Table, Paul expressly addresses both men and women in the first part of 1 Corinthians 11, and the same is true when he requires participants at the Lord's Table to examine themselves in the latter half of the same chapter (v. 15). His instructions with respect to the Lord's Supper are addressed to the same people to whom he has been speaking about hair length and submission. It is therefore absurd to say that there is no biblical evidence for women to take either the Passover or the Lord's Supper. There may be a legitimate use of silence as a hermeneutical principle for biblically based applications, but not where positive precept is given. To adopt a practice from silence is not the same as rejecting a practice never mentioned. It is my conclusion that the silent pearl-gate of paedobaptism is not large enough for saints to enter.

THE REGULATIVE PRINCIPLE OF WORSHIP

Though discussed previously, let me repeat and expand my argument from the regulative principle of worship in rejection of the erroneous argument from inferential silence. Baptists have held historically to the very same regulative principle of worship as paedobaptists, though many in both camps are forgetting that today. The fact is that Baptists ultimately practice the baptism of disciples alone because of a more consistent application of the regulative principle. I am convinced that one reason we are losing some Baptists to our Presbyterian friends is because Baptists no longer understand the regulative principle. However, one of us is right, and the other is wrong, concerning something so important as a sacrament instituted by Christ, though many try to diminish its importance. Those Baptists who are tempted to forsake our theologically troubled Baptist Zion for the more comfortable Presbyterianism may not realize that they must violate the Presbyterian (and Baptist) regulative principle of worship to do so.
In order to prove my thesis, I will further define "the regulative principle" using both Presbyterian and Baptist sources, and show why I believe that infant baptism is a clear violation of that principle.

What is the regulative principle of worship? This principle states, according to the Presbyterian *Westminster Confession* and the *1689 London Baptist Confession* (the mother confession of American and Southern Baptists):

> . . . the acceptable way of worshipping the true God is *instituted by himself,* and *so limited by his own revealed will,* that he may not be worshipped according to the imaginations and devices of men, or the suggestions of Satan, under any visible representation, or any other way *not prescribed in the holy Scripture* [WCF 21:1; emphasis mine; cf. 1689 22:1].

This regulative principle teaches that God-approved Christian worship only includes elements and practices "instituted by God Himself . . . limited by his own revealed will . . . [and not] any other way not prescribed in the holy Scripture." In other words, speculation, invention, imagination, and uncommanded practices, cannot be permitted to overrule written revelation; *this includes the argument of inferential silence.* Therefore, the only elements of worship permitted in the regulative tradition, according to Scripture, are:

> Prayers . . . The reading of the Scriptures with godly fear; the sound preaching, and conscionable hearing of the word, in obedience unto God, with understanding, faith, and reverence; singing of psalms with grace in the heart; as also the due administration and worthy receiving of *the sacraments instituted by Christ;* are all parts of the ordinary religious worship of God: besides religious oaths and vows, solemn fastings, and thanksgivings upon special occasions, which are, in their several times and seasons, to be used in a holy and religious manner [*WCF* 21:4–5; emphasis mine; cf. 1689 22:4–5].

Prayer, the reading and preaching of Scripture, singing, the sacraments, vows, thanksgivings, and the like, are the only authorized elements of Reformed worship. It should be noted that it is the sacraments instituted by Christ Himself, not by silence or supposed good and necessary inference, that are approved elements of worship.

In contrast, the "normative principle of worship" is practiced by Lutherans, Anglicans, Roman Catholics and, apparently, many charismatic and fundamental Baptists. They are joined by a growing number of Presbyterians and Southern Baptists who have turned from their theological heritage in the regulative principle and have, sometimes ignorantly, adopted the normative principle. This normative principle teaches that worship must consist of everything that is commanded by God and may also consist of anything *that is not specifically prohibited by Scripture.* This is the argument from silence and opens the door to the use of many uncommanded practices (which often limit the practice of those commanded elements so that we have "worship" consisting of less or no Scripture reading and twenty-minute sermons).

Obviously, the normative principle invites invention, creativity, and new elements of worship never commanded or mentioned in Scripture. It also permits practices prescribed in Old Testament worship to be included in New Testament Christian worship by a misuse of good and necessary inference, even if these practices are not prescribed for Christian worship. This accounts for the traditional differences in worship between those from a normative or regulative background. Those holding to a normative principle have historically been willing to include normative additions such as pageantry, altars, priesthoods, vestments, prayer books, mariolatry, prayers to saints, and other practices not instituted by Scripture for gospel worship. Others today add drama, dance, puppets, clowns, movies, magicians, comedians, weight lifters, the pressured invitation system, musical entertainment, and whatever else their heart desires by normative principles. When one holds to the normative principle, another must ask: "Where will it end?"

The regulative principle recognizes that:

> there are some *circumstances* concerning the worship of God, and government of the Church, common to human actions and societies, which are to be ordered by the light of nature and Christian prudence, according to the general rules of the word, which are always to be observed [*WCF* 1:6; emphasis mine].

However, according to G. I. Williamson, these circumstances of worship are limited in the Reformed regulated worship to time, place, order of worship, length of worship, language, pews, air conditioning, and other practical issues common to any human society.[201] Circumstances of worship under the regulative principle of worship have never included new uncommanded activities such as those just mentioned.

In summary, the Reformed regulative principle of worship allows only those elements of worship that have been positively instituted and commanded by God in Scripture, not those permitted by silence and possibly erroneous inference.

What has the regulative principle to do with infant baptism?
Simply this: Baptism is one of the sacraments instituted by Christ, governed by the regulative principle, instituted by God, limited by His revealed will, and prescribed by Holy Scripture. This includes the subjects of baptism as well as its mode and meaning, yet the only subjects of baptism instituted by God through Christ, limited by His revealed will, and actually prescribed by Scripture, as all agree, are professing disciples. If infants are included by an erroneous use of good and necessary consequence, then paedobaptism is a normative addition never commanded.

---

[201] G. I. Williamson, *The Westminster Confession of Faith for Study Classes* (Philadelphia, PA: The Presbyterian and Reformed Publ. Co., 1964), 161.

Pierre Marcel states that God gives us general instruction concerning the doctrine of baptism in Scripture and leaves it up to us to determine its practical application to infants by normative principles. He compares the application of infant baptism to legitimate application by normative principles in preaching, a very inadequate comparison to the regulative principle of worship for instituting a sacrament:

> The Church never confines herself merely to the letter, but, working from the data of Scripture and under the control of the Holy Spirit, *she affirms normative principles* and elaborates the consequences and applications which make her life and development possible and effective. Were it not so, the exercise of the pastoral ministry, the cure of souls, preaching, discipline, and so on, would be absolutely impossible! *It is thus that the Church operates when she passes from adult to infant baptism. Scripture affords general instruction on baptism, its meaning and value, and the Church applies it concretely in life* . . . since [Scripture] nowhere makes mention of a baptismal ministry which should have been applied to adults *born of Christian parents,* it has said sufficient on this point, *without needing to have prescribed literally the baptism of infants* [emphasis mine].[202]

It is astonishing that Marcel admits that infant baptism is practiced on normative principles of application and does not need to be prescribed literally by Scripture. This is clearly a return to the normative principle itself, not the regulative principle for a sacrament instituted by Christ. It is even more astonishing that he uses the lack of biblical instruction concerning the baptism of adult children born of Christian parents as a parallel justification for unmentioned infant baptism. Scripture does not need to mention these adult children as a special case simply because the commands to repent and believe already cover all adults! To put infant baptism, never mentioned at all in Scripture, into the same category is completely unwarranted. Such thinking can lead us anywhere we wish, even to the seven sacraments of Roman Catholicism. Further, there is a great deal of difference between applying revealed truth in preaching by legitimate normative principles and inventing new subjects for a sacrament instituted by Christ by the normative principle of worship.

---

[202]Marcel, *Infant Baptism,* 190.

The question remains: If Christ did not institute infant baptism, then how can it be a sacrament instituted by Christ? Marcel's explanation simply affirms from a paedobaptist perspective what has been maintained all along in this entire book, that infant baptism is a violation of the regulative principle of worship and is based upon the normative principle and the argument of silence. Only that which is expressly set down in Scripture fits the regulative principle of defining the elements of Christian worship.

When God instituted circumcision, He was very specific to identify its subjects. That is why infants were circumcised. That is the regulative principle. Now are we to assume that the subjects of the sacraments instituted by Christ (baptism and the Lord's Supper), limited by God's revealed will, and prescribed by Holy Scripture, are to be identified by normative principles of application or as an uncommanded circumstance of worship? If words defining the regulative principle mean anything, the answer is clearly no. According to the regulative principle, the only subjects of baptism instituted by Christ and prescribed in Holy Scripture are disciples alone.

Perhaps we all, paedobaptists and Baptists, need to wake up and to recommit ourselves to the regulative principle of worship and to follow it where it leads us. It may lead biblically minded paedobaptists to become Baptists—and let us hope that it will lead us both back to scripturally regulated worship, rejecting new normative additions such as drama, puppets, and dance. However, let neither of us violate the regulative principle of worship in order to practice never-prescribed, never-instituted, biblically silent infant baptism.

SUMMARY

This chapter has shown that the weight of precept, the more consistently read argument of silence itself, and the regulative principle of worship prohibit infant baptism by the positive institution of disciple's baptism. To maintain the hermeneutics of infant baptism opens the door for many uncommanded practices in New Testament worship. In a day when the church needs biblical reform, let us return to those principles of the Reformation that first established us. Only let us be more consistent and practice the baptism of disciples alone.

Chapter 11

The Argument of Expanded Blessings to "Covenant Children"

One of the great pearls that shines as brightly as the rest, from the paedobaptist perspective, is found in rhetorical questions such as: "If the Old Testament children were granted the covenant sign, in this New Covenant day of expanded blessing and fulfillment, shall we prohibit the covenant sign to believers' children?" "Are our New Covenant children less blessed and privileged than Old Testament children?" "What happens to our infants who die in infancy?" Such questions are certainly legitimate and lay at the heart of the matter of paedobaptism.

The primary power of these and similar questions resides in their rhetorical force. No one wants to prohibit little children from God's blessings or to limit God's goodness in granting salvation to infants. Infant and small-child salvation has a strong emotional pull. Undiscerning parents will believe or do almost anything to enhance the possibility of their child's salvation. These thoughts tug at our heartstrings and constrain many to say "yes" to covenant promises and to the covenant sign upon their infants. However, God's Word, not well-intentioned sentimentality toward our children, must define how we answer questions such as those just mentioned. We must trust God's Word, not attempt to reinvent it.

Before we discuss a covenantal Baptist view of the blessings upon the seed of believers, including the question of infant salvation, let us first examine the divergent views among paedobaptists regarding the covenant promises to believers' seed. Such disagreement has created confusion for parents about how or whether to evangelize their children as well as questions concerning the salvation of deceased infants.

PAEDOBAPTIST VIEWS OF COVENANT PROMISES TO BELIEVERS' SEED

Even though paedobaptists agree that the children of believers are members of the New Covenant and the visible church who should receive the covenant sign of infant baptism, there is wide disagreement among them about the promises of salvation to the children of believers. The classic covenantal view will be presented first, followed by a discussion of more extreme views. It will be seen that there is, by no means, unanimity among paedobaptists on these things. This reveals a real weakness in the paedobaptist position. If God has clearly revealed these covenant promises for the children of believers in the New Covenant, then why do conflicting views persist among those who hold to the same theological confessions (*Westminster, Heidelberg Catechism,* etc.)?

I once heard a very prominent Presbyterian pastor declare at an infant baptism:

> Infant baptism does not regenerate or save the child, it is only a promise by the parents that they will raise the child in the nurture and discipline of the Lord. We need to pray that God will bless their efforts and save the child.[203]

The same sort of explanation is common among Baptists who practice infant blessing or dedication. Therefore, Baptists who join Presbyterian churches have no problem with this explanation of the meaning of infant baptism. That is one reason, I believe, why so many Baptists are joining Presbyterian churches; it allows them to feel comfortable with infant baptism.

However, this is not the historic view of paedobaptists, nor is it an accurate presentation of covenantal paedobaptism to uninformed former Baptists. One of the questions asked of parents before infant baptism in the *PCA Book of Church Order* is:

---

[203] I was an eyewitness to this baptismal service in 1993. However, this appears to be a common explanation given by other Presbyterian pastors. I have heard it at other times, and several Baptist laymen, now Presbyterians, have also reported to me that this was the explanation of infant baptism given to them by their pastors.

Argument of Expanded Blessings to "Covenant Children"   **175**

> Do you claim God's covenant promises in (his) behalf, and do you look in faith to the Lord Jesus Christ for (his) salvation, as you do for your own?[204]

Such a question implies far more than either dedicating your child to the Lord or promising to raise him properly, praying, and hoping for his salvation.

Certainly parents are to pray to the Lord Jesus for the salvation of their children. Certainly they are to believe that God's Word does not return void and to have faith that He is able to save their children and willing to hear their prayers. However, how do parents "look in faith to the Lord Jesus Christ for [their child's] salvation as (*in the same way?*) [they] do for their own"? Christian parents "look in faith" to the Lord Jesus Christ and have assurance that they are justified because God's Word surely promises this. Are parents to have the same level of assurance that their child will be saved, if they "look in faith to the Lord Jesus Christ" for their child's salvation, as they have for their own salvation by faith in Christ?

Such a question asked of parents is far beyond their promising to raise their children faithfully, preach the gospel to them, and pray for their salvation. According to Scripture, even in the covenant family, God is the one who chooses whom He will save. Romans 9 addresses this very subject, using Jacob and Esau as an example. No one can look in faith to the Lord Jesus Christ for the salvation of another in the same way that he looks to Christ for his own. Salvation is entirely in God's hands, even in the covenant family.

The following discussion will reveal several diverse views that exist among paedobaptists, none of which are compatible with the just described pastoral explanation commonly heard in Presbyterian churches today.

Classic Paedobaptist Views

The first classic view is defined by William Hendriksen:

> Now God has *not promised that every child of believing parents would be saved,* but he has definitely promised to perpetuate his

---

[204]*PCA Book of Church Order,* ch. 57, par. 5, 80.

work of grace *in the line* of the children of believers considered as a group [emphasis mine].[205]

Hendriksen cites several Scripture references (Genesis 17:7; Psalm 103:17–18; Isaiah 59:21; Acts 2:38) in support of this position. Acts 2:38 says: "For the promise is to you, and to your children, and to all that are afar off, even as many as the Lord our God shall call to Himself." I explained in Chapter 7 how this Scripture is erroneously interpreted by paedobaptists.

Louis Berkhof essentially agrees with Hendriksen's view. According to him, there is a twofold involvement in the Covenant of Grace. First, all children of believers are in the covenant in a "legal sense," duty bound to live by that covenant. Second, although they all are in the physical line from which God promises to save, only the elect from among the covenant seed, that is, regenerated children, enter into "the covenant as a communion of life." Therefore:

> Is there any reasonable ground to expect that the covenant relation will issue in a living communion; that for the sinner, who is of himself unable to believe, the covenant will actually become a living reality? In answer to this question it may be said that God undoubtedly Himself guarantees by His promises pertaining to the seed of believers that this will take place, *not in the case of every individual, but in the seed of the covenant collectively*. On the basis of the promise of God we may believe that, under a faithful administration of the covenant, the covenant relation will, *as a rule,* be fully realized in a covenant life [emphasis mine].[206]

This explanation of covenant life upon the seed of believers "as a rule" (but not infallibly) is a much more sure hope of salvation than that expressed by some Presbyterian ministers during infant baptism. According to classic paedobaptist covenantalism, no particular child can be assured salvation by being in the covenant household, but parents should be assured that God will save their children "as a rule" if they raise them faithfully as they have promised. Therefore, infants are baptized on the basis of being in the covenant from which God usually saves the seed (children) of believers.

A second classic paedobaptist view, though much different from the first, is that infants are baptized upon the presumption

---

[205] Hendriksen, *Covenant of Grace,* 28–29.
[206] Berkhof, *Systematic Theology,* 281.

that they are regenerated or elect. Andrew Sandlin, a representative of this view (who cites Ursinus, Witsius, and others), would go so far as to say:

> We may baptize infants of Christian parents, in fact because there is *every reason to believe children of covenant parents are elect.* In Acts 2:37–39, for example, Peter assures his listeners that the promise of salvation extends to their children. In 1 Cor. 7:14 we note that the children of but one Christian parent are "holy", interestingly, in no case in the NT does the word translated "holy" in 1 Cor. 7:14 refer to merely "set apart" people; it is interchangeable with "saints", that is, saved individuals. In other words, the "holy" child is not comparable to the "sanctified" unbelieving spouse....
>
> Since the new covenant is inherently redemptive (Heb. 8:10–12), and since baptism is a sign and seal of the benefits of regeneration, we have *every reason to assume that the infants of Christian parents are regenerate and baptize them on that basis,* which is, after all, only a crucial aspect of the "all-comprehensive promise of God in the covenant."[207]

Sandlin errs when he states that the New Testament "in no case" translates the adjective *holy* as anything other than a saint. As mentioned in Chapter 7, Luke 2:23 speaks of Jesus' circumcision as an example of the Old Testament commandment that "Every firstborn male that opens the womb shall be called *holy* to the Lord" (Luke 2:23). This is, in fact, one case where an infant is called holy in the sense of set apart as a firstborn male beyond even circumcision, yet none would argue that this means that every firstborn male should be assumed regenerate to the neglect of the second born.

We have already seen the error of paedobaptist interpretations of Acts 2:37–39 and 1 Corinthians 7:14. Does Sandlin actually believe that the latter teaches that children of believers are to be presumed regenerate? And if the children are presumed regenerate, do you ever call them to repent and believe in Christ to salvation? Not according to some. This presumptive regeneration is, in principle, another form of baptismal regeneration and withholds the call to salvation from the child, giving them a false assurance that they are true Christians and endangering their

---

[207] Sandlin, "Reformed Paedobaptism," 6, 17.

eternal souls. Watson quotes William Cunningham, a paedobaptist, who warns against this doctrine:

> We believe that the notion of sacramental justification and regeneration, more or less distinctly developed, has always been, and still is, one of the most successful delusions which Satan employs for ruining men's souls, and that there is nothing of greater practical importance than to root out this notion from men's minds, and to guard them against its ruinous influence.[208]

Remember that Cunningham's statement is that of one paedobaptist warning another.

As we have seen, even classical covenantalists differ significantly on the blessings to covenant children and on the ground of infant baptism. Classical covenantal views promise much more than infant dedication or parental promises of faithfulness and prayer as stated by many modern Presbyterians. Baptists need to know this when they consider joining a paedobaptist church. False hope may be offered to parents concerning their children's salvation. This teaching even affects how many paedobaptists teach their children the gospel, possibly giving them a dangerous false assurance. Even more so, the following authors show the weakness of this divided position.

Extreme Paedobaptist Views

An extreme and minority application of paedobaptist covenant theology is proposed by Douglas Wilson. Wilson comes very close to saying that if parents are faithful to their responsibilities of raising their children in the nurture and discipline of the Lord, then they will inevitably see their children saved. If their children do not profess Christ or turn away from Him, then one must assume the parents have not been faithful to their covenant vows. This position is a step beyond even Berkhof's position that God saves believer's seed as a rule.

---

[208]Watson, *Babies Be Baptized?*, 112–113. In Watson's chapter on the evils of infant baptism, he charges that it betrays the Reformed cause of Scripture alone against Roman Catholicism, it alters the meaning of baptism for infants as applied to disciples, it destroys the appointed way of confessing Christ, and it is ruinous to the souls of thousands, 107–113.

Argument of Expanded Blessings to "Covenant Children" 179

This is an extremely attractive argument emotionally for the validity of covenant children and infant baptism. It is fed by the emotions and hopes of parents who will do or believe anything in order to assure that their children are or will be saved. I believe that this issue is at the root of the reason why infant baptism continues to hold such attraction despite its lack of biblical support.

Wilson applies his erroneous view (that parental faithfulness almost inevitably brings God's blessing in their children's salvation) to the essential qualifications of elders in Titus 1:6:

> If any man be above reproach, the husband of one wife, having children who believe [or having faithful children], not accused of dissipation or rebellion.

This passage certainly teaches that an elder's children should be "faithful children" and that the elder must "[keep] his children under control with all dignity" (1 Timothy 3:4). However, contrary to most interpreters, Wilson seems to interpret having faithful children as more than being under control, respectful to parents, respectful to the faith, and so forth. He states:

> . . . if he has children, they should be faithful children, children who cannot be accused of riotous living or disobedience. The phrase "faithful children" can also be rendered as "believing children"—in other words, *they should be Christians, whose lives match their profession.*
>
> But the basic meaning remains unchanged even if we leave the translation as "faithful children." In context, what are they to be faithful to? Clearly, they are to be faithful to the teaching and instruction of their father. Now do we want to require children to be faithful when they are told to make their beds or take out the trash, but leave them to their rebellion at the most important point—*when they are told to believe on the Lord Jesus Christ* [emphasis mine]?[209]

Wilson has so much confidence in the covenant promises to faithful parents that he concludes that unconverted children, or children who refuse their father's command to believe, show a man unfaithful and apparently unqualified to be an elder. Does Wilson really put professing faith in Christ in the same category

---
[209]Wilson, *Standing on the Promises,* 21.

as obeying a father's command to "make their beds or take out the trash"? Does he really equate the Holy Spirit's sovereign regenerating work in a child's heart to obeying their father "when they are told to believe on the Lord Jesus Christ"? And how old are these children? Such reasoning borders on decisional regeneration and high pressure tactics at their worse! What pressure may be put upon elders or potential elders to "convert" their children? And what pressure may be put upon children to please and obey parents by confessing faith prematurely and/or falsely?

Such extremism is beyond the descriptions of other leading covenantal theologians, as well as being a practical nightmare. Should a man not be an elder if he has a child who refuses to be coerced into a false profession so that his dad can enter or keep his office? Should a child be considered unfaithful if he refuses to confess Christ at his dad's command when he has not repented or believed and knows that God has not yet given him a new heart in Christ? The practical implications of Wilson's view are a nightmare to apply to the local church. In my experience, very few Presbyterians hold to Wilson's view of elder qualifications.

Lest I be accused of misunderstanding Wilson's intentions, he is even more specific in an article entitled "Transaction" in his magazine *Credenda Agenda*. Faced with the dilemma of explaining how some apparently faithful covenant parents can have unfaithful children and other less disciplined covenant parents have faithful children, he explains that the real solution to the dilemma is found in the faith of the parents to accept the promise of their child's salvation. This supposedly explains why one child is saved and another is not. He explains:

> We think that our children's salvation is dependent upon the turn of a cosmic roulette wheel, or we think that we control it by our own efforts and works. But neither is the case. God has given believers countless promises concerning the salvation of their children. And each, as a divine promise, can only be received, by one instrument. That instrument is *faith*. When such faith is present, parental good works will always be present, but as a result of the faith, not the cause of it. We must always remember our religion is not based upon good works. Salvation is by grace through faith—not by works lest anyone should boast. This includes the salvation of our children. This is the order of Christ's kingdom . . . God has promised us the salvation of our children. Do we believe Him? If we

do, then we bring up our children with confidence. . . . Parents lose their children to the world *because they do not believe God for them* (emphasis mine).[210]

"Believe God for them"? Wilson's view places the salvation of each child upon the responsibility of the parents to raise them well *enough* and to believe God's promise *enough* to save that child. This view runs entirely counter to Paul's explanation in Romans 9 of God's sovereign choice between Jacob and Esau, Isaac and Ishmael, and anyone else as examples of how God chooses to save whom He will. Even within the covenant family, God chooses as He will. Wilson's view veers alarmingly close to the "name it and claim it" charismatic theology characterized by having enough faith to be healed, to become rich, and so forth.

Some paedobaptists believe that the concept of covenant children is a great tool for evangelism, allowing their children to close with the covenant that they are in, or suffer greater condemnation as covenant breakers. However, Baptists believe that all are responsible to live according to God's commandments and to respond to the gospel call to repent and believe, whether they are baptized or not. All children belong to God as His creatures and are equally commanded to repent and believe in the Lord Jesus Christ, whether they are baptized or not (Acts 2:37–42; 17:30–31). All are commanded to honor their father and mother under God's law, whether they are in the covenant or not (Romans 2:14–16). All are born under the judgment of the failed Covenant of Works in Adam, needing to repent as creatures and to believe whatever revelation God has given.

Further, some paedobaptists believe that infant baptism removes a person from under the Covenant of Works and its condemnation. However, this is an untenable position that teaches that one may be removed from the Covenant of Works, placed in the New Covenant by baptism, and later return to the Covenant of Works in condemnation. This is true Arminianism! Marcel actually says that the baptized children of believers are removed from the Covenant of Works, are no longer under the condemnation of God, and are restored to an ability to decide for or against the covenant blessings. It is as if they are a third category of people

---

[210] Douglas Wilson, "Transaction," *Credenda Agenda,* 8, no. 3:14.

neither under the Covenant of Works nor full participants of the life of the Covenant of Grace.[211]

Nowhere in the New Testament are sinners, children or otherwise, called to repent and believe because they are already in the New Covenant and could become covenant breakers. Baptized children, like all children, already are covenant breakers of the covenant with Adam (Romans 5:12ff.). They already are "without excuse" (Romans 2:1–16) and need to repent. And just as those who refused to enter Abraham's Covenant by circumcision were called covenant breakers of that covenant, though they were never in it (Genesis 17:14), so those who refuse the call of the gospel to all to repent and believe in Christ might be called covenant breakers. Those who are truly in the New Covenant, however, can never be covenant breakers.

In summary, the overall view of classic covenantal paedobaptists is that God saves from among the covenant seed and that He blesses parental efforts, as he wills.[212] Covenantal Baptists believe this, too. In fact, Baptists feel very comfortable that God does indeed save from among the seed of believers, simply because His Word does not return void and because, even in the mystery of God's election, He hears the pleadings of faithful parents who try to raise their children in the nurture and discipline of the Lord.

The promises of salvation to *covenant children* cannot be used as an emotional appeal to justify infant baptism or to include infants in the Covenant of Grace. God saves whom He will, even from among believers' seed.

A COVENANTAL BAPTIST VIEW OF GOD'S PROMISES TO BELIEVERS' CHILDREN

The Baptist view is that, if God so chooses to grant the covenant sign to physical children in the Old Covenant shadow and to prohibit the covenant sign to physical children in the New Covenant fulfillment, He has the sovereign right to do so, without being accused of logical inconsistency. Neither does this necessarily

---

[211] Marcel, *Infant Baptism,* 108–10.
[212] Herman Hoeksema, *Believers and Their Seed,* trans. Homer C. Hoeksema (Grand Rapids, MI: Reformed Free Publishing Association, 1971), 158.

imply that our New Covenant children are less privileged or blessed simply because they may not take the New Covenant sign.

In response to the rhetoric of paedobaptists, I rhetorically reply: Are our Baptist children less blessed and privileged by being born to godly parents who reflect the fullness of the Spirit that was only partially tasted in the Abrahamic Covenant? Are our children less blessed in having Christ and Him crucified proclaimed to them from infancy as compared to the types and shadows preached to their Old Covenant counterparts? Are our children less privileged in being raised in the Israel of the Spirit as compared to the children raised in the Israel of the flesh? Are our children less likely to be saved when compared with the Old Testament children who never heard the fullness of the gospel, much less the uncountable ones who still perish in darkness? I think not.

Our Baptist and paedobaptist children, above all others in Old Testament Israel and on the present-day earth, have privileges above measure. They are being raised in homes and churches that set before them the now crucified and risen Lord of Glory as their daily fare. Our gracious God has chosen them above multitudes that perish in darkness to hear the same promise of the gospel He sovereignly used to bring their parents into the everlasting kingdom:

> Repent and let each of you be baptized in the name of Jesus Christ for the forgiveness of your sins; and you shall receive the gift of the Holy Spirit. For the promise is *to you* and *to your children,* and *for all who are far off, as many as* the Lord our God shall call to Himself [Acts 2:38,39; emphasis mine].

Deuteronomy 30:6 is an interesting passage when compared to Acts 2:38ff. It is God's promise to circumcise the hearts of the New Covenant Israelites and their seed after He returns them from the prophesied exile:

> And Jehovah thy God will circumcise thy heart, and the heart of thy seed, to love Jehovah thy God with all thy heart, and with all thy soul, that thou mayest live (Deuteronomy 30:6 ASV).

This is the same "return from captivity" context as Jeremiah 31:31–34 and Ezekiel 36:25ff. In these passages, God does promise to call His elect out of believers' children as well as from among those afar off, but we cannot say that any of them are in the New Covenant of heart-circumcision and should receive its outward sign until they repent and believe. Neither can we say that any of them are infallibly among the elect. This concept of election from believer's seed is akin to that of Herman Hoeksema, a paedobaptist, who finds comfort enough in it. Hoeksema believes that God saves out of the seed of believers, but does not promise to save every one of them. Therefore, in an infant's death, parents should hold to this promise and trust in God.[213] However, even with this comfort, the precepts of baptism and the application of the New Covenant sign as illustrated in Acts 2:38, 39, 41 prevent us from applying the sign of heart-circumcision until our children have shown evidence of having been heart circumcised and having entered the New Covenant (Jeremiah 31:31–34).

Our children have been blessed with hearing and memorizing the written Word of God from the cradle. They have been blessed with the tear-stained prayers of Spirit-filled parents pleading for their soul's regeneration and conversion. They have been blessed to live in a day where the gospel is proclaimed not in Old Testament types and shadows, but in its fulness in the New Covenant. The glory of Christ and His finished work of redemption upon the cross woo them to forsake their sin and flee to Him for salvation. Can we say that they have a less privileged position in growing up under the sown seed of the full revelation of God's sovereign plan? Of course not! They can never be considered less privileged when God has sovereignly chosen to preach the gospel of sovereign grace to them while so many of our fallen race perish each day in ignorance and darkness. Besides Deuteronomy 30:6, we also have this wonderful promise of God, in His sovereign good will, to plead before Christ our personal Advocate for our children:

> So shall My word be which goes forth from My mouth; it shall not return to Me empty, without accomplishing what I desire, and without succeeding in the matter for which I sent it (Isaiah 55:11).

Let us plead the goodness of God to His people and call down His Spirit to plant the word of life in the hearts of our children till they bear the fruit of a new creation in Christ Jesus. We know

---

[213]*Ibid.*, 159.

that He has and that He can regenerate the children of believers who die in infancy, saving them by the same grace whereby He saves any conscious believer (David's son, Jeremiah, John the Baptist). For this reason, we Baptists have great comfort should our children die in infancy. Many Baptists and Presbyterians believe that God has mercy upon all who die in infancy. We feel biblically comforted by King David's words when he lost his child: "I shall go to him, but he shall not return to me" (2 Samuel 12:23). We hold to the same position as paedobaptists stated in the exact same words both in the *Westminster* and *London Baptist Confessions'* chapters on Effectual Calling:

> Elect infants dying in infancy are regenerated and saved by Christ through the Spirit; who worketh when, and where, and how he pleaseth; so also are all elect persons, who are incapable of being outwardly called by the ministry of the Word (*WCF* 10:3; *LCF* 10:3).

Therefore, we Baptists have every reason to say that our children have expanded blessings in the New Covenant, even if they, in God's good pleasure, must not receive the outward sign till regeneration and conversion are evidenced.

Let us not appeal to the shiny pearl of sentimental rhetoric to set aside the revealed and commanded will of God in the New Covenant administration of sovereign grace. Let us not play on people's fears for their children's salvation by holding up infant baptism as some type of assurance that their children are in the Covenant of Grace. And let us not withhold from our children the joy and expanded privilege never granted to the children of circumcision: *that of obeying Christ's command to all men everywhere to be baptized as confessing disciples upon their own personal repentance.* Paedobaptist parents and pastors must realize that infant baptism robs infants of their responsibility and privilege to obey a clear command of Christ for themselves. Rather, let us proclaim the gospel of grace to our children, begging God for mercy upon them, trusting in His goodness, until they come to Christ on their own and receive the blessed baptism of disciples alone, publicly identifying themselves as followers of their dear Savior.

Chapter 12

The Testimony of Tradition and the Historical Argument of Silence

I have deliberately chosen tradition as the last pearl to add to the string, simply because it should be the smallest. I fear that often it has been the largest. However, if the Scripture is our only rule of faith and practice, then the role of tradition must be only to clarify and corroborate what Scripture clearly sets forth. Marcel laments:

> O the inconsistency of Protestants who wish to found baptism upon tradition or upon "the authority" of the Reformers.[214]

We cannot allow the unified testimony of the greatest of paedobaptist divines to overthrow our own consciences bound to Scripture alone, especially in regard to the sacraments supposedly instituted by Christ. Was this not the heartcry of the Reformation to begin with?

To paedobaptists, the two most attractive areas of tradition are the uncertain practice of Jewish proselyte baptism and the documented practice of the early church as testified by the Apostolic Fathers. In both of these testimonies, T. E. Watson and Paul K. Jewett have presented the most incisive summaries I have read.[215]

CHURCH TRADITION

Jewish Proselyte Baptism

First of all, Alfred Edersheim and Louis Berkhof both conclude that Jewish proselytes and their children up to age twelve were

---
[214]Marcel, *Infant Baptism,* 19.
[215]Watson, *Babies Be Baptized?,* 65–74; and Jewett, *Infant Baptism,* 13–46.

baptized into Judaism.[216] However, unborn children in the womb of the baptized mother were not baptized after birth as they were considered already clean and a part of Israel.[217] So, even if proselyte baptism existed in New Testament days, it lends no real support to baptism of newly born infants. Further, if we appeal to any part of the Judaistic practice, we have to contend with the late age of household children receiving baptism, up to twelve years old, as well as the prohibition of post-partum baptism to unborn children in the womb. Both of these difficulties undermine any support Jewish proselyte baptism may otherwise lend to infant baptism.

Further, the practice of Jewish proselyte baptism is not well attested in the first century. Most of the evidence comes primarily from Rabbinical writings that are not well attested until circa 200 A.D.[218] Christian baptism could easily have influenced such a development, so it is not a dependable resource. This was discussed in Chapter 6 under the *oikos* formula debate between Joachim Jeremias and Kurt Aland. Aland contends there is no solid evidence for Jewish proselyte baptism in the first century A.D. or for infant baptism until the third century A.D.

Apostolic and Church Fathers

Second, the very earliest explicit mention we have of infant baptism in the didactic writings of the early church is from Tertullian, circa 200 A.D. In this passage he urges the delay of baptism, especially of little children, so that its significance might be fully realized. This, of course, admits that children, possibly including infants, were

---

[216] Alfred Edersheim, *The Life and Times of Jesus the Messiah,* vol. 2 (Grand Rapids, MI: William B. Eerdmans Publishing Co., 1970), 746; and Berkhof, *Systematic Theology,* 622.

[217] This may be yet another explanation of 1 Corinthians 7:14. Perhaps Jewish proselyte baptism, if it existed in Paul's day, caused questions of clean and unclean children to arise in the minds of the Corinthians. Paul declared them "clean" as the children of believers, not because of baptism.

[218] A. T. Robertson, *The Pharisees and Jesus,* (1920; reprint, Eugene, OR: Wipf and Stock Publishers, 1999), 4–10. Robertson warns against using later Jewish sources to reject the picture of Rabbinic Judaism in the New Testament. This sane advice is needed today in the "new perspective" on Paul and James concerning the issue of justification by faith alone.

being baptized in his day, but this is far from granting that it was an apostolic tradition. Tertullian considered it an erroneous practice, even though he often defended apostolic traditions.

Origen, Augustine, and many others following say that it was the apostolic custom to baptize infants. It is probable that Origen was baptized as an infant around 185 A.D., and he claims that this was the tradition handed down from the apostles. Irenaeus mentioned the stages of life from infancy to old age as the stages that Christ went through to save all those who are born again at every age, thus possibly alluding to infant baptism via the tendency of the church fathers to identify baptism with regeneration. It has further been pointed out that Tertullian's objections to infant baptism led to clinical baptism, the unbiblical postponement of baptism till the deathbed. This error supposedly eliminates his objection to infant baptism. Therefore, it appears on the surface that, from the end of the second century to the Reformation, infant baptism has been accepted by some as an apostolic tradition.

However, Irenaeus also claimed in his possible reference to infant baptism that he had received an apostolic tradition that Jesus was forty to fifty years old in His active ministry, contradicting the scriptural record. It is well known that the church fathers have claimed many other apostolic traditions that are unfounded. Furthermore, Tertullian is often recognized as a staunch defender of apostolic traditions. But why did he not defend infant baptism, if it was in fact an apostolic tradition? Such confusing testimony must not be regarded as conclusive unless well-founded in Scripture.

The Didache

Against infant baptism as an apostolic tradition, the *Didache* (100 to 125 A.D.) gives instruction only for the baptism of catechumens (disciples), an awesome silence regarding infant baptism in such a significant post-apostolic church manual:

> 1. Now concerning baptism. Baptize as follows, when you have rehearsed the aforesaid teaching [to catechumens]: Baptize in the name of the Father and of the Son and of the Holy Spirit, in running water. 2. But if you do not have running water, use whatever is available. And if you cannot do it in cold water, use warm. 3. But

if you have neither, pour water on the head three times—in the name of the Father, Son, and Holy Spirit.[219]

The *Didache* simply says, "Now concerning baptism," as if the baptism of catechumens (disciples) is the only kind of baptism practiced. Much teaching was required of candidates before baptism. This is especially significant because the church was more established than the supposed *missionary* church of Matthew 28:18–20. The *Didache* only commands catechumen's baptism; there is no mention of infant baptism in the later church's manual. The *Didache* also requires baptism in running water or tri-pouring only if necessary. *See* Appendix B for a more thorough discussion of the *Didache* and the mode of Christian baptism.

Such confusing testimony in the apostolic and church fathers concerning the tradition of paedobaptism should not serve to build our doctrine of baptism but only support what is clearly revealed in the written word. As the *Westminster Confession of Faith* says:

> The whole counsel of God concerning all things necessary for His own glory, man's salvation, faith and life, is either expressly set down in Scripture, or by good and necessary consequence may be deduced from Scripture, unto which nothing at any time is to be added, whether by new revelations of the Spirit, or *traditions of men* [*WCF* 1:6; emphasis mine].

An interesting study of baptism in the early church was written by two paedobaptist authors, H. F. Stander and J. P. Louw, professors at the University of Pretoria, South Africa. They claim:

> The truth is that modern-day authors misinterpret and sometimes misrepresent the statements of the Church Fathers.[220]

These authors point out that many references used by paedobaptists from the church fathers to support infant baptism are really dealing with the baptism of small children, not infants.

---

[219]Robert M. Grant, ed., *The Apostolic Fathers* (New York: Thomas Nelson & Sons, 1965), vol. 3, *Barnabas and the Didache,* by Robert A. Kraft, 163–64 (*Didache* 7).
[220]H. F. Stander and J. P. Louw, *Baptism in the Early Church* (Garsfontein, South Africa: Didaskalia Publishers, 1988), 1.

They demonstrate that the link between the Abrahamic Covenant, circumcision, and infant baptism is a later development from the third to fourth century A.D. They find no widespread practice of infant baptism until the fourth century.[221]

In summary, the use of tradition is no certain authority for the apostolic practice of infant baptism. It is post-biblical, extra-biblical, and disputed. In fact, the *Didache* seems to prescribe catechumen's baptism alone.

THE ERRONEOUS HISTORICAL ARGUMENT OF SILENCE

One of the fathers of American Presbyterianism is Archibald Alexander, famous president of the Log College that later became Princeton University. From 1797 to 1799, while president of the Log College, he began to question the validity of infant baptism and refrained from performing the practice for a season. Oddly, one of the most convincing proofs to him of its apostolic authority was the early church's silence about it in the first few centuries A.D. He reasoned that if it were an apostolic practice, there would have been no reason to oppose it in the first through third centuries. This is why it was mentioned as universal only in the fourth and fifth centuries. On the other hand, if it were not an apostolic practice, then he believed there would have been a great opposition to its introduction in the third century, for which there is no significant evidence. Therefore, he reasoned, because of historical silence, infant baptism must have been an apostolic practice.[222]

Dr. Alexander stated that, during this uncertain period of his life, two things kept him from becoming Baptist. One was the mentioned universal practice of infant baptism after the fourth and fifth centuries A.D. Let it be said upfront that this historical argument of silence can justify any speculation one wishes to invent. However, the other reason was:

> ... that if Baptists are right, they are the only Christian church on earth, and all other denominations are out of the visible

---
[221]*Ibid.*, 4, 168.
[222]James W. Alexander, *Life of Archibald Alexander*, 204–224.

church. Besides, I could not see how they could ever obtain a valid baptism.[223]

Once again, these reasons are not founded on biblical exegesis. Although I do not agree that all paedobaptist churches are outside the visible church, at least Dr. Alexander's extreme statement should awaken Baptists and paedobaptists who tend to diminish the importance of baptism while seeking a place to worship and to serve. Finally, his statement that Baptists could not "ever obtain a valid baptism" simply ignores the professors' baptisms of the New Testament (Acts 2:41). Such illogical and extreme statements by one of history's most respected Reformed leaders reveals the weakness of the paedobaptist position.

This historical argument of silence is widely held among paedobaptists. Again, Stander and Louw refute this argument in the following quotation. They are refuting the statement of Oetting that there is no mention of infant baptism in the *Didache* because it was always assumed to be practiced:

> Oetting is employing here a rather haphazard form of argumentation based on the fact that if a matter was not recorded in a writing, one can assume that it is taken for granted. *But one is on very shaky ground when one argues that an author is actually giving his tacit approval of infant baptism, or any other issue for that matter, when he does not mention it in his work.* If this form of argumentation were allowed, one might as well argue that because rebaptism or even the baptism of non-human beings for that matter is not mentioned, "the literature seems to assume it." Oetting, too, prefers not to mention the explicit references to believer's baptism in Justin's writings [emphasis mine].[224]

This historical argument of silence is an erroneous hermeneutical method used to establish the subjects of a sacrament. Once again, to ignore a practice because it is not mentioned in Scripture (the regulative principle) is not the same as adopting a practice never mentioned (the normative principle).[225]

---

[223]*Ibid.*, 205.
[224]Stander and Louw, *Baptism,* 7.
[225]This concept which has been stated throughout this book was suggested to me by Pastor Walter Chantry, pastor of Grace Baptist Church, Carlisle, Pennsylvania.

Paedobaptists use this normative principle argument of silence, not only when dealing with Scripture, but also when dealing with history. Neither are trustworthy authorities when establishing a sacrament instituted by Christ.

Stander and Louw also refute the argument that we should not expect infant baptism to be mentioned in the New Testament:

> Finally, it needs to be remarked that the contention often found in modern literature, viz. that adult baptism in the early Church entailed a missionary situation, cannot be substantiated by the relevant patristic literature, since the transition from adult baptism to infant baptism occurred at a time when Christianity was already a widespread phenomenon in the ancient Church. Therefore, it is also unsound to scrutinize the New Testament writings for allusions to infant baptism, since the latter involved a historical development. Moreover, no distinction was ever made between persons coming from a heathen or Christian family. In fact, the reason for the transition to infant baptism was one of theological perspective and had nothing to do with a missionary situation.[226]

None of this takes away from the unvarnished fact that the earliest clear didactic reference to infant baptism is in the negative. One cannot let uncertain and disputed evidence regarding tradition to trump Scripture and apostolic teachings. Tradition, as many paedobaptists agree, can offer corroborating proof of this argument of infant baptism only if it is first found in Scripture, but as I gaze through the eyes of Scripture, I find the small pearl of tradition shrinking in size and fading from sight.

SUMMARY

The baptism of disciples alone is the only baptism instituted by Christ and His apostles. Catechumen's baptism is the earliest referenced baptism in post-apostolic writings. The baptism of disciples is the only baptism prescribed by Holy Scripture. The weight of an erroneous inference from silence, whether biblical or historical, cannot overturn such testimony from Scripture or history. The baptism of disciples alone is the only prescribed baptism that fits the evidence.

---

[226]Stander and Louw, *Baptism,* 168–69.

Chapter 13

What Difference Does It Make?

Having gone to such lengths to prove that credobaptism is the only authorized baptism prescribed and instituted in Scripture, now we must ask: "What difference does it make?" This is a question I have heard repeatedly from pastors and laymen of Presbyterian and Baptist churches. "As long we are saved and worshipping God in spirit and truth and are evangelizing our children and living holy lives, why make such a big deal about baptism?"

Good question. The answer is that the ordinances of the church of Jesus Christ are important. Baptism illustrates an individual's union with Christ and entrance into His visible church. The subjects of this sacrament of necessity determines one's concept of and ministry in the visible church.

PRACTICAL IMPLICATIONS

There are many practical implications to this belief in credobaptism, the baptism of disciples alone. *First, the New Testament church is called repeatedly "the disciples"* (Acts 6:1–7, 9:26; 11:26). This means that the local church must be composed of baptized disciples alone who give evidence of regeneration by their repentance and faith in Christ before their baptism. That is why Peter commanded people to "repent and be baptized" at Pentecost. There is no room in the New Testament for a church made of believers and their seed as members without a profession of faith before a disciple's baptism. This is an ecclesiastical implication that automatically divides Christian brethren between paedobaptist and Baptist churches.

Second, the baptism of disciples alone affects evangelism. It means that candidates (catechumens) for baptism should have adequate understanding of the person and work of Jesus Christ, the gospel of repentance and faith, and be committed followers of the Lord Jesus Christ. Jesus *made* disciples first, then baptized them (John 4:1–2). A prerequisite to baptism is Lordship salvation and a disciple's commitment. Baptismal candidates should know what they are committing to—a submission to Christ and His commandments as Lord of their lives. This requires that the faith and salvation experience of an individual must be examined before baptism. Instead of baptizing immediately anyone who "walks the aisle" or "raises a hand" or "prays a prayer," this Baptist distinctive requires the pastor to meet with and examine the beliefs and commitment of baptismal candidates. Endeavoring to ensure that a candidate understands what it means to be a disciple of Jesus Christ would greatly remedy the problem of inflated church rolls of uncommitted members; at the same time, it would help make sure that we do not mislead one precious eternal soul that he or she is saved when they may not understand the gospel before being baptized and accepted as a Christian.

Third, the church as an assembly of baptized disciples demands that the worship and teaching ministry of the church on the Lord's Day be geared toward disciples, people of faith, not "seekers." The Great Commission requires that baptized disciples be taught "to do all that [Christ] commanded [His disciples]." Systematic expository teaching and preaching is a commandment of the Great Commission. This is what is missing in many of our Baptist churches today, though commanded by Jesus Christ. I believe that the expository preaching of the PCA has attracted many former Southern Baptists who are hungry for the Word of God. Oh, that Baptist churches would follow the Great Commission and teach the whole counsel of God to people! Because faith comes by hearing, and hearing by the Word of Christ, systematic expository preaching will edify the saints and evangelize the sinner at the same time. Those Baptist churches that commit themselves to an expository, teaching ministry to the saints will see the fruit of obedience to Christ in the method by which He builds His church. The method of Christ is as clearly revealed in Scripture as the message.

Fourth, the church as an assembly of baptized disciples demands that the priority and autonomy of the local church be emphasized over denominationalism. The local church is the only earthly, visible organization that has Jesus Christ as its Head, carrying His authority. Although we believe in the church universal, Baptists do not believe in ecclesiastical authority beyond the local church. In Revelation 2 and 3, Jesus is seen as the Head of each of the seven churches. No church was more important to Him than another because it was bigger or richer or had fewer problems. They all had problems, and He dealt directly with each one as Head. This means that each local church has Christ as its Head and has all the authority of His Word to govern its life without being dictated to by another church or association of churches. If churches choose voluntarily to associate with one another, they must agree on the doctrines and practices concerning the purpose of their association, such as missions, literature, and ministerial preparation (Acts 15). However, no association or employees thereof, should presume authority over a local church or churches in associational cooperation, because that authority is reserved only for the leaders of Christ's local church. Associations and their employees are servants of the local churches, not masters.

Fifth, the church as an assembly of baptized disciples must recognize the priesthood of the believer as each disciple approaches God through Christ alone. Every Christian is a disciple of Christ, not of the church. However, this does not mean that peopld can believe anything they wish and still be a member of a local Baptist church. The church must examine the beliefs of potential members and make sure that they believe the gospel of Jesus Christ as stated in the Scripture and the articles of faith of that church. Neither a Mormon, nor a Jehovah's Witness, nor a Muslim can be a member of a Baptist church, no matter how sincere each may be. The priesthood of the believer does not mean that a Baptist church member can believe anything he or she wishes and remain a member of a Baptist church. It simply means that each one approaches God through Christ, not the church. Each one is a disciple of Christ.

Sixth, the church as an assembly of baptized disciples requires the practice of church discipline. Besides the fact that Jesus commanded this of each local church (Matthew 18:15–17), it is obvious that someone who professes to be a disciple of Jesus Christ, yet who stubbornly refuses to live by His teachings (Matthew 28:19–20), is not really a disciple and is in spiritual danger of false conversion (Matthew 7:22–23). It is an act of love and obedience for the local church to confront and discipline its baptized members. This should be understood at the beginning of church membership.

Seventh, the church as an assembly of baptized disciples requires the church to practice biblically regulated worship. The Great Commission of Christ calls the church to teach baptized disciples to do whatever Jesus commanded His disciples to do. Worship must be in spirit and in truth, not in spirit and in creativity. To invent new forms of worship not instituted by Christ and His apostles in the New Testament is to disobey His commandments as professed disciples. The approved elements of worship in the New Testament are reading the Scriptures, preaching and teaching them, congregational singing (of psalms, hymns and spiritual songs), prayer, baptism, the Lord's Supper, and collections. Such additions as drama, dance, rock bands, puppets, gospel monkeys, high-wire acts, and power-lifting demonstrations are violations of the biblical and historical regulative principle of worship believed by historical Baptists. Further, such unbiblical practices push out time given to commanded practices. An assembly of baptized disciples must follow their Lord's commandments, not their own inventions, in His worship.

The ecclesiastical implications of credobaptism, a disciple's baptism alone, are not insignificant. They are formative to the establishment of biblical Baptist churches that will stand before the next generation holding forth the biblical gospel of Jesus Christ. We pray that God will raise up a new generation of covenantal Baptist churches that will stand in the front line as outposts of the Kingdom of God, as cities of light for the lost, and as cities of refuge for the weary believers who are looking for Bunyan's House Beautiful as a spiritual haven and armory for battle.

THE STRING WITHOUT PEARLS

As I have examined each pearl on the string, I come away with the mirage of a necklace of discolored and missing jewels and the reality of an empty string called good and necessary inference that does me no good in showing the beauty of instituted Christian baptism. It is as a string of twine around the neck of a princess. This illegitimate use of legitimate good and necessary inference opens the door to unrestrained inference that will ultimately undermine the doctrine of *sola Scriptura*.

One cannot build a doctrine of sacraments upon an empty string of inferences. Sacraments must be instituted by Christ and expressly set down in Scripture. Therefore, I accept the one priceless pearl of credobaptism, a disciple's baptism alone, as that which is prescribed by Holy Scripture, and wear it upon my hand as a sign of my marriage to Christ.

It is now my clear understanding that baptism is the outward sign of entrance into the New Covenant by the inward circumcision of the heart, the circumcision of Christ. This inward circumcision is exhibited outwardly by one's personal repentance and confession of Christ as Lord and is signified to others by the baptism of disciples alone. This is credobaptism. As the Old Testament children entered the Abrahamic Covenant through circumcision of the flesh, sealed individually by the righteousness of faith, so our New Covenant children enter the New Covenant by the individual circumcision of the heart, sealed by the Holy Spirit, revealed in their confession of faith, and signified by the sign of the baptism—the baptism of disciples alone.

Chapter 14

Postlude: A Final Appeal to Build Baptist Churches

It is my earnest and sincere prayer that this fruit of my studies is true to Scripture and brings glory to Christ. It has not been my intention to be controversial or uncharitable toward other positions. I simply ask that all who would question my conclusions would study my work and the two excellent books on the subject by Watson and Kingdon, both of which are referenced herein, to do justice to my position.

It greatly saddened me long ago that my position on this subject affected my sphere of service in Christ's paedobaptist church, which I still dearly love, but our consciences must be held in bondage to the Word of God. Yet I rejoice to see a revival of Reformed beliefs in our Baptist churches across the land. Baptists of every stripe are rediscovering their Reformed roots in the *1689 London Baptist Confession* and the writings of men like James P. Boyce and John L. Dagg. However, the cost of restoring biblical truth has cost many pastors their jobs and their family's peace of mind. In love, I challenge those of a Baptist background not to accept too quickly a welcome refuge in paedobaptist churches. Stand fast with Reformed Baptists and reforming Southern Baptists to build for future generations instead of fleeing to calmer paedobaptist waters!

It is unworthy of Baptist pastors and laymen to consider baptism a secondary matter in order to serve in a paedobaptist church. The right administration of the sacraments is not secondary. It is one of the three Reformed marks of a true church governed by the regulative principle.

It is unworthy as well of laymen to leave a Baptist church in trial where a faithful pastor is bringing reform, fleeing to a good paedobaptist church simply to find a more peaceful environment. Baptists today need sacrificial Bunyans, Careys, Judsons, Rices, and Spurgeons of conscience in the pulpit and in the pews to count the cost of building biblically Reformed and Baptistic churches of faithful disciples, for the sake of truth and the next generation. If our Reformed forefathers had chosen the easiest path, Protestantism never would have gotten off the ground. Now let us finish the course.

It is my belief that infant baptism will lead to a presumption of salvation for children by those children and their parents, ultimately leading to a decline in experiential religion in each succeeding generation of paedobaptists, at least until a revival restores born-again Christianity for another season. This is one reason why, in my opinion, we often see a cycle of decline, revival, and decline in paedobaptist churches throughout history. Already there is an organization, Concerned Presbyterians, in the PCA calling for a return to Reformed theology and to the regulative principle. I wish my paedobaptist brothers could see that the regulative principle is fundamentally compromised by the misuse of good and necessary inference for paedobaptism and will inevitably infect other doctrines. Paedobaptist churches have been a welcome temporary relief for ailing Baptists, but they are no safe and permanent refuge for their future generations.

Although there has been a decline in theology and a rejection of historical Baptist theology in Baptist churches in the last century, along with the introduction of shallow evangelism, still the repetitive cycle of decline and revival has not been as characteristic of Baptist denominations. The Baptist emphasis upon the need of personal repentance and faith before every baptism—credobaptism—has kept many from falsely presuming their special status or salvation upon the basis of covenantal blessings.[227]

Finally, having gone through so many struggles on the question of Christian baptism, I can only heartily plea for unity and understanding between Baptist and paedobaptist brethren who hold the great Doctrines of Grace in common. Let us fellowship first on these things. Let us preach the gospel to every creature— and let us hold to our convictions concerning baptism because

---

[227]Howell, *Evils of Infant Baptism,* 302–3. Howell lists nineteen reasons why infant baptism leads to a decline in biblical Christianity. He even supplies statistics gathered from various paedobaptist denominations in his day showing a decline in the evangelization of children compared to the Baptist churches, (*see* Ibid., 218).

they are our own convictions, not those of others, and because they are clearly revealed in the Scriptures. To do less is unworthy of the blood shed by One who called Himself *the Truth* and who came to build His church as the pillar and ground of the truth.

Therefore, I call Baptists in conscience to hold fast to credobaptism, the baptism of disciples alone, and to band together to start Reformed and Baptist churches across our nation, true to the Scriptures, instead of seeking a welcome refuge in paedobaptist churches as pastors or laymen.[228] I call them to endure hardship while supporting a Reformed and Baptist pastor in church reformation and revival. I call them to commit themselves to be Bunyan's hero "Valiant for Truth" and to build faithful Baptist churches for their children and grandchildren.

Finally, I call the reader to add one more *sola* to your Reformed theology: credobaptism, the baptism of disciples alone. *Solis discipulis!* To God be the glory in His church.

---

[228] The Web sites of the Association of Reformed Baptist Churches of America (www.reformedbaptist.com) and of Founders Ministries, Inc. (www.founders.org) can assist those interested in starting Reformed and Baptist churches and put you in contact with like-minded believers in your area.

Appendix A

Spurgeon on Baptism[229]

THE MODE OF BAPTISM

Baptism is, we doubt not, immersion. This is taught by all Greek usage of the terms chosen by the spirit of inspiration to designate this action. It is admitted by almost every learned paedobaptist that until the time of Christ the word *baptizo* had no other meaning. It required that "the element encompass its object." Nor does the use of this word by heathen or Christian Greeks, in the ages immediately succeeding apostolic times, encourage the idea of a changed import adopted by inspired penmen, which some vainly imagine. Anyone maintaining this change of import in inspired writ, is bound to prove that, in one or more instances, the word is divinely used in another sense, the previous import (immersion) being certainly inadmissible. There is not such an occurrence. On paedobaptist testimony, the immersion of "pots, cups, brasen vessels," yea, of beds, was a Jewish custom, in order to cleanliness, or purification from ceremonial defilement. So also immersion on returning from the market, or from a crowd, and often by many before eating. Facts, on paedobaptist testimony, prove that the rich Pharisee, who expected our Saviour to baptize himself before eating, might have ample provision for immersion, and that the climate, clothing, and habits of Syrian Jews, made them ever

---

[229] Charles H. Spurgeon. *Spurgeon on Baptism*. London: Henry E. Walter, Ltd., n.d. Spurgeon wrote this appendix when he republished Thomas Watson's *Body of Divinity* in 1890 for use as a textbook at his Pastor's College. Rev. George Rogers, the principal of the college edited it for modern use. However, instead of removing Watson's chapter teaching paedobaptism, Spurgeon added this appendix on believer's baptism.

ready for the practice of immersion without indelicacy or injury. Consequently the record of great numbers baptized by John, or by the disciples of Jesus, and the non-record as to whether or how they changed their garments, proves nothing against immersion. Bathings in the Jordan, now annually and more frequently taking place, testify its present suitability for immersion; nor can the idea that a river, flowing hundreds of miles, was either too deep or too shallow for immersion, be rationally entertained. The sufficiency of water and baths in Jerusalem, Samaria, and Damascus, for the immersion of those whose baptism in the oracles of God is recorded, has abundant paedobaptist and every other acknowledgement.

The baptism of Israel in the cloud and in the sea, and the baptism of the Spirit by Christ, are not literal baptisms in water. By the sea and the cloud unitedly the children of Israel were covered. That the disciples as to their bodies, on the day of Pentecost, were not encompassed with the emblematic fire, is incapable of proof, whilst all admit that their souls were, as it were, immersed in the divine Spirit. The fulfillment of a predicted and abundant pouring might therefore constitute an immersion as to body and soul, or that which by no other word can be more properly designated. A prediction of the sprinkling of water, or pouring out of the Spirit by the divine Being on men, is no proof that the word which, in the New Testament, describes the divinely enjoined action of man towards man, is either sprinkling, or pouring, or immersion. The expression of Peter, "Can any man forbid water?" cannot be proved to mean more than, "Can any man forbid Baptism?" nor dare any who are regardful of truth affirm that the jail at Philippi was not, like other Eastern jails, supplied with a bath.

The fact that the Greek words *baptizo, baptisma, and baptismos,* underwent no change of import when used by the inspired writers, is evident from such expressions as, that John baptized "in Jordan," and "in Aenon, near to Salim, because there was much water there"; that Philip and the eunuch "went down both into the water"; that after Philip had baptized the eunuch, they came up "out of the water"; that we are buried with Christ "by baptism," and "in baptism," in which also we "are risen with him." If the words buried and risen are here used figuratively, there is an allusion to the literal immersion and emersion which had taken place. The calling of the overwhelming sufferings of Christ and his apostles, a baptism, is consistent only with its being immersion. The common and necessary use of a word meaning to immerse, and the marked distinction of this from sprinkling or pouring, would necessarily prevent its change from one to the others or to meaning the use of a liquid, as some have maintained, "in any way."

If inspired writers had used the Greek word in another sense, surely the practice among Christians of immediately subsequent times would have corroborated this. But neither the Greeks, who are supposed best to understand their own language, nor the Latins, nor any barbarians, afford the slightest support to a supposed alteration by divine or any other warrant of the import of *baptizo* and the words derived from it. Nor does Jewish proselyte baptism, whether it originated before, or, as many eminent Paedobaptists believe, after apostolic times, give the least countenance to anything short of immersion as baptism. The first recorded departure from immersion for baptism is an acknowledged deviation—an acknowledged imperfection—which, it was believed, required God's mercy and special necessity for its adoption. This took place at about the middle of the third century. Baptism was then believed requisite in order to have the certainty of salvation. A dying man might be incapable of being baptized. A substitute for baptism in such circumstances was admitted, with allowed disadvantages if life should be spared. This at length has been palmed off as baptism, as the very thing that God requires, or all that from any he demands! And while there is such a cross in being once immersed for Christ's sake, especially in these cold and northern regions, the convenience and decency of sprinkling are lauded to the skies. And by some who speak of immersion as if it could not be performed without a breach of delicacy, it is maintained that immersion is one of the actions embraced in the word divinely chosen when "baptizing" is enjoined.

The idea of necessary indecency in the "one immersion," or of the danger unless in affliction, or special circumstances, the practice of our own land and other countries is continually and loudly condemning. Where danger or incapacity really prohibit, we believe God does not demand; but he authorizes no substitute in these circumstances. Nor is a more paltry subterfuge conceivable than that the sprinkling or pouring of a little water on the face is substantially baptizing a person. However great or little the importance we attach to baptism, we are bound in observing it, to practise what God enjoins. For the servant of an earthly master to perform his own likings, instead of his master's biddings, it would be an insult which none would brook. The pretext, for sprinkling and pouring that they are not forbidden, is a scandalizing of what God has enjoined, by choosing a human invention to the rejection of a divine appointment. If God is infinite in wisdom and love, a stern adherence to his precepts is our wisdom and profit. "This is the love of God, that we keep his commandments; and his commandments are not grievous."

THE SUBJECTS OF BAPTISM

On the subjects of baptism, greater length, and some reference to our worthy author's erring assertions, are requisite. The divinely approved subjects of Christian baptism can be ascertained only from the New Testament. Christ's commission, confirmed as to its import by previous and especially by subsequent practice, and by every reference to this ordinance in the oracles of God, is "the law," and "the testimony." An attempt to prove the rightful subjects of Christian baptism from God's word and Jewish proselyte baptism, is to imitate the Popish appeal to Scripture and tradition. Besides, no man upon earth knows that proselyte baptism had an existence in apostolic times, whilst every one may know that its origin is "of men," not "from heaven"; and that the Bible alone is man's rule of faith and practice. Every legitimate inference from every part of Holy Writ we admit.

We maintain that the only proper subjects of Christian baptism are believers in Christ, those proselyted to Christ, disciples of Christ; or, since we have not, and are not required to have access to the heart, those who make a credible profession of faith in Christ. This we believe to be taught in the divine precept, "Go ye therefore and teach [make disciples of] all nations, baptizing them in [into] the name of the Father, and of the Son, and of the Holy Ghost: teaching them to observe all things whatsoever I have commanded you"; and to be confirmed by the record, "Go ye into all the world, and preach the gospel to every creature. He that believeth and is baptized shall be saved; but he that believeth not shall be damned." We maintain the sufficiency of the first Scripture, independently of the latter, on which we lay not stress in this controversy, knowing that in some manuscripts it is wanting, yet believing with almost all our opponents, that it belongs to the word "by inspiration given." The first quoted passage, the commission of Christ for the guidance of his disciples, "unto the end of the world," does not say, first disciple, and then baptize, and then teach to observe all things, etc.; but that this is an import we maintain, from the construction of the entire precept, from what the apostles had before witnessed and practised, from their subsequent practice, and from every reference to baptism in their writings.

In understanding this passage, if we follow order, where, above all places, the most precise order might be expected, we must understand Christ's will to be, that we first make disciples, then baptize, etc. That [this] order is not here to be regarded it devolves on the opponents of [this] order to prove. In making disciples, the communication and the acceptance of truth, the teaching and the receiving of the good news, are requisite. After this and baptism, teaching is not to cease, "teaching them to observe all things whatsoever I have commanded you." Nor is there anything in the passage demanding another interpretation. It has indeed been said, that "them" after "baptizing" has "all nations" for its antecedent, that the discipling and baptizing are of equal extent, embracing the same persons, even every individual in all the nations; but that the discipling of all nations means the discipling of infants is no more apparent than that infants are included where we are taught that all nations shall call our Redeemer blessed, or when he predicted, "Ye shall be hated of all nations." Nor is the antecedent, as maintained, although grammatically admissible, a grammatical requirement. Also, that the inspired writers, any more than other men, do not use the pronouns with such scrupulous exactness, is manifest from an examination of the New Testament. It is, however, maintained, and by some who denounce immersion as inconvenient and dangerous, that the commission teaches that we are to make disciples by baptizing and teaching, these present participles, following the command to disciple, certainly including the accomplishment of the discipling, and necessarily involving a contemporaneous act. The word "by" is, however, no more in Christ's words than are firstly and secondly. The word "by," though frequently admissible in such sentences, without obscuring or altering the sense, is also frequently inadmissible, as involving the most obvious perversion of a writer's meaning. No one will doubt on reading, "He spake, saying," etc., or, "They cried, saying," etc., that the speaking or crying is accomplished by saying; but when we read, "The men marvelled, saying" (Matt. 8:27), does anyone doubt that the marvelling preceded and caused the saying, and that the marvelling was not accomplished by the saying? When our Saviour said, "Lend, hoping for nothing again" (Luke 6:35), did he mean that the lending would be accomplished by hoping for nothing again? When we read, "Then came to him a man, kneeling down to him" (Matt. 17:14), do we understand that the coming of Christ was accomplished by kneeling, or that the kneeling was contemporaneous with the coming? No rule demands this absurdity. A thousand instances of such a construction in our own and the Greek language, could be adduced as disproving the necessity of so understanding Christ's words. Moreover, were "by" admissible before the participles "baptizing" and "teaching," infants would be excluded as incapable of being taught; or if admitted because in them it is the first part of discipling, it must be continued, if baptizing and teaching are contemporaneous with discipling and the fulfilling of it, until the baptizing commenced as soon as convenient after birth, its continuance would be, as we maintain, until Christ should be in them "the hope of glory," until they became believers in Christ, or made a credible profession of this faith. Any rule that would unite the participle "baptizing" to the verb disciple, and make it the accomplishment of discipling and a contemporaneous act, would also unite the participle "teaching." Nor is there a noted Paedobaptist commentator, or controversialist, whom we remember, who does not interpret baptism into the name of Father, Son, and Spirit, baptism into Christ, or into Moses, as involving a profession and consecration; which interpretation necessarily excludes infants.

Dr. Martensen says that, "baptism, as a human ceremony, is an act of confession, by which a person is admitted into Christ's church"; that "the sacraments, as acts of the church, are chiefly to be viewed as acts of profession (notae professionis), visible, sensible acts, by participating in which, each person indeed confesses his Lord and the church." Mr. Watson says: "That Christ is formed in us (Gal. 4:19); that our nature is changed; that we are made holy and heavenly; this is to be baptized into Jesus" (Rom. 6:3). He further speaks of an "oath of allegiance" which we make to God in baptism. Yet it is also said by him on Christ's commission, "The Greek is, 'Make disciples of all nations.' If it be asked how should we make them disciples? it follows, 'Baptizing them and teaching them.' In a heathen nation, first teach, and then baptize; but in a

Christian church, first baptize, and then teach them" (p. 217). Not only has Christ given no intimation of two ways of discipling, not only do the inspired writings contain no record of apostolic discipling in two ways, but the very records of discipling and baptizing the heathen, as at Philippi and Corinth, are the records from which our opponents advocate their first baptizing, and then teaching.

We admit that in accordance with human phraseology the word "disciples" is used in Scripture in application not only to those who were really, but also to those who were professedly disciples. Yet assuredly the Saviour did not wish his apostles, nor does he wish us, to make hypocrites; although, not having access to the heart, we may sometimes baptize the unworthy, as Philip baptized Simon. This inevitable fallibility we deem no more condemnable in ourselves than in the evangelist. From this necessary weakness of humanity, we may not only sometimes receive the unworthy to baptism and the Lord's Supper, but may also induce such into the highest office in the Church of Christ. We are not justified for this reason in altering the import of a disciple of Christ, solemnly and explicitly given by the Saviour himself. The tendency of paedobaptism, as we could clearly show, is to pervert the import of a disciple of Christ, by teaching that an unconscious babe, that a child who can answer certain questions, yea, that a man or woman known to be ungodly, may by baptism, become a disciple of Christ! Thus while certain conformists, maintaining justification by faith, are inconsistently teaching that baptism regenerates and converts into a child of God, certain nonconformists, maintaining the divine truth of salvation by grace through faith, teach that baptism is reserved for disciples of Christ! A correct interpretation of discipling excludes infants from the commission.

According to this natural import of Christ's words, namely, that we are to disciple him, to baptize into the name of the Father, Son, and Holy Spirit, and to teach obedience in all things to Christ's commands, we further conceive the apostles must have understood Christ, on account of the baptism they had already witnessed and practised. They knew not, so far as we are aware, any other baptism than John's, and that of Jesus through themselves. Were we to bind with the Bible all the Rabbinical lumber and all the condemned (or approved) Jewish traditions that the world contains, we should, while dishonouring the sufficiency of inspired writ, be in the same destitution of evidence that the apostles knew of any other baptisms than those recorded in the oracles of God. John "baptized with the baptism of repentance, saying unto the people, that they should believe on him who should come after him, that is, on Christ Jesus" (Acts 19:4). They "were baptized of him in Jordan, confessing their sins," (Mark 1:5). It was a baptism "into repentance," as this was the state professed by them while confessing their sins and being baptized. Until our Lord's commission, the Scriptures speak of no baptism from heaven in addition to John's except that of Christ, by means of his disciples. Concerning this the inspired record is, first, that "He baptized" (John 3:22), and secondly, that "He made and baptized more disciples than John, though Jesus himself baptized not, but his disciples" (John 4:1, 2). He baptized disciples. He made AND baptized them. The instruction from this baptism can only be in favour of first making disciples, and then baptizing them. The whole of divine revelation respecting every baptism from heaven which the apostles had previously witnessed or practised, confirms our belief that they would certainly understand Christ's words according to their natural import already indicated.

We finally maintain that our view of the commission is correct, because the apostles so understood it, as their subsequent conduct and writings abundantly evidence. Peter, on the day of Pentecost, first preached the gospel of Christ, and then taught the anxiously inquiring to repent and be baptized in the name of Jesus Christ. They must change their minds, having been unbelieving in regard to Jesus as the Messiah and Saviour, and on this faith in Christ, to which God's Spirit was drawing and helping them, be baptized, thus in obedience to Christ, avowing their belief in him as the Messiah and their Saviour. And after further exhortation and instruction from Peter, "Then they that gladly received his word were baptized: and the same day there were added unto them about three thousand souls. And they continued steadfastly in the apostles' doctrine and fellowship and in breaking of bread, and in prayers." The next record of baptism thus reads: "But when they believed Philip preaching the things concerning the kingdom of God and the name of Jesus Christ, they were baptized, both men and women. Then Simon himself believed also: and when he was baptized, he continued with Philip, and wondered, beholding the miracles and signs which were done." The next recorded baptism is that of the praying "brother Saul," whom the Lord had met on his way to Damascus. The next recorded baptism is that of Cornelius and "his kinsmen and near friends," of whose baptism Peter judged all would approve, since, while hearing Peter's words of divine instruction, the Lord had baptized them with the Holy Ghost, and they were heard to "speak with tongues, and magnify God." The next baptisms on record are those at Philippi and Corinth, adduced by Mr. Watson as proving that the apostles, in baptizing "whole families," baptized "little children" and "servants" (p. 219). We admit that, in Lydia's case, we have the record that "she was baptized, and her household" and the previous record respecting her, "whose heart the Lord opened, that she attended unto the things which were spoken of Paul," while nothing is said respecting the character of "her household." This proves not that Lydia had either husband or child. The household of this "seller of purple, of the city of Thyatira," might consist wholly of servants. Silence here neither proves nor confirms anything in favour of paedobaptism. Having no record respecting the character of this household, we are bound to believe that apostolic practice here accorded with previous and subsequent apostolic practice. The next baptism, that of the jailor "and all his," is one from which infants are clearly excluded. Paul and Silas "spake unto him the word of the Lord, and to all that were in his house"; and after baptism, "he set meat before them and rejoiced, believing (having believed) in God with all his house." The next record is equally explicit, and opposed to the baptism of infants or unbelievers. "And Crispus, the chief ruler of the synagogue, believed on the Lord, with all his house; and many of the Corinthians hearing, believed, and were baptized." The baptism of "certain disciples" at Ephesus, of whom we read, "And all the men were about twelve," equally refuses its aid to the baptism of infants; while "the household of Stephanas," of whom Paul says, "They have addicted themselves to the ministry of the saints," cannot be brought to the rescue of our opponents.

Arguments from references to baptism in God's word are as futile as those from precepts and examples in favour of baptizing infants. The apostle of the Gentiles appeals to all the "saints" in "Rome," that as "dead to sin," they had been "baptized into Jesus Christ," "baptized into his death," and "buried with him by baptism into death." Their having been baptized, demanded that they "should walk in newness of life." Is this applicable to infants? To the churches of Galatia he wrote, "For as many of you as have been baptized into Christ, have put on Christ." Of the Colossians he writes, "Buried with him in baptism, wherein also ye are risen with him through the faith of the operation of God, who hath raised him from the dead." The last mention of baptism is by Peter, who speaks of baptism as "the answer of a good conscience towards God." Thus condemnatory to paedobaptism is the entire New Testament.

But to another refuge the advocates of paedobaptism usually resort. Hence, in answer to the question, "How does it appear that children have a right to baptism?" we read, "Children are parties to the Covenant of Grace. The covenant was made with them. 'I will establish my covenant between me and thee, and thy seed after thee, for an everlasting covenant, to be a God unto thee, and to thy seed after thee' (Gen. 17:7). 'The promise is to you and to your children.' The Covenant of Grace may be considered either: (1) More strictly, as an absolute promise to give saving grace; and so none but the elect are in covenant with God. Or (2) More largely, as a covenant containing in it many outward glorious privileges, in which respects the children of believers do belong to the Covenant of Grace," and "cannot justly be denied baptism, which is its seal. It is certain the children of believers were once visibly in covenant with God, and received the seal of their admission into the church. Where now do we find this covenant interest, or church membership of infants, repealed or made void? Certainly Jesus Christ did not come to put believers in a worse condition than they were in before. If the children of believers should not be baptized, they are in worse condition now than they were in before Christ's coming" (p. 219).

In this extract from Watson, God's gracious covenant with Abraham, or one of God's covenants with him, is styled "the Covenant of Grace." But the Covenant of Grace commenced with Adam, whether we restrict it to "the elect," those chosen for salvation, or regard it, "more largely," as referring to "outward glorious privileges." Again, God's covenant with Abraham was not a covenant with the elect of mankind, nor with the whole race, nor with Abraham and the elect descending from him, nor with Abraham and exclusively the children of believers, nor with any children for the sake of their parents, excepting Abraham's own children. Nor can the Pentecostal promise of Peter be proved to have any connection with, or reference to, the Abrahamic covenant, admitting that, as some promises resemble others, this and the immediately following may remind us of the predictions that in Abraham and his seeds all the nations, all the families, of the earth shall be blessed. That all Abraham's descendants were elected to salvation, no one believes; nor is it less apparent that the children of wicked parents received the token of the covenant, as well as the children of believing parents; and in every instance beyond that of Abraham's children, not from filial relationship, but from relationship to Abraham. "The sons of David," as says Dr. Halley, "were circumcised according to the same law, and therefore for the same reason as the sons of that worshipper of Baal, Ahab, and of that wicked woman, Jezebel." Nor was the covenant of God with Abraham and his seed a covenant with his seed as infants, but with his descendants. If the token of the covenant had been disobediently neglected, it might at any age, and irrespective of character in its recipient or the parent, be performed from relationship to Abraham. Not one of Abraham's natural seed is another Abraham, nor is one believer. But all believers may be spoken of as the (believing) children of faithful Abraham. That God graciously entered into covenant with all Abraham's descendants for his sake, and instituted a sign to be fixed on every male, is no evidence that God has entered into covenant with the natural children of every believer, and with each child, for the parent's sake, and that the baptism of male and female infants of believers is the appointed sign of this covenant. Where is such a law but in the writings of Paedobaptists?

The "covenant interest" of "the children of believers" as such, or of "infants" of believers, or the "church membership of infants," and "the seal of their admission into the church," giving to the word "church" any idea resembling its New Testament use in application to the church, or a church of Christ, needed not to be "repealed or made void," because they had never existed. If God's covenanting with Abraham and his seed, and instituting the sign of circumcision in males, proves the church membership of the seed of Abraham, it proves an Ishmaelitish as well as an Israelitish church of God, and a church to which ungodly adults, equally with infants of believers, belonged. If circumcision is the seal of admission into the church, there has been not only a Jewish church, but an Edomite, a Moabite, an Ammonite church. Did Episcopalians and all others who believe a church of Christ to be "a congregation of faithful men," always speak consistently with this, we should hear less of any nation at any period, or of any building in any place, as a church. Why should we not, except where the idea of assembly exists, after the manner of inspired writers, speak of those who anciently enjoyed the divine favour, as saints, as the people of God, as those that feared the Lord, as the righteous, etc., instead of confoundingly speaking of the church before the flood, the patriarchal, the Abrahamic, the Mosaic, the Jewish (etc.) church?

The children of believers, if not baptized, are not in "a worse condition" than were the circumcised children of believers before the Christian dispensation. Grace is not, and never was hereditary. The "sons of God" have ever been those "born not of blood, nor of the will of the flesh, nor of the will of man, but of God." In every age have men become "the children of God by faith." This faith has been stronger, and has shone more conspicuously and gloriously, in some than in others; but "without faith it is impossible to please" God, and it ever has been (Heb. 11:6, etc.). The application of this to those only who are capable of believing, none can doubt. It is equally clear that the faith of some must have had reference to a Messiah who had appeared. We doubt not that the children of believers, they and their parents being spared, have had, and to the end of prevailing and parental ungodliness will have, advantages not possessed by the children of unbelievers. Parental piety superadded to parental affection necessitates this. Nor can there be hindrance—we shall not now speak of the encouragement and help—from him who has left it on record, "Train up a child in the way he should go: and when he is old he will not depart from it." There is not, however, the slightest intimation in God's word that "the children of believers," or "the infant seed of believers," in distinction from the children or infant seed of unbelievers, constitute or belong to "the election of grace." The attempt to found such an hypothesis on the covenant with Abraham and his seed, requires the belief that grace is hereditary; that all Abraham's posterity were in infancy the children of God and heirs of heaven through their relationship to Abraham, whatever their subsequent piety or ungodliness, salvation or damnation; that divine grace through Abraham naturally and efficaciously descended through all his seed, or, if it is preferred, through all his seed in the line of Isaac and Jacob, until the coming of Christ, when the infant seed of believers have the same "claim to the Covenant of Grace as their parents; and having a right to the covenant, they cannot justly be denied baptism." What inference is possible from this reasoning, but that the infant seed of all from Abraham to Christ, who descended not from Abraham, were heirs of hell? And that it is now, and from the time of Christ has been, the condition of all infants having unbelieving parents? Besides, unless circumcision introduced into the Covenant of Grace, or confirmed spiritual blessings, or promoted spiritual along with its temporal good, and unless the baptism of infants secures temporal or spiritual good to the same extent, which also the lack of baptism by infants prevents, the implied retaining of the same blessings since by baptism, and the inferred diminution of blessings by the omitted infant baptism, fall to the ground. We might also inquire of some, can the blessings of the covenant, to those born in the covenant, and who have its blessings signed and sealed to them, slip out of their hands?

It has probably been reserved to Dr. Bushnell, while saying many good things on parental influence and obligations, in advocating the baptism of infants, to carry filial relationship and its effects to their most absurd and monstrous extent. He teaches, in his *Christian Nurture,* that "until the child comes to his will, we must regard him still as held within the matrix of the parental life" (p. 97); that the covenant with Abraham "was a family covenant, in which God engaged to be the God of the seed as of the father. And the seal of the covenant was a seal of faith, applied to the whole house, as if the continuity of faith were somehow to be, or somehow might be maintained in a line that is parallel with the continuity of sin in the family" (p. 106); "the old rite of proselyte baptism, which made the families receiving it Jewish citizens and children of Abraham, was applied over directly to the Christian uses, and the rite went by "households" (p. 107); that by "organic unity in families," we have "the only true solution of the Christian church and of baptism as related to membership" (p. 108); that "baptism is applied to the child on the ground of its organic unity with the parent, imparting and pledging a grace to sanctify that unity, and make it good in the field of religion" (p. 110); that the child "is taken to be regenerate, not historically speaking, but presumptively, on the ground of his known connection with the parent character, and the divine or church life, which is the life of that character" (p. 110); and "that the child is potentially regenerate, being regarded as existing in connection with powers and causes that contain the fact before time, and separate from time" (p. 110). Thus the "seal of faith" has belonged to infants and unbelievers, and now belongs, and is restricted to, believers and their children! If Jewish "proselyte baptism" is made "over directly to the Christian uses," this is, of course, taught in God's word, or we are expressly or by implication taught, that the Jewish Talmud, a Rabbinical composition of the third century of the Christian era, belongs wholly, or in some specified part, to the oracles of God! We deny not "an organic unity" in any man, or any animal, having head, heart, lungs, liver, etc.; nor do we deny a union between Christ and his people, so that he lives in them; but we deny a union between children and parents, so that when father and mother is converted, the child becomes potentially regenerate, not through organic unity with any believing man, but as belonging to those for whom God has instituted an economy of grace, no man becoming potentially regenerate but through the sacrifice of the Son of God, which atones for sin and secures the bestowment of the divine Spirit. Well may Dr. B. piteously exclaim on his "doctrine of organic unity," "as a ready solvent for the rather perplexing difficulties of this difficult subject," that "one difficulty remains, namely, that so few can believe it" (p. 111). There is as much evidence that a child is baptized in the baptism of the parent, as that it is regenerated in the regeneration of the parent; yea, that the whole life and character of the child, and its eternal salvation or damnation, are that of the parent.

We believe that the circumcision, not only of male adults, but of male infants, was divinely enjoined, and that the unconsciousness of the latter constituted no hindrance to an accomplishment of the design of this institution; and we doubt not God's right, if he had seen it good, to institute a rite under the Christian dispensation that should embrace the unconscious, both males and females; but we deny the shadow of evidence that he has so enacted. The existence of circumcision from Abraham proves it not. Nor are we taught that baptism is in the place of circumcision, although in some things there is a resemblance in one to the other. The antitype of circumcision, or spiritual, Christian circumcision, is the renewal of the heart (Rom. 2:28, 29; 1 Cor. 7:19; Gal. 6:15; Phil. 3:3; Col. 2:11). The apostles and elders gathered together at Jerusalem to consider the necessity of circumcision, which some of the baptized Jewish believers maintained, drop not a single hint to the erring, that baptism is in the place of circumcision. The apostle of the Gentiles, warning the Colossian believers, and rebuking those in the churches of Galatia who held the destructive error, instead of teaching that baptism occupies the place of circumcision, teaches that Christian circumcision, the circumcision of Christ, is a circumcision "without hands, in putting off the body of the sins of the flesh." Nor is there in the fact that all children, or all the children of believers, are of "the Kingdom of God," a particle of evidence that God has commanded their baptism. The Scriptures which speak of baptism, recording its appointment, its practice, its nature, design, or benefit, are those from which its divinely approved subjects can be learned. These speak of confession of sin, repentance, faith in Christ, discipleship, a good conscience, as characteristic of the baptized. Not a word is recorded respecting parents or others as proxies for "the child's personal engagement" (p. 220). Ourselves, our children, and all we possess, are God's property; and with all, as "his servants," God has a sovereign right to deal. The duty of baptism is not learnt from this fact, but from the revelation of God's will. The apostle Paul, speaking of the marriage bond, when one partner has become a Christian, and the other remains an unbeliever, teaches a sacredness in the children, and the unbelieving partner that forbids a dissolution of the connection; but, while attributing the same holiness to the children and the unbelieving partner, he says not a syllable implying a "right and title to baptism" (p. 220). Everything really included in parental dedication is as much the privilege of the Baptist as Paedobaptist. It is a benefit to the child when no deceptive substitute has been performed on him, preventing, or helping to prevent, his personal, conscious, voluntary, and acceptable obedience to God's command. The obtaining by infants, through baptism, of entrance into the church, of "a right sealed to the ordinances," that is, to the Lord's Supper, etc., and of "the tutelage of angels to be the infant's lifeguard," may be in the imagination of the Paedobaptists; but these are not in the word of God, any more than that baptism is to elected infants "a seal of the righteousness of faith, a laver of regeneration, and a badge of adoption" (p. 218).

Not only are the Scriptures silent respecting infant baptism, but every record relating to baptism forbids its existence in apostolic times, and its right to a subsequent existence. Nor does Irenaeus, or any of the earliest fathers, say one word favouring the supposition of its existence, notwithstanding the inference that is drawn by some of the Paedobaptists from one passage in Irenaeus. What authority has a practice that can be proved as possibly beginning to exist at the close of the second, or in the early part of the third century? For Tertullian, dissuading from the baptism of children, may not refer to infants. The existence of infant baptism in the third century is certain. The existence in the third, and in the preceding century, of sentiments on the efficacy of baptism, and of various practices, which have no foundation in Holy Writ, is easily and abundantly proved. But neither infant baptism nor any other practice could be sanctioned by evidence of existence in the age immediately succeeding the apostolic period, or existence in apostolic times, if destitute of apostolic sanction; and especially if opposed to, and destructive of, what is divinely enjoined. The fact that inspired writers, in recording baptisms, except where the baptism of parents and other members of the family take place at the same time, say nothing as to parental piety, accords with and corroborates our view of baptism as a personal and voluntary profession and engagement. Every record of baptisms in Holy Writ, and every reference to baptism, is a confirmation of believers" baptism as the "one baptism" for parents and children, for every generation, and for all alike, to the end of time.

Nor are we ashamed of the Baptist, as compared with the Paedobaptist history, tracing it through every age, and in every country, from apostolic to the present times, although we are not disposed to boast of our own righteousness. We justify not "the doing of the Anabaptists in Germany," though Paedobaptists were united with them, and all were then but emerging from the darkness and errors of Popery. We believe in what has just fallen from the lips of the Rev. W. Walters respecting the Baptists of this country. "From the beginning," says Locke, 'they were the friends and advocates of absolute liberty—just and true liberty, equal and impartial liberty.' The claim which we make to have been the first expositors and advocates in modern times of religious liberty, is based on the surest foundation, and is capable of the most satisfactory proof." Instead of exalting believers' baptism above measure, we say in the words of our honourable and Rev. brother Noel, "It is not separation from the church of Rome, or from the Church of England, nor a scriptural organization, nor evangelical doctrine, which can alone secure our Saviour's approbation." They who speak of infant baptism as a putting of the child's name in a will by the parent, need to be reminded of God's prerogative, and of the character of his government as revealed in the words: "All souls are mine; as the soul of the father, so also the soul of the son is mine: the soul that sinneth, it shall die." Who, believing this testimony, can also believe that unbaptized infants are "sucking pagans," while those kindly baptized through parental influence are sucking Christians?

The baptism of believers, we believe to be a reasonable, scriptural, and profitable service, calculated to strengthen and perpetuate every right feeling and conduct. But in whatever esteem we hold the erring Paedobaptist, and however cordially we say, and hope ever to say, "Grace be with all them that love our Lord Jesus Christ in sincerity," we are obliged to think and speak of infant baptism according to a writer before quoted. "In it there is no conscience, no will, no reasonable service. It allies persons without their consent, or even their intelligence, to a religious creed; it forces upon them an unreasoning and unwilling service; it imposes upon them an unconscious profession: it anticipates the conduct of riper years to a degree which both nature and Scripture condemn; and is therefore a violation of their just rights."

Appendix B

The Proper Mode of Biblical Baptism

It was not my original intention to address the mode of baptism in this work. However, due to the influence of John Murray and Duane Spencer upon some students and pastors encountered while writing this book, I decided to address briefly the issue of mode in this appendix. Murray and Spencer vigorously defend the position that the mode of baptism in the New Testament clearly is sprinkling or pouring, not dipping or immersion. John Calvin and Herman Witsius, however, both affirm that the early church practiced immersion.[230] This is just another example of the lack of uniformity among paedobaptists. Such disagreement does not engender confidence in Murray's and Spencer's arguments.

I will attempt to examine the biblical mode of baptism as practiced by John, Jesus, and the apostles, and to examine and refute Murray's and Spencer's arguments for pouring and sprinkling as the proper modes of baptism. Inevitably, some of Murray's and Spencer's erroneous arguments will be exposed in the first part. The reader will see that they set aside several commonly accepted hermeneutical principles such as the literal-grammatical-historical method of exegesis in order to establish their position. The reader will also see that they generally ignore the tenses, voices, and moods of the Greek verb *baptizo* in context; these provide clear grammatical evidence regarding its proper translation as "to dip; to immerse." It is a serious oversight that such an important part of biblical exegesis such as

---

[230]Calvin, *Institutes,* 4:15:19 (1320); and Herman Witsius, *The Economy of the Covenants Between God and Man,* vol. 2 (Reprint, Escondido, CA: The den Dulk Christian Foundation, 1990), 425–27.

verb forms could be so completely ignored by some paedobaptists, as we shall see.

THE BIBLICAL MODE FOR CHRISTIAN BAPTISM

The primary New Testament verb used to describe the act of baptism is *baptizo*. It is agreed in many lexicons that *baptizo* is the intensive form of *bapto,* which itself means *to dip* or *to dye.* Most Greek lexicons define *baptizo* as "to dip; to immerse."[231] *Baptizo* is used in secular Greek to describe the sinking (immersion by dipping) of ships, to be drowned in water, to be overwhelmed or flooded with fear, or to dye. The main idea is to dip, to be dipped or immersed, or to be put into union with or covered by some substance (i.e., by dyeing). The nouns *baptismos* or *baptisma* (translated *baptism* and *washing* respectively) describe the event of the verb *baptizo.*

Josephus

We have other sources besides lexical definitions to consult. For example, Josephus, the Jewish author of the first century and a contemporary of the apostles, used *baptizo* in several instances. He always used it as the idea of dipping or immersion into some kind of substance.

First, when describing the cleansing of a dead body, Josephus distinguished between sprinkling (*raino*) and dipping (*baptizo* as immersing): "and dipping (*baptizo*) part of these ashes in [spring water], they sprinkled (*raino*) them. . . . "[232] It would be nonsensical to distinguish between baptizing and sprinkling if baptizing meant sprinkling, especially when it is also possible to sprinkle "part of these ashes" in water. Second, when Josephus spoke of Jonah's ship in the storm, he said, "The ship was in danger of sinking [being baptized as an immersion]."[233] Third, while

---

[231] Arndt and Gingrich, *Greek-English Lexicon,* 131–32; and Colin Brown, ed., *The New International Dictionary of New Testament Theology* (Grand Rapids, MI: Zondervan Publishing House, 1967), 144–50. Many others could be added.
[232] Josephus, *Josephus: Complete Works, The Antiquities of the Jews,* trans. William Whiston (Grand Rapids, MI: Kregel Publications, 1960), 4:4:6.
[233] *Ibid.,* 9:10:2.

describing how Herod commanded his young men to swim playfully with Aristobulus, his son-in-law, and then to baptize (*baptizo*) him until he drowned, Josephus said:

> . . . while such of Herod's acquaintance as he had appointed to do it, dipped [baptized as an immersion] him as he was swimming, and plunged him under water, in the dark of the evening, as if it had been done in sport.[234]

The last instance is clear that the young men baptized, or immersed, Aristobulus by dipping him under water until he drowned.

In all of these instances and more it is obvious that Josephus understood the simple root meaning of *baptizo* as *to dip* or *to immerse (by dipping)*. Josephus distinguished between dipping part of the ashes and then sprinkling the dipped ashes. According to Josephus, ships and people are dipped or immersed.

It is a serious oversight that neither Murray nor Spencer use Josephus, a standard reference tool for New Testament historical exegesis, when attempting to define *baptizo*. Such an oversight does not engender confidence in their method or objectivity.

Old Testament

In light of this preliminary definition of *baptizo* from etymology and historical Greek as *to dip* or *to immerse (by dipping)*, we now examine the Greek Old Testament, the Septuagint, to see if it generally uses *baptizo,* or *bapto,* in the same sense of dipping (or immersing in a substance) or as the paedobaptist claims, *to pour, to sprinkle.*

Baptizo

The verb *baptizo* is used twice in the Septuagint, once figuratively and once literally, both times to translate the Hebrew verb *tabal, to dip.* As Berkhof explains, one has to determine whether a word is being used figuratively or literally to determine its meaning. In figurative uses, Berkhof warns that one

---

[234]*Ibid.*, 15:3:3.

must discover the principal idea without putting much emphasis upon details.[235] However, placing too much emphasis upon details is a mistake paedobaptists make when explaining the figurative uses of *baptizo* (Isaiah 21:4; Romans 6:3–4; 1 Corinthians 10:2; 1 Peter. 3:21; Colossians 2:12). Instead of focusing upon the central principle and simple idea of the figure, they focus upon the details to invent new modes of *baptizo*. In so doing, they redefine the literal usage by the supposed figurative usage. This is a major error in their hermeneutical approach.

In Isaiah 21:4, *baptizo* is used figuratively: "Horror overwhelms [falls upon, startles, terrifies] me." The Piel (intensive) form of the Hebrew verb *tabal* means *to be suddenly and intensively fallen upon, startled, or overwhelmed*. The literal translation reads "horror [baptizes] me." This figurative use makes it difficult at first reading to understand how the Septuagint's *baptizo* carries the idea of *to dip or to immerse,* yet the idea may be to be covered over by a sudden deluge or flood, seized by horror as one grasps an object to dip it, or immersed in horror: "Horror floods or immerses me." Any of these are real possibilities.

However, some paedobaptists use this figure to define baptism as *pouring or falling upon*. Yet according to standard principles of interpretation, we must be careful not to use figures to define the literal meaning of words. Instead, we must hold to the literal meaning if possible in order to explain the figure, being careful not to place too much emphasis upon the details to create a new definition. Remembering that the direct object receives the action of the active verb, Isaiah 21:4 certainly falls within the literal idea of being dipped or immersed in horror. Even if one accepts the idea of "horror [pours] me," one is left with no explanation of how "horror pours me," or what horror pours upon me, unless one wishes to say nonsensically that "horror actually pours me." Yet one easily may say "horror actually dips me." The translation of *baptizo* as *to pour, to sprinkle* does not hold in this text.

The one literal use of *baptizo* in the Septuagint is the account of Naaman's experience in the Jordan River: "So he went down and dipped *himself* (baptized himself) seven times in the Jordan, according to the word of the man of God; and his flesh was restored

---

[235]Berkhof, *Principles,* 84–86.

like the flesh of a little child, and he was clean" (2 Kings 5:14). This is a literal baptism in water.

In this case, as in several New Testament texts, the grammar of *baptizo* clearly indicates something about the mode. Here the aorist middle (reflexive) form of *baptizo* translates the Hebrew Qal intransitive (reflexive) verb *tabal, dipped himself.* The word "himself" is not in the text itself, but is so translated as a Qal intransitive with reflexive meaning. The subject receives the action of the verb performed upon himself. Thus, Namaan dipped *himself* in the Jordan; he did not dip, pour, or sprinkle *water upon himself* from the Jordan. If pouring or sprinkling were possible translations, a strict literal translation would require us to say that "Namaan [actually poured or sprinkled] himself" in the Jordan, a nonsensical idea. Water can be poured or sprinkled, but men cannot; they can only be dipped or immersed. Namaan dipped himself in the Jordan.

Duane Spencer reflects the typical paedobaptist oversight of the verb form by saying that "himself" is not even in the text. So, according to Spencer's own words, Namaan must have dipped *water* from the Jordan and poured it upon himself.[236] Such negligence of the Hebrew and Greek reflexive verbs is not worthy of serious consideration. Likewise Murray conveniently dismisses Naaman's experience as evidence for any mode of baptism, ignoring the verb form.[237]

According to both the Hebrew Qal intransitive verb and the corresponding Greek aorist middle form in the Septuagint, Naaman baptized (dipped or immersed) *himself* in the Jordan River. Any other view ignores the very grammatical forms of the verbs.

Bapto

The root word for *baptizo,* which is *bapto,* is also used in various ways to translate the Hebrew word *tabal, to dip.* Paedobaptists go through various strategies to try to prove that *bapto* does not always mean to immerse completely under a substance. For instance, Spencer and Murray maintain that the priests feet may

---

[236]Spencer, *Holy Baptism,* 31–32. Spencer particularly ignores Hebrew and Greek verbal forms and their influence on translation. His book is flawed in a number of hermeneutical and exegetical ways.
[237]Murray, *Christian Baptism,* 13.

not have been covered when they were dipped (*bapto*) in the edge of the Jordan River (Joshua 3:15).[238] Of course, they both overlook the fact that God promised the stopping of the flow when the "*soles* of the feet of the priests" rested in the waters (3:13). All that was required for complete immersion was for the *soles* to be dipped, or immersed, in the edge of the water. Neither do they explain how pouring or sprinkling would define *bapto* in this case.

The same sort of oversight is found in the paedobaptist explanation of Jonathan's dipping (*bapto*) the tip of his staff into the honeycomb (1 Samuel 14:27). Murray ridicules the idea that the whole staff was immersed, even though no Baptist claims such an act.[239] All that is required is that the *tip* of the staff be dipped (immersed by dipping) in the honeycomb, which obviously occurred. *Bapto*'s usages support the idea of *baptizo* as dipping, rather than pouring or sprinkling.

Another example of faulty exegesis comes from Murray's argument that *bapto* cannot mean completely to immerse in Leviticus 14:6, 51. On this occasion, directions are given for cleansing a person or a house from leprosy. One bird is to be slain in an earthenware vessel over running water. The live bird is to be dipped (*bapto*) in the blood of the first bird. Murray claims that there could not have been enough blood from the first bird completely to immerse the second. Therefore, according to Murray, to dip (*bapto*) does not necessarily mean to immerse; in fact, it cannot be so in this text.[240]

The problem with Murray's position is that he discounts his own footnote that lists the many commentators such as Keil and Delitzsch, tested Hebrew experts, who believe that the text supports a mixture of water and blood in the vessel in which the second bird is dipped.[241] Such a mixture certainly could have contained enough liquid to completely immerse the second bird. Even if the second bird was not completely immersed over its head, the point is that the bird was *dipped* into the liquid, or perhaps completely dyed in the liquid. Liquid was not poured or sprinkled upon the bird. To be so dogmatic as is Murray about the

---

[238]Spencer, *Holy Baptism,* 31; and Murray, *Christian Baptism,* 13.
[239]Murray, *Christian Baptism,* 13.
[240]*Ibid.,* 11–12.
[241]*Ibid.,* 11–12. See footnote 6a.

amount of liquid, as well as discounting a real exegetical alternative in the text as far-fetched, is reaching for straws. It misleads the unskilled reader. *Bapto* as dipping is maintained.

The Septuagint's use of *baptizo* still clearly indicates the dipping of Naaman in water, not the pouring or sprinkling of water upon him. Paedobaptists usually ignore the evidence from the verb forms for *baptizo* and *bapto*.

New Testament

The New Testament use of *baptizo* as immersion by dipping is even clearer. Very simply, in the passive forms of *baptizo,* the subject of the verb is baptized; that is, people are baptized (dipped or immersed), not water (poured or sprinkled). There is no instance in the New Testament description of baptisms in which water is the subject of the passive form of *baptizo,* which would be necessary if it means pouring or sprinkling. As A. H. Strong says:

> The absence of any use of [*baptidzo*] in the passive voice with "water" as its subject confirms our conclusion that its meaning is "to immerse." Water is never said to be baptized upon a man.[242]

The passive verbs are particularly instructive, as A. H. Strong affirmed. For instance, Mark records the imperfect passive: "[they] were baptized by [John] in the Jordan River" (1:5). No mention of water is made as the receiver of the action of the verb. John baptized the people, not the water. Nor is water described as the means of pouring or sprinkling, only the location is mentioned—"in the Jordan River."

Another example is the aorist passive of *baptizo* in Mark 1:9: "Jesus . . . was baptized (dipped or immersed, not poured or sprinkled) by John into (*eis*) the Jordan River." Again, no mention is made of water as the subject of *baptizo*—and it is ridiculous to think of Jesus Himself, as the receiver of the action of the verb, being poured or sprinkled into the Jordan River by John. However, it is perfectly natural to think of Jesus being dipped or immersed by John into the Jordan River as the location and/or medium of the baptism. To accept the literal and historical meaning of *baptizo* as

---

[242] Augustus Hopkins Strong, *Systematic Theology* (Old Tappan, NJ: Fleming H. Revell Company, 1907), 935.

to dip or *to immerse* is the most natural reading of the passive verbs and does not require complicated explanations by paedobaptists about why *eis* should be translated "in the Jordan" instead of "into the Jordan." Paedobaptists argue that such a change, making *into* read as *in,* only requires the Jordan as the location of the sprinkling or pouring, not the medium *into* which one is baptized. However, even a change from *into* to *in* (as the locative sense alone) cannot negate the passive idea. Very simply, "Jesus [Himself] . . . was dipped or immersed by John into (or even *in*) the Jordan River."

Many other examples of the passive verb could be given, but John 4:1–2 is very instructive in the active form of *baptizo:* "Jesus was making and baptizing more disciples than John (although Jesus Himself was not baptizing, but His disciples were). . . . " Disciples themselves were baptized, not water baptized upon disciples, lending further support to people being dipped rather than water being poured or sprinkled. It is as if the paedobaptist reads the text to say: "Jesus was making more disciples than John and baptizing (pouring) water upon them." Yet to make this claim, they must continue to assume that water is the understood subject or direct object of the verb, or the instrument of baptism as a pouring or sprinkling, without textual support. The grammar of John 4:1–2 supports dipping much more than sprinkling. Disciples can be dipped or immersed in water, but they cannot themselves be poured or sprinkled as water can be. Here we find that Jesus dipped or immersed disciples alone.

This is exactly the same kind of baptism in the Great Commission's use of the active verb: "Go [or having gone] therefore and make disciples of all the nations, baptizing [dipping, immersing, pouring, or sprinkling?] *them* in [*eis,* into] the name of the Father . . . (Matthew 28:19–20)." Here the idea is to dip or immerse *disciples,* not pour or sprinkle *water,* into union with the name of the Father, Son, and Holy Spirit as the body is dipped into union with water. Them, not water, is the direct object of *baptizo.* Further, if *baptizo* means to sprinkle or to pour, then one must explain once again why *eis* does not mean *into.* In the New Testament, only disciples are baptized or immersed by dipping them in/into water and into union with the name of the Father, Son, and Holy Spirit.

If not for Josephus and the clear passive forms of *baptizo,* it might be possible to translate the active *baptizo* in some cases as pouring or sprinkling, because water is not designated the subject or direct object of the verb in those passages. Matthew 3:11 says: "As for me, I baptize you *en* [in, with, or by] water for repentance, . . . He Himself will baptize you *en* [in, with, or by] the Holy Spirit and fire." Here, ignoring other evidence, *baptizo* could mean either dipped in water or sprinkled with water. Recognizing this, Duane Spencer argues from Matthew 3:11–12 that John sprinkled "with [*en*] water," then uses Ezekiel 36:25 as an example: "I will sprinkle clean water upon you and you shall be clean."[243] However, Spencer does not recognize that this construction in Ezekiel makes water the direct object and the receiver of the action of the verb, contrary to the construction in Matthew 3:11 which makes the subject of baptism the receiver of the action. The Ezekiel example actually weakens his argument. Although Matthew 3:11 conceivably could be translated either "I dip you in [locative] water" or "I sprinkle you with [instrumental] water," the fact is that there is no such parallel construction in Ezekiel with the use of water as the stated subject or direct object of *baptizo* in the New Testament. Once again, Spencer misunderstands the grammar.

The critical point is that all of the passive forms clearly refer to dipping, some active constructions also clearly refer to dipping, and those fewer uncertain active alternatives cannot overrule them. The grammatical construction surrounding *baptizo* and its verb forms, especially the passive forms, has generally been overlooked by those who advocate pouring and sprinkling. This is an amazing oversight for those who claim to base their case upon Scripture.

Paedobaptists sometimes try to undermine the case for dipping or immersion by quoting obscure and disputed texts (Hebrews 9:10), or figurative uses (1 Corinthians 10:2; 1 Peter 3:21; Romans 6:4). However, it is a poor interpretation that must depend upon obscure, few and disputed texts, or figurative usages, to redefine the simple literal-historical-grammatical meaning of a word.

The clear and simple meaning of *baptizo* in the New Testament, when describing the physical baptism of disciples, is to dip or to immerse. This understanding is based upon consistent etymology, historical usage in Josephus, and the internal grammar of both the Old and New Testaments. This definition also provides a clearer concept of being baptized "*into* the name of the

---

[243]Spencer, *Holy Baptism*, 81.

Father . . . baptized *into* Christ . . . buried with Him through baptism *into* death" (Matthew 28:18–20; Romans 6:3–4; Colossians 2:12). To be dipped or immersed into Christ is to be put "in union with" Christ. Sprinkling and pouring do not bear sufficiently the idea of in union with. The figurative usage must be built upon the literal usage, not vice-versa.

Further paedobaptist objections will be addressed later, but for now, *baptizo* is best defined as dipping or immersing (by dipping) disciples in or into water. In this process, disciples are introduced into union with the water or covered by water as dye covers an object, thus explaining the figurative uses of *baptizo* as *in union with* in Romans 6:3–4, Colossians 2:12, 1 Corinthians 10:2, and 1 Peter 3:21.

Church History

Church history after the New Testament must only corroborate what the Bible teaches, as Marcel states.[244] We must be cautious in its use, as I demonstrated in arguing against infant baptism. The earliest reference to Christian baptism outside of the New Testament is from the *Didache* (100 to 125 A.D.), commonly called *The Teaching of the Twelve Apostles.* According to *Didache* 7:

> 1. Now concerning baptism. Baptize as follows, when you have rehearsed the aforesaid teaching [to catechumens]: Baptize in the name of the Father and of the Son and of the Holy Spirit, in running water. 2. But if you do not have running water, use whatever is available. And if you cannot do it in cold water, use warm. 3. But if you have neither, pour water on the head three times—in the name of the Father, Son, and Holy Spirit.[245]

Obviously, in this passage, ordinary baptism is not the same as pouring on the head. It is a strong support for dipping or immersion. Robert A. Kraft, a recognized scholar on the Apostolic Fathers, comments on this passage from the *Didache:*

> Immersion in a river or a spring (cold flowing water) was preferred practice, but still water (pools, cisterns, fonts) could be used

---
[244]Marcel, *Infant Baptism,* 19.
[245]Robert M. Grant, ed., *The Apostolic Fathers* (New York: Thomas Nelson & Sons, 1965), vol. 3, *Barnabas and the Didache,* by Robert A. Kraft, 163–64.

if necessary (cf. Tert., *Bapt.* 4). As a last resort, affusion was permissible—this is probably the earliest reference to that practice in Christianity (cf. Tert. *Poen.* 6; *Bapt.* 12; *Acts of Thaddeus* 4).[246]

From these resources, apparently pouring (affusion) was permitted by the end of the first century in extreme cases of scarce water resources, or perhaps even illness. However, this permission in difficult circumstances only bolsters the case that dipping, or immersion by dipping, was the norm for baptism in the first century. Pouring is a distinctly different practice from ordinary baptism by dipping.

Other sources in church history that affirm dipping or immersion as the main practice of the early church into the seventh century are well documented by Francis Wayland, Philip Schaff, John L. Dagg, and Alexander Carson in their respective works.[247] Furthermore, the historical testimony of the Greek Orthodox church is that immersion by dipping has been the proper mode of baptism from the beginning, even of their infants. Apparently, the Greek church understands *baptizo* in the Greek language to be immersion by dipping.

In summary, dipping or immersion was the practice of the New Testament and the earliest record we have in church history. Such consistent testimony for immersion by dipping must not be overlooked to justify pouring or sprinkling as normative baptism.

JOHN MURRAY AND DUANE SPENCER'S VIEW OF MODE REJECTED

To the layman and to those ignorant of major Baptist works, Murray's and Spencer's arguments seem reasonable at first glance. However, upon closer exegetical examination, they make several errors that are essential to sustaining their position for pouring and sprinkling.

---

[246]*Ibid.*, 164; Stander and Louw, *Baptism,* 20–21.
[247]Edward T. Hiscox, *Principles and Practices for Baptist Churches* (Grand Rapids, MI: Kregel Publications, 1980), 386–444. Hiscox marshals quotations from church history to support the established practice of immersion in the first seven centuries.

Etymology

First, because of their misinterpretation of the Baptist position, together with their complete oversight of Greek verb forms, both Murray and Spencer claim that the mode of *baptizo* cannot be determined from secular Greek usage or verb forms. Rather, they say, only its usage in the Scripture can determine its real import or mode. Both warn against the use of Greek lexicons and examples from secular literature to define a scriptural word.

Even though Murray and Spencer discount etymology and the secular usage of *baptizo* for defining its biblical meaning, the literal-grammatical-historical method that they profess to follow includes the study of the common and contemporary usage of Bible words to help understand the root idea from which God chose a specific word to express His revelation. Perhaps this is why they do not even mention Josephus, a glaring omission for scholarly works. We agree that the Bible usage of a word has final authority, including that for *baptizo*, but only the prejudiced or uninformed would think that we can translate and understand the Bible while completely ignoring the literal and historical background of those words. If we did that, how could we define the many *hapax legomena* (single occurrences) in the New Testament? We could not. Such selective application of hermeneutics is prejudicial.

Louis Berkhof, a paedobaptist, explains that the Bible is written in human language and must be interpreted grammatically first. He explains that interpretation does not spend much time on etymology, not because it is unimportant as some seem to imply, but simply because it is a very technical area and needs to be left to those who have an expert knowledge of the biblical languages. Furthermore, he explains, etymology does not always show the current signification of a word in Scripture, but it is advisable to take notice of the established etymology of a word to help determine its real meaning. He advocates that a concordance be used to check the usage of biblical words in their contexts, but he does not mean that one may completely ignore etymology![248]

The literal-grammatical-historical method of interpretation recognizes that God established Hebrew and Greek as languages before inspiring men to write down His revelation using those

---

[248] Berkhof, *Principles,* 67–68.

languages. To treat the Bible as if it were dropped out of heaven with detached meanings from the surrounding culture and languages reveals ignorance of the verbal plenary method of inspiration and literal-grammatical-historical exegesis. Josephus is neither an insignificant, optional, or a minor secular resource. His Judaism, his familiarity with Koine Greek and the Septuagint, his awareness of the Christian movement, and his discussion of biblical passages in Greek all give major corroboration to the accuracy of most Greek lexicons in their definition of *baptizo: to dip, or to immerse.*

Conservative paedobaptists agree with the literal-grammatical-historical method of interpretation, yet they are inconsistent with their own hermeneutical method of determining the meaning of words when they deal with *baptizo*. They do not ignore etymology, grammar, and history when defining other biblical words. Why do so with *baptizo?* It is an accepted principle of translators that the commonly accepted meaning of a word in a language be considered a priority unless the immediate Scriptural context indicates a different usage. The burden of proof is upon the translator to show why a word should not be translated according to its literal, historical, grammatical and normal use—and that proof must be literal, historical and grammatical, not wishful imagination.

Verb Forms

A second common error of paedobaptist hermeneutics, as just discussed, is to ignore the verb forms of *baptizo.* In order to go outside the normal use of *baptizo* (to dip or to immerse by dipping) the paedobaptist overlooks the subject of the passive forms. Never is water the subject of the passive verb *baptizo:* "Jesus [Himself, not water] was baptized [dipped or immersed, not poured or sprinkled] by John into the Jordan River" (Mark 1:9). To ignore Jesus as the subject of the passive verb is to ignore the grammatically determined mode of dipping rather than pouring or sprinkling. It is as if the paedobaptist wants the text to say: "Water was baptized (poured, sprinkled) upon Jesus by John in the Jordan River," but it does not.

As discussed, some active forms of *baptizo* conceivably could support either dipping or sprinkling because of the imprecise Greek grammar: "I baptize [dip or sprinkle] you in/with water" (Matthew 3:11). However, the clearer passive forms cannot support either sprinkling or pouring as an alternative translation and must, therefore, determine the translation of the less clear active forms. This procedure is fundamental to sound biblical hermeneutics and exegesis. Matthew 3:11 must read "I baptize [dip or immerse] you in water."

This oversight of passive verb forms causes the paedobaptist further to mistranslate the prepositions *en* (in, with, by) and *eis* (into, in) to make them fit the idea of "with water" (*en*) or "in water" (*eis*) as the means of or location of pouring or sprinkling. Instead, the passive verbs dictate the understanding in or into water with the active verb as the location of where one is dipped. Sound hermeneutics dictates that the passive verb's sure meaning and form control how to translate attached prepositions, which may have more than one meaning, rather than using prepositions to violate the meaning of the passive verb.

Obscure Texts

Third, both Murray and Spencer appeal to the use of *baptismois* in Hebrews 9:10 as "various washings (baptisms)" to claim that the Old Testament pourings and sprinklings are also biblical forms of Christian baptism. This supposedly defines New Testament baptism as pouring or sprinkling through prior Old Testament usage. Spencer leaps from this assumption to the conclusion that Jesus' baptism was by pouring, as the High Priest was anointed by pouring.[249] However, such an argument is by eisegesis, not exegesis, and ignores the clearer texts of the Gospels.

Despite paedobaptist claims that the sprinklings of Hebrews 9:13, 21 are examples of various baptisms, thus validating sprinkling as a legitimate Christian baptism, several hermeneutical principles are violated to support this theory. First, various baptisms in Hebrews 9:10 is by no means a clear translation. That is why it is usually translated in our English versions as *various washings*. Second, just because some sprinklings are mentioned in Hebrews 9:19 does not mean that they are the same *various washings* of Hebrews 9:10. Hebrews 9:10 could be referring to the Old Testament washings of hands, cups, and so forth by dipping (Mark 7:4–5), or to the dipping of a bird in leprous cleansings.

---

[249]Spencer, *Holy Baptism,* 11–12, 34–38.

Neither are Murray's and Spencer's arguments against dipping in Mark 7:4–5 convincing. Are we really to believe that "the baptism of cups . . . " means the sprinkling or pouring of water upon cups rather than the dipping of cups themselves in water? Once again, if *baptisma* means sprinkling or pouring, then how does one understand the pouring of cups? Can cups themselves be poured? No, but they can be dipped or immersed. It is a poor hermeneutic that uses difficult texts to explain the clearer ones that actually deal with the baptism of people.

Berkhof, a paedobaptist, warns against using an obscure text to build a doctrine. He says that such a practice is of "dubious value." Further, he adds, the analogy of faith cannot be contradicted by an obscure passage. He references Revelation 20:4–5 as an example of how eschatology may be ruled in an unbalanced way by one text.[250] In other words, an obscure passage such as Hebrews 9:10 cannot overrule the many clearer passages on baptism in the New Testament, especially those that institute baptism, such as Mark 1:8–9, John 4:1–2, and others.

Figures

Fourth, the way Murray and Spencer deal with the figurative uses of *baptizo* is hermeneutically unsound. Berkhof warns that in figurative texts, one must stick to the main principle, not trying to interpret every detail of the figure.[251] There are five instances where figures are used by Murray and/or Spencer to deny that *baptizo* or its noun form means dipping or immersion by dipping.

Romans 6:3–4

Murray and Spencer deny that Romans 6:3–4 has any reference to immersion as the symbol for being baptized into Christ or raised up with Him. They do this by trying to make each detail of the figure incompatible with dipping or immersion. Their emphasis upon Jesus' burial in a tomb instead of into the ground enables them to overstate the importance of tomb burial and thereby reject the figure of immersion as a burial and resurrection.

---

[250]Berkhof, *Principles*, 165–66.
[251]*Ibid.*, 84–86.

For example, Spencer claims that Romans 6:3–4 could not refer to immersion because, he claims, burial in the Bible always occurred in tombs, never in the ground. In fact, Spencer ridicules Baptists for being ignorant of this supposed fact:

> Ignorance of meaning of key words and oriental customs common to people of the Bible lands during the period during which the Scriptures were written, is the breeding ground of much heresy . . . lowering the body into the ground was totally foreign to Paul's thinking.[252]

I hope Spencer is not ungraciously accusing Baptists of "heresy" in their views. However, one has to do little biblical research to discover burial in the ground against Spencer's view (Genesis 35:8, 2 Kings 23:6, Jeremiah 26:23, Luke 7:11–17, Luke 11:44, and Matthew 27:7). Those of wealth were usually buried in tombs, but many common people were buried in the ground in graveyards. Even if one claims that Jesus was buried in a tomb instead of the ground, so that immersion is not clearly pictured in His burial and resurrection, one still has the problem that the Psalms picture His descent into death or Hades as a burial and His resurrection to life as a raising up (Acts 2:29–32). Spencer's splitting of hairs between tomb burial and ground burial suggests a larger problem with his view.

In any case, Spencer's ridicule of Baptists for ignorance must be turned upon himself. One friend of mine, influenced by Spencer's book, concluded:

> If the Jewish burial customs were to lower the body down into the earth, and the context of Romans 6 was pointing to water baptism, then the Baptist position would be correct. But the New Testament does not recognize burial methods of lowering the body into the earth.[253]

According to my friend's own words, erroneously influenced by Spencer's ignorance of biblical burial customs in the ground, the Baptist position must be correct on Romans 6:3–4.

---

[252]Spencer, *Holy Baptism,* 149.

[253]I have chosen to refrain from referencing this quotation by my friend, who since has become Presbyterian. It is my hope that he will reconsider his position one day.

Tomb burial versus earth burial aside, Baptists agree with paedobaptists that the primary emphasis of these verses is union with Christ. However, we also believe that dipping or immersion as defined in the Gospels' baptisms better illustrates the idea of union than does pouring or sprinkling. This is seen in the following parenthetical alternatives quoted in the Scripture text:

> Or do you not know that all of us who have been baptized [dipped or immersed, not poured or sprinkled] into Christ Jesus have been baptized [dipped or immersed, not poured or sprinkled] into His death? Therefore we have been buried with Him through baptism [dipping or immersing, not pouring or sprinkling] into death, in order that as Christ was raised from the dead through the glory of the Father, so we too might walk in newness of life]Romans 6:3–4; parenthetical comments mine].

The parentheses that I've inserted show that the only fitting mode of being baptized into (*eis*) Christ and buried with Him through baptism into [*eis*] death is dipping or immersing. This corresponds either to dipping into union with Christ in His death and out again in His resurrection, or simply to a burial and resurrection from a grave as a spiritual comparison to conversion. One is hard pressed to see how sprinkling or pouring symbolizes burial. Once again, the paedobaptist ignores the passive form of *baptizo*. Christians, not water, are baptized as the subject of the verb into Christ Jesus. The mode of dipping or immersing into water perfectly corresponds to this figure of people being baptized into Christ. In any case, the literal usage takes priority over the figurative usage when defining a word, not vice-versa.

1 Corinthians 10:2

Paedobaptists also cite another figurative use of *baptizo* in 1 Corinthians 10:2 to deny that the word refers to dipping or immersion:

> Moreover, brethren, I would not that ye should be ignorant, how that all our fathers were under the cloud, and all passed through the sea; And all were baptized unto Moses in the cloud and the sea; And did all eat the same spiritual meat; And did all drink the same spiritual drink; for they drank of that spiritual Rock that followed them; and that Rock was Christ (1 Corinthians 10:1–4; KJV).

Obviously, this historical event is used as a figure in which details must not be pressed too far in order to define words. The idea of this text is that when the Israelites passed through the Red Sea, covered by the cloud, they were baptized into union with Moses somehow. Even though they walked on dry ground, Paul emphasizes the cloud covering and passing through the sea as if they were covered all around by water.

Spencer goes to ridiculous ends to show how the people did not get wet, except possibly by sprinkling from the glory cloud over them (Psalm 77:17), so that immersion cannot be meant.[254] However, such speculation still ignores the verb form of *baptizo* in the text. The aorist middle indicates that the people baptized themselves (dipped or immersed, not sprinkled or poured) into Moses; even stronger, some accept the aorist passive reading. Water is never mentioned as the subject of "baptized themselves" or "were baptized," nor does it say that all were sprinkled with water from the cloud into Moses. Only "dipped or immersed into Moses" sustains the idea of the people being put into union with Moses as their mediator and leader (Hebrews 3:2–4, 16), just as Romans 6:3–4 does with Christ. Dipping or immersion also sustains the idea of confessing their faith as the basis for crossing the sea as one confesses his faith in baptism (Hebrews 11:29).

1 Corinthians 10:2 is a figurative text in which the phrase were baptized into Moses is sufficiently explained by the meaning of to dip, to immerse according to the literal-grammatical-historical usage in the Gospels and Acts. This figure cannot be used to deny the literal meaning of *baptizo* as to dip, to immerse.

Colossians 2:11–12

Colossians 2:11–12 contains a use of *peritome* [circumcision] and *baptisma* in a figurative sense:

> . . . and in Him you were also circumcised with a circumcision made without hands, in the removal of the body of the flesh by the circumcision of Christ; having been buried with Him in [the] baptism, in which you were also raised up with Him through faith in the working of God, who raised Him from the dead.

---

[254]Spencer, *Holy Baptism,* 153.

This text teaches that Christians have been circumcised already, having been co-buried with Christ in *"the [tow]* baptism," and co-raised with Christ through *faith* in the operation of God who raised Him from the dead. To be buried with Christ in baptism is sustained only by the translation of dipping or immersion as a burial. Pouring or sprinkling does not carry the idea of burial and resurrection in this text, whether in the ground or in a tomb. Further, the baptism refers to a specific occasion of baptism in which the co-raising of the Christian is coincident with their personal faith, once again affirming disciples alone.

The baptism of Colossians 2:11–12 is a figure of having been buried and raised with Christ through the exercise of faith in Him. Only the dipping or immersion of disciples fits such a figure.

1 Peter 3:18–22

Another figurative use of *baptisma* is found in 1 Peter 3:18–22. After describing how Christ was put to death but raised by the Spirit, he explains how he went and preached to the spirits in prison:

> ... which sometime were disobedient, when once the long-suffering of God waited in the days of Noah, while the ark was preparing, wherein few, that is, eight souls were saved by water. The like figure whereunto *even baptism* doth also now save us [not the putting away of the filth of the flesh, but the answer of a good conscience toward God] by the resurrection of Jesus Christ . . . [1 Peter 3:20–21, KJV; emphasis mine].

It is clear that this is a figurative use of *baptisma* simply because the text says so. But *how* is it a "like figure" or antitype [*antitupos*]? The comparison is between eight souls who were saved "through water [*di hudator*]" while on the ark and the "baptism that does now save us . . . by the resurrection of Christ." The latter is the like figure, or antitype, of the former. Peter says that, in some way, baptism saves us by the resurrection of Christ in the same way the eight souls were saved on the ark "through water."

Spencer attempts to use the figure of the ark riding on top of the water and poured upon from above in order to redefine the meaning of baptism as "to pour, to sprinkle."[255] However, in so

---

[255]*Ibid.*, 154–55.

doing, he tries to make every element of the figure take on meaning to define baptism's mode, rather than sticking to the main principle as Berkhof instructs.

The comparison is not to the modes between the ark and baptism, but simply to the likeness of being saved through water. If one wanted to establish mode in this text, the "putting away of the filth of the flesh" indicates more than sprinkling or pouring. Dipping or immersion would better fit the description of putting away the filth of the flesh. If one wanted to be as imaginative as Spencer, he might argue that the water of the flood represented burial to death in immersion, or being saved from death by drowning, while the ark represented being saved by Christ's resurrection out of the waters. In reality, however, how does "baptism now save us . . . through the resurrection of Christ" except that it pictures a burial and resurrection like that of Romans 6:3–4 consistent with dipping or immersion, not pouring or sprinkling?

The figure of 1 Peter 3:21 is sufficiently compared to the truth that salvation through water is the simple type-antitype comparison in the flood and in baptism. Through water is not attempting to decide between sprinkling or pouring and immersion, it is simply exalting the salvation of Christ portrayed in baptism and signified in the ark experience. It is wrong to think Peter is defining the mode of baptism in the ark figure in a way that would overthrow the clearer literal definition established in the Gospels and Acts, that of dipping or immersion. It is the duty of the interpreter to determine the meaning of the figurative from the literal, not vice-versa.

Matthew 3:11

The figurative language used by John the Baptist is claimed by Murray and Spencer to describe baptism as a pouring or sprinkling: "I baptize you with water . . . he will baptize you with the Holy Spirit and with fire" (Matthew 3:11). They then go to Old Testament passages that speak of the sprinkling of clean water upon the heart and the pouring out of the Spirit from above (Ezekiel 36:25–27; Joel 2:28–30; Acts 2:17), claiming that sprinkling and pouring have to be the mode of baptism in John the Baptist's figure. They attempt to bolster their argument by referring to the Holy Spirit descending in the form of a dove upon Jesus in His baptism as an anointing to His high priesthood, using the anointing of Aaron by pouring to prefigure Jesus' anointing to His high priesthood at John's baptism. Thus, they say, the mode of baptism is proven to be sprinkling or pouring.

The problem with this argument is that it is, again, a violation of basic interpretive principles. Like their interpretation of Hebrews 9:10, this argument is interpretation by association rather than by literal-grammatical-historical principles. We again refer to Berkhof's warning about making too much of the details of figures rather than sticking to the main principle or idea. Grammatically, *en hudati . . . en pneumati hagio kai puri* may be translated either as dative of means, "with water . . . with the Holy Spirit and fire," or as locative of place, "in water . . . in the Holy Spirit and fire."

However, due to the fact that people are *themselves* baptized (dipped or immersed, not sprinkled or poured), and that water is never used as the subject or object of the active verb, we must allow the dipping or immersing of people to determine the locative meaning of *en* rather than choosing the dative of means in order to support pouring or sprinkling. Even if one were to choose the dative of means alternative, "with water . . . Spirit . . . fire," the verb still cannot be translated to sprinkle or to pour simply because people are the objects of the verb, not water or Spirit or fire. To justify Spencer's idea, the text should read: "He will baptize [sprinkle] the Holy Spirit and fire upon you . . ." or "The Holy Spirit and fire will be baptized [sprinkled] upon you." However, these translations are improper simply because the verb, including its subject and object, determines the translation of the prepositional phrase, not vice-versa.

Even though Old Testament passages describe the Spirit's outpouring or sprinkling, it does not follow that John's baptism had to be by pouring or sprinkling. It is still permissible for God to introduce an additional figure to describe baptism in the Spirit as an immersion into union with the Holy Spirit or an immersion into union with the fire of judgment (Matthew 3:12; i.e., the lake of fire).

A SUMMARY REJECTION OF MURRAY'S AND SPENCER'S POSITION

It has been demonstrated that Murray and Spencer violate several principles of literal-grammatical-historical exegesis. Their subtle manipulation of the Old Testament examples of *bapto* and *baptizo* sounds convincing to the undiscerning reader, but is quite unconvincing to those who know how to use the languages. Furthermore, their complete ignoring of etymology, the historical use in Josephus and the *Didache,* the verb forms, and grammatical constructions of *baptizo* in the Old and New Testament is almost unforgivable to those who claim to base their conclusions on biblical exegesis. Finally, their use of figurative and obscure texts to redefine the literal and historical mode of *baptizo* in the baptisms of individuals recorded in the Gospels and Acts is a serious violation of basic interpretive principles.

In summary, Murray's and Spencer's position that pouring or sprinkling are the primary or exclusive modes of Christian baptism is untenable and biblically unsupportable. Their misunderstanding and misstatement of Baptist positions, as well as their misinterpretation of biblical texts, makes their position very difficult to follow by the untaught and impossible to accept by Baptist scholars.

The primary mode of disciple's baptism in the New Testament is immersion by dipping: "Jesus was baptized (dipped) by John into the Jordan." To permit some other mode, there would have to be some extenuating circumstances such as the lack of water or the presence of illness (*see Didache* 7), and Spurgeon would not even do this. He argued that immersion is a command of God (*see* Appendix A).

Appendix C

Book Review of *The Biblical Doctrine of Infant Baptism*

Considered a classic work on infant baptism for decades, Pierre Marcel's *The Biblical Doctrine of Infant Baptism* is a must read to understand the strengths and the weaknesses of the paedobaptist position. Marcel was a pastor of the French Reformed Church, editor-in-chief of *La Revue Reformee,* vice-president of the Calvinist Society of France, and lectured in the Free Faculty of Theology at the University of Paris. His purpose in writing was to refute the attacks upon infant baptism led by Karl Barth and F. J. Leenhardt. He takes them on in vigorous style. Highly respected as a defender of the Reformed Faith in France, Marcel's work is respected by paedobaptists worldwide as a classic argument and is recommended by Philip Edgcumbe Hughes, Marcel's equally esteemed translator. Marcel rejects the voice of tradition in the second and third centuries, used by many paedobaptists, as having any validity in the argument. As we all wish to do, he desires his argument to be based upon *sola Scriptura*.[256]

Divided into three parts, the book covers a general study of the sacraments, the Covenant of Grace, and baptism as a sacrament of the Covenant of Grace. The first part sets forth Marcel's premises and presuppositions, while the second and third parts explain his theology of the covenants and of infant baptism. As Marcel states throughout the book, "The Covenant of Grace is the foundation of baptism." From this premise, he argues that the Covenant of Grace is the historical outworking of the Covenant of Redemption and, by biblical definition, includes the organic

---

[256]Pierre Marcel, *The Biblical Doctrine of Infant Baptism.* Translated by Philip Edgcumbe Hughes (London: James Clarke & Co. Ltd., 1959).

seed of believers. Therefore, because the Covenant of Grace to Abraham included his organic seed who received circumcision as a sign and seal of the covenant, so the Covenant of Grace in the New Covenant administration automatically includes the organic seed of believers who may receive infant baptism. For Marcel, the only biblical evidence that he would accept not to include the organic seed in the New Covenant administration of baptism would be a positive statement in the New Testament that specifically prohibits the baptism of infants. His primary argument against Baptists is that they hold to *a priori* notions that color the way they read Scripture and interpret clear biblical texts on the covenants, thus coming to a different position in the end. He believes that *a priori* notions least affect the paedobaptist position.

As a Baptist who once was convinced by Marcel's book to become a Presbyterian, and who now has read his book many times, the reviewer now notices a number of weaknesses in Marcel's presentation. There are exegetical errors, hermeneutical mistakes, and contradictory language that bother the close reader.

First, there are exegetical errors of great significance. Marcel erroneously uses Ephesians 1:13–14 and 4:30 to establish baptism as a seal of the Covenant of Grace corresponding to Abraham's circumcision, which was a seal of the righteousness of the faith that he had while uncircumcised. He states that "the exegetes" understand "after having believed you were sealed with the Holy Spirit of promise" to refer to baptism as a seal of the Covenant of Grace. However, "the [paedobaptist] exegetes" such as Charles Hodge and William Hendriksen do not even mention baptism in these texts, understanding the seal to be the Holy Spirit's sealing of the heart. This is what Baptists have contended all along, that the only seal of the New Covenant mentioned in the New Testament is the Holy Spirit who seals the heart of every New Covenant member. Thus, the typological fulfillment of circumcision as the sign and seal of Abraham's faith is not baptism, but antitypical Holy Spirit regeneration, the seal of the New Covenant. The sign of that antitypical sealing is baptism. Therefore, those "disciples" alone who exhibit outward repentance and faith as evidence of Holy Spirit regeneration are baptized (Matthew 28:18–20; John 4:1; Acts 6:1; 9:26, 38; 11:26, 29; 13:52; 14:20, 22, 28).

A second exegetical error identifies the parable of the wheat and the tares as a justification for including the unregenerate in the kingdom of God, the church, and the Covenant of Grace (i.e., the unregenerate children of believers, thus entitling them to baptism, pp. 126–127). Marcel erroneously joins this parable with the root and branches metaphor of Romans 11, thus condemning efforts to separate the wheat and the tares in building the church. However, the parable of the wheat and the tares is clear. The field is the world, not the church, as paedobaptists often claim (Matthew 13:38). This attempt to refute the Baptist argument of baptizing disciples alone confuses the issue. We all agree that one may be baptized and yet unregenerate in the church. The issue is that certain New Testament texts are misinterpreted by paedobaptists to fit their *a priori* theology of infant baptism. Marcel's accusation that Baptists approach texts with *a priori* prejudice does not stand when compared with his own exegesis.

A third exegetical error concerns Colossians 2:11–12. This passage is often used by paedobaptists as a proof-text that the fulfillment of circumcision is baptism, thereby permitting infant baptism by an erroneous use of good and necessary inference. Baptists challenge the faulty exegesis of this text by such proponents as Marcel. Marcel states:

> The text of Colossians ii. 11 f. plainly links circumcision to baptism and teaches that *the circumcision of Christ,* that is to say, the circumcision of the heart, signified by the circumcision in the flesh (cf. Rom. ii. 28 f.), is achieved *by baptism,* that is to say, by that which baptism signifies. . . . They are grafted into Christ by means and in virtue of the circumcision which Christ Himself endured at His death for sin, at the same moment as they are buried and resurrected with Christ *by baptism* (p. 156).

On the one hand, Marcel wants to say that the circumcision of Christ in the heart is the fulfillment of physical circumcision. On the other hand, he actually says that the fulfillment is "by baptism." Does he really mean to say that one is "grafted into Christ" at the same moment that he is buried and resurrected "by baptism"? Does he mean physical baptism or spiritual baptism at regeneration? His language is so imprecise that one wonders if he is teaching hardcore sacramentalism. Marcel is so intent on identifying circumcision and baptism, thus permitting the same infant subjects, that he says the circumcision of Christ "is achieved *by baptism*, that is to say, by that which baptism signifies." Well, which does he mean? By physical baptism? Or by that which it signifies, the circumcision of the heart by Christ? It cannot be both. Baptists say that it is fulfilled by that which baptism signifies; Marcel says by baptism itself. Such imprecise exegesis and language is typical of the paedobaptist position, subtly leading the reader astray. Other examples such as Act 2:38–39 or 1 Corinthians 7:14 could be cited.

Besides exegetical errors, Marcel makes a number of hermeneutical mistakes. First, as so often happens in paedobaptist theology, he completely identifies the Abrahamic Covenant as the Covenant of Grace, thereby including an organic element in the very definition of a covenant. This is a hermeneutical mistake simply because there are other divine covenants described in the Scripture that have no organic element attached (i.e., the Noahic Covenant). If one wishes to include Noah's family as an organic element, then one must ask if in-laws should be included in the covenant concept and signs. The definition of a covenant must be defined from scriptural usage first as a promise, oath, or bond (Hebrews 6:13–18). Then each covenant's stipulations must be determined by written revelation, not unfettered good and necessary inference. This is John Owen's view (*see* his Hebrews 8 commentary).

For instance, the Abrahamic Covenant included the organic seed of Abraham, heart changed or not. However, the New Covenant, by self-definition, shifts to a more individual, effectual membership that only includes those who have a changed heart and the forgiveness of sins (Jeremiah 31:27–34; 32:40). Marcel's *a priori* definition of a covenant automatically including organic seed in the New Covenant is a major hermeneutical mistake that, absurdly, would require a New Testament statement to prohibit infant baptism, even if it were never practiced (pp. 121–122). To Marcel, the positive commands and examples that define the New Covenant and institute baptism in the New Testament are not enough to define baptismal candidates as those who repent and believe alone. The *a priori* assumption of organic seed in the Covenant of Grace carries more authority to Marcel than stated revelation.

Marcel's view is a violation of the Reformed regulative principle of worship and a violation of the hermeneutical principle that the New is the final interpreter of the Old. Marcel actually states that God gives "general instruction" to the church concerning baptism in the New Testament and, like preaching, applies it concretely to life by baptizing infants according to normative principles of application (p. 190). This astonishing admission that infant baptism is established on normative principles of application reveals that it violates the regulative principle of sacraments *instituted* by Christ. Thus, the regulative principle is transformed by normative principles of application into *the* normative principle itself, allowing one to go beyond scriptural elements of worship into unprescribed practices, as long as the church calls it application. John Frame has justified drama and dance in just this same manner (*Worship in the Spirit and Truth,* p. 93). What can come next by such inference and application?

Finally, there is a lot of confusing, unsubstantiated, and contradictory language in Marcel's work. He actually states that it is more likely that infant-baptized children will be converted than those baptized in proselyte baptism (p. 232). He offers no evidence for this, which is an appalling conclusion in the light of the existence of widespread nominal Christianity among paedobaptists around the world today, both Protestant and Catholic.

Other confusing language surrounds his discussion of the efficacy of baptism. Although stating that the Covenant of Grace does not promise the salvation of every seed, but only in a collective sense, he also says:

> *Beyond doubt the promises of the covenant will be fulfilled* when parents, clinging to these promises by faith, entreat and supplicate God, in the name of these promises, to be faithful to His promises in regard to their posterity [p. 113; emphasis mine].

He blames the lack of salvation among children of the covenant upon parental failure. They have believed only for themselves, not for their children as well (pp. 113–114). Well, which is it? Does the Covenant of Grace only promise salvation in the collective seed alone, or is it each parent's fault when a particular child is not saved? It cannot be both. What guilt and burden this places upon faithful parents, much less the ignoring of God's sovereign distinction between Jacob and Esau (Romans 9).

Because of this confusing and contradictory language, one is baffled by the difficult position parents and children are placed in when they reach the age of discretion, which is twelve according to Marcel (p. 99). If they do not commit themselves to the covenant by that age, they may be subject to the discipline of the church for covenant breaking (p. 131; this concept is so stated in the PCA *Book of Church Order*). If they do not commit, the testimony of the parents is placed in jeopardy. Such confusing and contradictory language can only place enormous pressure upon parents and children to conform without true conversion.

Another instance of confusing language surrounds Marcel's definition of the position of believer's children in the covenant. Though he may mean "that which baptism signifies," he actually says,

> Original sin is, indeed, partially and in principle nullified by baptism, though not totally so (p. 147) . . . [they are] separate from the profane world and are placed neither under God's judgment nor under Satan's power. God regards them as members of His kingdom (p. 191) . . . He says that He has removed [condemnation] for the children of the covenant (p. 108). . . . God, according to the promise, restores liberty of choice to the children of the covenant, with the result that, confronted with the alternative of life or death, they are able voluntarily and freely to embrace the one or the other (p. 110).

Such confusing language seems to remove covenant children from the Covenant of Works, the blinding damage of original sin, the condemnation of God, and to place them in a new third category of people who have more ability than rank unbelievers.

If this is Marcel's way of assuring parents when their underage children die that they are safe, or if it is his way to pressure twelve-year-olds to acquiesce to the covenant or else enter a new condemnation, it is a weak attempt biblically. There is no biblical basis for such confusing language. Children of believers are just as much under the Covenant of Works as pagan children; everyone is either in Adam or in Christ (Romans 5). There is no third way. In addition, they are just as responsible to repent and believe on the basis of their sins, not their covenant position, as pagan children are. Such confusing language may attract parents to baptize their babies to assure their salvation, but it may also prevent parents from calling their children to repent and to believe in Christ, assuming they are safe, thus condemning their souls.

Pierre Marcel's arguments sound convincing to the novice reader and intellectually stimulating to the convinced paedobaptist. However, the faulty exegesis, logical inconsistencies, confusing language, and theological speculation is too unbiblical to be taken seriously as a challenge to the informed Baptist position. That is, of course, unless one *a priori* wants to believe it.

Appendix D

Appendix to the 1689 London Baptist Confession[257]

Whoever reads, and impartially considers what we have in our forgoing confession declared, may readily perceive, that we do not only agree with all other true Christians on the Word of God (revealed in the Scriptures of truth) as the foundation and rule of our faith and worship. But that we have also industriously endeavored to manifest, that in the fundamental Articles of Christianity we mind the same things, and have therefore expressed our belief in the same words, that have on the like occasion been spoken by other societies of Christians before us.

This we have done, that those who are desirous to know the principles of Religion which we hold and practice may take an estimate from ourselves (who jointly concur in this work) and may not be misguided, either by undue reports, or by the ignorance or errors of particular persons, who going under the same name with ourselves, may give an occasion of scandalizing the truth we profess.

And although we do differ from our brethren who are paedobaptists in the subject and administration of Baptism, and such other circumstances as have a necessary dependence on our observance of that ordinance, and do frequent our own assemblies for our mutual edification, and discharge of those duties, and services which we owe unto God, and in His fear to each

---

[257]This presentation of the *Appendix to the 1689 London Baptist Confession* has removed Elizabethan printing styles but has retained the awkward grammar of the original document, for historical interest. However, I have changed some spellings and updated some words for the modern reader. This appendix was included in the original 1677 publication of the confession, although its authorship remains unknown. I am indebted to Dr. Mike Renihan for supplying a copy of the original document.

other: yet we would not be from hence misconstrued, as if the discharge of our own consciences herein, did anyway disoblige or alienate our affections, or conversation from any others that fear the Lord; but that we may and do as we have opportunity participate of the labors of those, whom God hath endued with abilities above ourselves, and qualified, and called to Ministry of the Word, earnestly desiring to approve ourselves to be such, as follow after peace with holiness, and therefore we always keep that blessed Irenicum, or healing Word of the Apostle before our eyes, if in anything you be otherwise minded, God shall reveal even this unto you, nevertheless whereto we have already attained; let us walk by the same rule, let us mind the same thing (Philippians 3:15–16).

Let it not therefore be judged of us (because much hath been written on this subject, and yet we continue this our practice different from others) that it is out of obstinacy, but rather as the truth is, that we do herein according to the best of our understandings worship God, out of a pure mind yielding obedience to His precept, in that method which we take to be most agreeable to the Scriptures of truth, and primitive practice.

It would not become us to give any such intimation, as should carry a semblance that what we do in the service of God is with a doubting conscience, or with any such temper of mind that we do thus for the present, with a reservation that we will do otherwise hereafter upon more mature deliberation; nor have we any cause so to do, being fully persuaded, that what we do is agreeable to the will of God. Yet we do heartily propose this, that if any of the Servants of our Lord Jesus shall, in the Spirit of meekness, attempt to convince us of any mistake either in judgment or practice, we shall diligently ponder his arguments; and account him our chiefest friend that shall be an instrument to convert us from any error that is in our way, for we cannot wittingly do anything against the truth, but all things for the truth.

And therefore we have endeavored seriously to consider, what hath been already offered for our satisfaction in this point; and are loath to say any more lest we should be esteemed desirous of renewed contests thereabout: yet forasmuch as it may justly be expected that we show some reason, why we cannot acquiesce in what hath been urged against us we shall with as much brevity as may consist with plainness, endeavor to satisfy the expectation of those that shall peruse what we now publish in this matter also.

1. As to those Christians who consent with us, *That Repentance from dead works, and Faith towards God, and our Lord Jesus Christ, is required in persons to be Baptized;* and do therefore supply the defect of the infant being incapable of making confession of either by others who do undertake these things for it. Although we do find by Church history that this has been a very ancient practice; yet considering, that the same Scripture which does caution us against censuring our brother (Romans 14:4–10; 12:23), with whom we shall all stand before the judgment seat of Christ, does also instruct us, *That every one of us shall give an account of himself to God, and whatsoever is not of Faith is sin.* Therefore we cannot for our own parts be persuaded in our own minds, to build such a practice as this, upon an unwritten tradition: But do rather choose in all points of Faith and Worship, to have recourse to the holy Scriptures, for the information of our judgment, and regulation of our practice; being well assured that a conscientious attending thereto, is the best way to prevent, and rectify our defects and errors (2 Timothy 3:16–17). And if any such case happens to be debated between Christians, which is not plainly determinable by the Scriptures, we think it safest to leave such things undecided until the second coming of our Lord Jesus; as they did in the Church of old, until there should arise a Priest with *Urim* and *Thummim*, that might certainly inform them of the mind of God thereabout (Ezra 2:62–63).

2. As for those our Christian brethren who do ground their arguments for Infant baptism, upon a presumed federal Holiness, or Church-Membership, we conceive they are deficient in this, that albeit this Covenant-Holiness and Membership should be as is supposed, in reference unto the infants of believers; yet no command for infant baptism does immediately and directly result from such a quality, or relation.

All instituted worship receives its sanction from the precept, and is to be thereby governed in all the necessary circumstances thereof.[258]

---

[258]This sentence illustrates a major argument of my position, that infant baptism is a violation of the regulative principle of worship. Such a clear statement by our Baptist forefathers, often missing from today's discussions, shows the consistency of my position historically.

So it was in the covenant that God made with Abraham and his seed. The sign whereof was appropriated only to the male, notwithstanding that the female seed as well as the male were comprehended in the covenant and part of the Church of God; neither was this sign to be affixed to any male infant till he was eight days old, albeit he was within the covenant from the first moment of his life; nor could the danger of death, or any other supposed necessity, warrant the circumcising of him before the set time, nor was there any cause for it; the execution of being cut off from his people, being only upon the neglect, or contempt of the precept. Righteous Lot was nearly related to *Abraham* in the flesh, and contemporary with him, when this covenant was made; yet inasmuch as he did not descend from his loins, nor was of his household family (although he was of the same household of faith with Abraham) yet neither Lot himself nor any of his posterity (because of their descent from him) were signed with the signature of this covenant that was made with Abraham and his seed.

This may suffice to show, that where there was both an express covenant, and a sign thereof (such a covenant as did separate the persons with whom it was made), and all their offspring from all the rest of the world, as a people holy unto the Lord, and did constitute them the visible church of God, (though not comprehensive of all the faithful in the world) yet the sign of this covenant was not affixed to all the persons that were within this covenant, nor to any of them till the appointed season; nor to other faithful servants of God, that were not of descent from Abraham. And consequently that it depends purely upon the will of the law-giver, to determine what shall be the sign of His covenant, unto whom, at what season, and upon what terms, it shall be affixed.

If our brethren do suppose baptism to be the seal of the covenant which God makes with every believer (of which the Scriptures are altogether silent) it is not our concern to contend with them herein; yet we conceive the seal of that covenant is the indwelling of the Spirit of Christ in the particular and individual persons in whom he resides, and nothing else, neither do they or we suppose that baptism is in any such manner substituted in the place of circumcision, as to have the same (and no other) latitude, extent, or terms, then circumcision had; for that was suited only for the male children, baptism is an ordinance suited for every believer, whether male or female. That extended to all the males that were born in Abraham's house, or bought with his money, equally with the males that proceeded from his own loins; but baptism is not so far extended in any true Christian church that we know of, as to be administered to all the poor infidel servants, that the members thereof purchase for their service, and introduce into their families; nor to the children born of them in their house.

But we conceive the same parity of reasoning may hold for the ordinance of baptism as for that of circumcision (Exodus 12:49) *viz.* one law for the stranger, as for the home born. If any desire to be admitted to all the ordinances, and privileges of God's house, the door is open; upon the same terms that any one person was ever admitted to all, or any of those privileges, that belong to the Christian church, may all persons of right challenge the like admission.

As for that text of Scripture, Romans 4:11, "He received circumcision a seal of the righteousness of the faith which he had yet being uncircumcised," we conceive if the Apostle's scope in that place be duly attended to, it will appear that no argument can be taken from thence to enforce infant baptism; and forasmuch as we find a full and fair account of those words given by the learned Dr. Lightfoot (a man not to be suspected of partiality in this controversy) in his *Hor. Hebrai,* on the 1 Corinthians 7:19, p. 42, 43. We shall transcribe his words at large, without any comment of our own upon them.

> Circumcision is nothing, if we respect the time, for now it was without use, that end of it being especially fulfilled; for which it had been instituted: this end the Apostle declares in these words, *Rom. 4:11.* But I fear that by most translations they are not sufficiently suited to the end of circumcision and the scope of the Apostle which something of their own is by them inserted.

And after the Doctor hath represented diverse versions of the words agreeing for the most part in sense with that which we have in our Bibles he thus proceeds.

> Other versions are to the same purpose; as if circumcision was given to Abraham for a seal of that righteousness which he had being yet uncircumcised, which we will not deny to be in some sense true, but we believe that circumcision had chiefly a far different respect.
>
> Give me leave thus to render the words; *And he received the sign of circumcision, a seal of the righteousness of faith, which was to be*

in the uncircumcision, which was to be (I lay) not *which had been,* not that which Abraham had while he was yet uncircumcised; but that which his uncircumcised seed should have, that is the Gentiles, who in time to come should imitate the faith of Abraham.

Now consider well on what occasion circumcision was instituted unto Abraham, setting before thine eyes the history thereof (Gen. 17).

This promise is first made unto him, "Thou shalt be a father of many nations" (in what sense the Apostle explains in that chapter) and then there is subjoined a double seal for the confirmation of the thing, to wit, the change of the name Abram into Abraham, and the institution of circumcision (v. 4). "Behold as for me, my covenant is with thee, and thou shalt be the father of many nations." Wherefore was his name called Abraham? For the sealing of this promise. "Thou shalt be the father of many nations." And wherefore was circumcision instituted to him? For the sealing of the same promise. "Thou shalt be the father of many nations." So that this is the sense of the Apostle, most agreeable to the institution of circumcision; he received the sign of circumcision, a seal of the righteousness of faith which in time to come the uncircumcision (or the Gentiles) should have and obtain.

Abraham had a twofold seed, natural, of the Jews, and faithful, of the believing Gentiles: his natural seed was signed with the sign of circumcision, first indeed for the distinguishing of them from all other nations while they as yet were not the seed of Abraham, but especially for the memorial of the justification of the Gentiles by faith, when at length they should become his seed. Therefore circumcision was of right to cease, when the Gentiles were brought in to the faith, forasmuch as then it had obtained its last and chief end, and thenceforth "circumcision is nothing."

Thus far he, which we earnestly desire may be seriously weighed, for we plead not his authority, but the evidence of truth in his words.

3. Of whatsoever nature the holiness of the children mentioned (1 Corinthians 7:4) be, yet they who do conclude that all such children (whether infants or of riper years) have from hence an immediate right to baptism, do as we conceive put more into the conclusion, than will be found in the premises.

For although we do not determine positively concerning the Apostle's scope in the holiness here mentioned, so as to say it is this, or that, and no other thing; yet it is evident that the Apostle does by it determine not only the lawfulness but the expedience also of a believer's cohabitation with an unbeliever, in the state of marriage.

And we do think that although the Apostle's asserting of the unbelieving yokefellow to be sanctified by the believer, should carry in it somewhat more than is in the bare marriage of two infidels, because although the marriage covenant has a divine sanction so as to make the wedlock of two unbelievers a lawful action, and their conjunction and cohabitation in that respect undefiled, yet there might be no ground to suppose from thence, that both or either of their persons are thereby sanctified; and the Apostle urges the cohabitation of a believer with an infidel in the state of wedlock from this ground that the unbelieving husband is sanctified by the believing wife; nevertheless here you have the influence of a believer's faith *ascending from an inferior to a superior relation;* from the wife to the husband who is her head, *before it can descend to their offspring.* And therefore we say, whatever be the nature or extent of the holiness here intended, we conceive it cannot convey to the children an immediate right to baptism, because it would then be of another nature, and of a larger extent, than the root, and original from whence it is derived. For it is clear by the Apostle's argument that holiness cannot be derived to the child from the sanctity of one parent only, if either father or mother be (in the sense intended by the Apostle) unholy or unclean, so will the child be also, therefore for the production of an holy seed it is necessary that both the parents be sanctified; and this the Apostle positively asserts in the first place to be done by the believing parent, although the other be an unbeliever; and then consequentially from thence argues, the holiness of their children. Hence it follows, that as the children have no other holiness than what they derive from both their parents, so neither can they have any right by this holiness to any spiritual privilege but such as both their parents did also partake of: and therefore if the unbelieving parent (though sanctified by the believing parent) has not thereby a right to baptism, neither can we conceive that there is any such privilege derived to the children by their birth-holiness.

Besides if it had been the usual practice in the Apostles days for the father or mother that did believe, to bring all their children with them to be baptized, then the holiness of the believing Corinthian's children would not at all have been in question when this Epistle was written, but might have been argued from their passing under that ordinance, which represented their new birth, although they had derived no holiness from their parents by their first birth, and would have lain as an exception against the Apostle's inference "else were your children unclean." But of the sanctification of all the children of every believer by this ordinance, or any other way, then what is before mentioned, the Scripture is altogether silent.

This may be also added, that if this birth holiness do qualify all the children of every believer, for the ordinance of baptism, why not for all other ordinances? For the Lord's Supper as was practiced for a long time together? For if recourse be had to what the Scriptures speak generally of this subject, it will be found, that the same qualities which do entitle any person to baptism, do so also for the participation of all the ordinances, and privileges of the house of God, that are common to all believers.

Whosoever can and does interrogate his good conscience towards God when he is baptized (as every one must do that makes it to himself a sign of salvation) is capable of doing the same thing, in every other act of worship that he performs.

4. The arguments and inferences that are usually brought for, or against infant baptism from those few instances which the Scriptures afford us of whole families being baptized, are only conjectural, and therefore cannot of themselves be conclusive on either hand. Yet in regard most that treat on this subject for infant baptism, do (as they conceive) improve these instances to the advantage of their argument. We think it meet (in like manner as in the cases before mentioned so in this) to show the invalidity of such inferences.

Cornelius worshipped God with all his house, the Jailor, and Crispus the chief ruler of the Synagogue, *believed God with each of their houses. The household of* Stephanas *addicted themselves to the ministry of the saints,* so that thus far worshipping and believing runs parallel with baptism. And if Lydia, had been a married person, when she believed, it is probably her husband would also have been named by the Apostle, as in like cases, inasmuch as he would have been not only a part, but the head of that baptized household.

Who can assign any probable reason why the Apostle should make mention of four or five households being baptized and no more? Or why he does so often vary in the method of his salutation (Romans 1:6), sometimes mentioning only particular persons of great note, other times such, and the church in their house? The Saints that were with them, and them belonging to Narcissus, who were in the Lord, thus saluting either whole families, or part of families, or only particular persons in families, considered as they were in the Lord, for if it had been a usual practice to baptize all children with their parents, there were then many thousands of the Jews which believed, and great number of the Gentiles in most of the principal cities in the world and among so many thousands it is more than probable there would have been some thousands of households baptized. Why then should the Apostle in this respect signalize one family of the Jews and three or four of the Gentiles, as particular instances in a case that was common? Whoever supposes that we do willfully debar our children from the benefit of any promise or privilege, that of right belongs to the children of believing parents; they do entertain over severe thought of us. To be without natural affections is one of the characteristics of the worst of persons, in the worst of times. We do freely confess our selves guilty before the Lord, in that we have not with more circumspection and diligence trained up those that relate to us in the fear of the Lord, and do humbly and earnestly pray that our omissions herein may be remitted, and that they may not redound to the prejudice of our selves, or any of ours. But with respect to that duty that is incumbent on us, we acknowledge ourselves obliged by the precepts of God, to bring up our children in the nurture and admonition of the Lord, to teach them His fear, both by instruction and example. And should we set light by this precept, it would demonstrate that we are more vile than the unnatural heathen, that like not to retain God in their knowledge, our baptism might then be justly accounted as no baptism to us.

There are many special promises that do encourage us as well as precepts that do oblige us to the close pursuit of our duty herein. That God whom we serve, being jealous of His worship, threatens the visiting of the fathers transgression upon the children to the third and fourth generation of them that hate Him: yet does more abundantly extend His mercy, even to thousands (respecting the offspring and succeeding generations) of them that love Him, and keep His commands.

When our Lord rebuked His disciples for prohibiting the access of little children that were brought to Him, that He might pray over them, lay His hands upon them, and bless them, does declare "that of such is the Kingdom of God." And the Apostle

Peter in answer to their enquiry, that desired to know what they must do to be saved, does not only instruct them in the necessary duty of repentance and baptism, but does also thereto encourage them, by that promise which had reference both to them and their children. If our Lord Jesus, in the aforementioned place, do not respect the qualities of children (as elsewhere) as to their meekness, humility, and sincerity, and the like, but intend also that those very persons and such like appertain to the Kingdom of God, and if the Apostle Peter in mentioning the aforesaid promise, do respect not only the present and succeeding generations of those Jews that heard Him (in which sense the same phrase doth occur in Scripture) but also the immediate offspring of his auditors, whether the promise relate to the gift of the Holy Spirit, or of eternal life, or any grace or privilege tending to the obtaining thereof, it is neither our concern nor our interest to confine the mercies and promises of God to a more narrow or less compass than He is pleased graciously to offer and intend them; nor to have a light esteem of them, but are obliged in duty to God and affection to our children, to plead earnestly with God and use our utmost endeavours that both ourselves and our offspring may be partakers of His mercies and gracious promises. Yet we cannot from either of these texts collect a sufficient warrant for us to baptize our children before they are instructed in the principles of the Christian religion.

For as to the instance in little children, it seems by the disciples forbidding them, that they were brought upon some other account, not so frequent as baptism must be supposed to have been, if from the beginning believers children had been admitted thereto: and no account is given whether their parents were baptized believers or not. And as to the instance of the Apostle, if the following words and practice, may be taken as an interpretation of the scope of that promise we cannot conceive it does refer to infant baptism, because the text does presently subjoin, "Then they that gladly received the word were baptized."

That there were some believing children of believing parents in the Apostles' days is evident from the Scriptures, even such as were then in their father's family, and under their parents tutelage and education, to whom the Apostle in several of his Epistles to the churches gave command to obey their parents in the Lord and does allure their tender years to hearken to this precept, by reminding them that it is the first command with promise.

And it is recorded by him for the praise of Timothy, and encouragement of parents betimes to instruct, and children early to attend to godly instruction, that from a child, he had known the holy Scriptures.

The Apostle John rejoiced greatly when he found of the children of the elect lady walking in the truth. And the children of her elect sister join with the Apostle in his salutation.

But that this was not generally so, that all the children of believers were accounted for believers (as they would have been if they had been all baptized) may be collected from the character which the Apostle gives of persons fit to be chosen to eldership in the church which was not common to all believers; among others this is expressly one, *viz.*, "If there be any having believing, or faithful children," not accused of riot or unruly. And we may from the Apostle's writings on the same subject collect the reason of this qualification, *viz.*, that in case the person designed for this office to teach and rule in the house of God, had children capable of it, there might be first a proof of his ability, industry, and success in this work in his own family and private capacity, before he was ordained to the exercise of this authority in the church in a public capacity, as a bishop in the house of God.

These things we have mentioned as having a direct reference unto the controversy between our brethren and us. Other things that are more abstruse and prolix, which are frequently introduced into this controversy, but do not necessarily concern it we have purposely avoided that the distance between us and our brethren may not be by us made more wide. For it is our duty and concern so far as is possible for us (retaining a good conscience towards God) to seek a more entire agreement and reconciliation with them.

We are not insensible that as to the order of God's house and entire communion therein there are some things wherein we (as well as others) are not at a full accord among ourselves, as for instance the known principle and state of the consciences of diverse of us that have agreed in this Confession is such, that we cannot hold church-communion with any other than baptized believers, and churches constituted of such. Yet some others of us have a greater liberty and freedom in our spirits that way; and therefore we have purposely omitted the mention of things of that nature that we might concur in giving this evidence of our agreement, both among ourselves and with other good Christians in those important articles of the Christian religion mainly insisted on by us. And this is notwithstanding we all esteem it our chief concern, both among ourselves, and all others that in every place call upon the name of the Lord Jesus Christ our Lord, both theirs and ours, and love Him in sincerity, to endeavor to keep the unity of the Spirit in the bond of peace, and in order thereunto to exercise all lowliness and meekness with long-suffering, forbearing one another in love.

And we are persuaded if the same method were introduced into frequent practice between us and our Christian friends who agree with us in all the fundamental articles of the Christian faith (though they do not so in the subject and administration of baptism) it would soon beget a better understanding and brotherly affection between us.

In the beginning of the Christian church, when the doctrine of the baptism of Christ was not universally understood, yet those that knew only the baptism of John were the disciples of the Lord Jesus, and Apollos an eminent minister of the gospel of Jesus.

In the beginning of the reformation of the Christian church, and recovery from that Egyptian darkness wherein our forefathers for many generations were held in bondage, upon recourse had to the Scriptures of truth, different apprehensions were conceived, which are to this time continued, concerning the practice of this ordinance.

Let not our zeal herein be misinterpreted: that God whom we serve is jealous of his worship. By his gracious providence the Law thereof is continued amongst us, and we are forewarned by what happened in the church of the Jews, that it is necessary for every generation, and that frequently in every generation to consult the divine oracle, compare our worship with the rule, and take heed to what doctrines we receive and practice.

If the ten commands exhibited in the popish idolatrous service books had been received as the entire law of God because they agree in number with his ten commands, and also in the substance of nine of them, the second commandment forbidding idolatry had been utterly lost.

If Ezra and Nehemiah had not made a diligent search into the particular parts of God's law, and His worship; the Feast of Tabernacles (which for many centuries of years, had not been duly observed, according to the institution, though it was retained in the general notion) would not have been kept in due order.

So may it be now as to many things relating to the service of God, which do retain the names proper to them in their first institution, but yet through inadvertency (where there is no sinister design) may vary in their circumstances, from their first institution. And if by means of any ancient defection, or of that general corruption of the service of God, and interruption of His true worship, and persecution of his servants by the anti-Christian bishop of Rome, for many generations, those who do consult the Word of God cannot yet arrive at a full and mutual satisfaction among themselves, what was the practice of the primitive Christian church, in some points relating to the worship of God: yet inasmuch as these things are not of the essence of Christianity, but that we agree in the fundamental doctrines thereof, we do apprehend, there is sufficient ground to lay aside all bitterness and prejudice, and in the spirit of love and meekness to embrace and own each other therein; leaving each other at liberty to perform such other services (wherein we cannot concur) apart unto God, according to the best of our understanding.

FINIS

Selected Bibliography

Aland, Kurt. *Did the Early Church Baptize Infants?* Translated by G. R. Beasley-Murray. Philadelphia, PA: The Westminster Press, 1963.

Alexander, James W. *The Life of Archibald Alexander.* Reprint, Harrisonburg, VA: Sprinkle Publications, 1991.

Alexander, Joseph Addison. *The Acts of the Apostles.* 1857; reprint, London: The Banner of Truth Trust, 1963.

"An Appendix," in *The 1689 London Baptist Confession,* 109–142. 1677; facsimile edition, Auburn, MA: B&R Press, 2000.

Arndt, William F. and F. Wilbur Gingrich. *A Greek-English Lexicon of the New Testament.* Chicago, IL: The University of Chicago Press, 1957.

Bahnsen, Greg. *By This Standard.* Tyler, TX: Institute for Christian Economics, 1985.

Berkhof, Louis. *Principles of Biblical Interpretation.* Grand Rapids, MI: Baker Book House, 1950.

———. *Systematic Theology.* Grand Rapids, MI: William B. Eerdmans Publishing Company, 1941.

Blaising, Craig A. and Darrell L. Bock. *Progressive Dispensationalism.* Wheaton, IL: Victor Books, 1993.

Bolton, Samuel. *The True Bounds of Christian Freedom.* London: The Banner of Truth Trust, 1964.

The Book of Church Order. Printed for the General Assembly of the Presbyterian Church in America. Montgomery, AL: Committee for Christian Education and Publications, 1975.

Booth, Abraham. *Paedobaptism [Infant Baptism] Examined.* 1787; reprint, Choteau, MT: Gospel Mission, 1980.

Booth, Robert R. *Children of Promise.* Phillipsburg, NJ: Presbyterian and Reformed Publishing Company, 1995.

Selected Bibliography

Brown, Colin, ed. *The New International Dictionary of New Testament Theology.* Grand Rapids, MI: Zondervan Publishing House, 1967.

Brown, John. *An Exposition of the Epistle of Paul the Apostle to the Galatians.* 1853; reprint, Minneapolis, MN: James Family Christian Publishers, 1979.

———. *Hebrews.* 1862 reprint, Edinburgh: The Banner of Truth Trust, 1976.

Calvin, John. *Commentary on the Acts of the Apostles.* Translated by Christopher Fetherstone. 1585; reprint, Grand Rapids, MI: Baker Book House, 1981.

———. *Institutes of the Christian Religion.* Edited by John T. McNeill. Translated and indexed by Ford Lewis Battles. Philadelphia, PA: The Westminster Press, 1967.

Cunningham, William. *The Reformers and the Theology of the Reformation.* Edinburgh: The Banner of Truth Trust, 1967.

Darby, John. *Synopsis of the Books of the Bible.* Vol. 5, *Colossians-Revelation.* New York: Loizeaux Brothers, n.d.

Edersheim, Alfred. *The Life and Times of Jesus the Messiah.* Vol. 2. Grand Rapids, MI: William B. Eerdmans Publishing Co., 1970.

Ferguson, Sinclair. *John Owen on the Christian Life.* Edinburgh: The Banner of Truth Trust, 1987.

Frame, John A. "The Lordship of Christ and the Regulative Principle of Worship" Tms [photocopy]. Class handout provided by a student in Dr. Frame's class on Christian Worship at Westminster Theological Seminary West, 1996.

———. *Worship in Spirit and Truth.* Phillipsburg, NJ: Presbyterian and Reformed Publishing Company, 1996.

Grant, Robert M., ed. *The Apostolic Fathers.* Vol. 3, *Barnabas and The Didache,* by Robert A. Kraft. New York: Thomas Nelson & Sons, 1965.

Grosheide, F. W. *Commentary on the First Epistle to the Corinthians. The New International Commentary on the New Testament.* Grand Rapids, MI: William B. Eerdmans Publishing Co., 1964.

Henderson, Robert T. "Is the Lord's Supper a Passover Feast for [the] Whole Congregation?" *The Open Letter,* 8, no. 1 (January, 1977): 1–4.

Hendriksen, William. *The Covenant of Grace.* Grand Rapids, MI: Baker Book House,1984.

Hiscox, Edward T. *Principles and Practices for Baptist Churches.* 1894; reprint, Grand Rapids, MI: Kregel Publications, 1980.

Hoch, Carl B., Jr. *All Things New.* Grand Rapids, MI: Baker Book House, 1995.

Hoeksema, Herman. *Believers and Their Seed.* Translated by Homer C. Hoeksema. Grand Rapids, MI: Reformed Free Publishing Association, 1971.

Howell, R. B. C. *The Covenants.* Charleston, SC: The Southern Baptist Publication Society, 1855.

———. *The Evils of Infant Baptism.* 1852; reprint, Watertown, WI: Baptist Heritage Press, 1988.

Jeremias, Joachim. *Infant Baptism in the First Four Centuries.* Translated by David Cairns. Philadelphia, PA: The Westminster Press, 1962.

Jewett, Paul K. *Infant Baptism and the Covenant of Grace.* Grand Rapids, MI: William B. Eerdmans Publishing Co., 1978.

Josephus. *Josephus: Complete Works, The Antiquities of the Jews.* Translated by William Whiston. Grand Rapids, MI: Kregel Publications, 1960.

Kingdon, David. *Children of Abraham.* Sussex: Carey Publications, Ltd., 1973.

Kistemaker, Simon. *Exposition of the Epistle to the Hebrews.* New Testament Commentary. Grand Rapids, MI: Baker Book House, 1984.

Kline, Meredith G. *By Oath Consigned.* Grand Rapids, MI: William B. Eerdmans Publishing Company, 1975.

Malone, Fred A. *A Critical Evaluation of the Use of Jeremiah 31:31–34 in the Letter to the Hebrews.* Doctoral dissertation, Southwestern Baptist Theological Seminary, 1989.

———. *A String of Pearls Unstrung.* Cape Coral, FL: Founders Press, 1998.

Marcel, Pierre. *The Biblical Doctrine of Infant Baptism.* Translated by Philip Edgcumbe Hughes. London: James Clarke and Company, Ltd., 1959.

Marston, George W. *Are you a Biblical Baptist?* Philadelphia: Great Commission Publications, 1977.

Mathison, Keith A. *Dispensationalism: Rightly Dividing the People of God?* Phillipsburg, NJ: Presbyterian and Reformed Publishing Company, 1995.

McCarney, Dan and Charles Clayton. *Let the Reader Understand.* Wheaton, IL: Victor Books, 1994.

Murray, John. *Christian Baptism.* Nutley, NJ: Presbyterian and Reformed Publishing Company, 1970.

———. *The Epistle to the Romans.* The New International Commentary on the New Testament. Edited by F. F. Bruce. Grand Rapids, MI: William B. Eerdmans Publishing Company, 1968.

———. *The Covenant of Grace.* Grand Rapids, MI: Baker Book House, 1954.

The New Geneva Study Bible. Edited by R. C. Sproul. Nashville, TN: Thomas Nelson Publishers, 1995.

Owen, John. *An Exposition of the Epistle to the Hebrews.* Edited by W. H. Gould. Vol. 6, *Hebrews 8:1–10:39.* Grand Rapids, MI: Baker Book House, 1980.

Ramm, Bernard. *Protestant Biblical Interpretation.* Grand Rapids, MI: Baker Book House, 1970.

"Report of the Ad-interim Committee to Study the Question of Paedocommunion Majority Report." General Assembly of the Presbyterian Church in America, 1986.

Ridderbos, Herman. *The Coming of the Kingdom.* Philadelphia: The Presbyterian and Reformed Publishing Company, 1962.

Robertson, A. T. *The Pharisees and Jesus.* 1920; reprint, Eugene, OR: Wipf and Stock Publishers, 1999.

Robertson, O. Palmer. *The Israel of God.* Phillipsburg, NJ: Presbyterian and Reformed Publishing Company, 2000.

———. *The Christ of the Covenants.* Phillipsburg, NJ: Presbyterian and Reformed Publishing Company, 1980.

Sandlin, Andrew. "A Support for Reformed Paedobaptism (with a Reformed Baptist Reply by Fred Pugh)," Tms [photocopy], position paper. Painesville, OH: Church of the WORD, 1996.

The Scofield Reference Bible. Edited by C. I. Scofield. New York: Oxford University Press, 1917.

Spencer, Duane. *Holy Baptism: Word Keys Which Unlock the Covenant.* Tyler, TX: Geneva Ministries, 1984.

Spurgeon, Charles H. *Spurgeon on Baptism.* London: Henry E. Walter, Ltd., n.d.

Stander, H. F. and J. P. Louw. *Baptism in the Early Church.* Garsfontein, South Africa: Didaskalia Pub., 1988.

Strong, Augustus Hopkins. *Systematic Theology.* Old Tappan, NJ: Fleming H. Revell Company, 1907.

Trench, R. C. *Notes on the Parables of Our Lord.* Grand Rapids, MI: Baker Book House, 1971.

Van Horn, Leonard T. "The Reformed Pastor and His Vows." *The Banner of Truth,* 412 (January 1988): 19.

Warfield, B. B. *Studies in Theology.* 1932; reprint, Grand Rapids, MI: Baker Book House, 1981.

Watson, Thomas E. *Should Babies Be Baptized?* London: Grace Publications Trust, 1995.

Williamson, G. I. *The Shorter Catechism*. Nutley, NJ: Presbyterian and Reformed Publishing Company, 1975.

———. *The Westminster Confession of Faith for Study Classes*. Philadelphia: The Presbyterian and Reformed Publishing Co., 1964.

Wilmot, John. *Inspired Principles of Prophetic Interpretation*. Swengel, PA: Reiner Publications, 1965.

Wilson, Douglas. *Standing on the Promises*. Moscow, ID: Canon Press, 1997.

———. *To a Thousand Generations*. Moscow, ID: Canon Press, 1996.

———. "Circumcision in the New Covenant." *Christianity and Society* 4, no. 4 (October 1994).

———. "Transaction." *Credenda Agenda* 8, no. 3: 14.

Author Index

A
Aland, Kurt, 129, 148, 188
Alexander, Archibald, 191–192
Alexander, J. A., 131–133

B
Bahnsen, Greg, 41–42, 46
Bannerman, James, 127
Barnes, Albert, 144
Barth, Karl, 245
Baxter, Richard, 127
Berkhof, Louis, 25, 29, 31, 52, 59, 64, 67–68, 74, 84, 107, 127, 150, 176, 187–188, 225–226, 234, 237
Blaising, Craig A., 89
Bock, Darrell L., 89
Boettner, L., 38
Bolton, Samuel, 43n. 100, 87
Booth, Abraham, 38–39, 88n. 147, 102n. 156
Booth, Robert R., 57, 86–90
Boston, Thomas, 127
Boyce, James P., 201
Brown, John, 87, 108

C
Calvin, John, 43n. 100, 75, 88, 223
Carson, Alexander, 233
Clayton, Charles, 33–34
Cunningham, William, 16n. 71, 178

D
Dagg, John L., 201, 233

E
Edersheim, Alfred, 187–188

F
Ferguson, Sinclair, 59–60
Frame, John, 39–40, 249

G
Grosheide, F. W., 143–144

H
Hendriksen, William, 63, 175–176
Henry, Matthew, 75–76
Hoch, Carl B., Jr., 84n. 138
Hoeksema, Herman, 184

J
Jeremias, Joachim, 127–130, 148, 188
Jewett, Paul K., 187

K
Kingdon, David, 38
Kistemaker, Simon, 107–108

Kline, Meredith, 73, 146
Kraft, Robert A., 232–233

L
Leenhardt, F. J., 245
Louw, J. P., 190–193

M
Marcel, Pierre, 3, 9n. 47, 40, 127, 148, 170, 181, 187, 232, 245–251
Mathison, Keith, 105
McCartney, Dan, 33–34, 106
Murray, John, 1–19, 24–26, 42n. 100, 78, 105, 127, 138n. 186, 154, 157, 223, 227–229, 233–244

O
Owen, John, 59–60, 62, 64–65, 86, 90–91, 107

P
Poole, Matthew, 154

R
Ramm, Bernard, 28, 32, 89
Ridderbos, Herman, 58, 77–78, 95
Robertson, A. T., 105n. 159, 188n. 218
Robertson, O. Palmer, 52, 56, 59, 69, 75, 78, 87, 104–105, 122–123

S
Sandlin, Andrew, 21, 177
Schaff, Philip, 233
Spencer, Duane, 6n. 33, 223, 227
Spurgeon, Charles H., 205–221
Stander, H. F., 190–193
Stauffer, E., 128, 148
Strong, A. H., 229

W
Walters, W., 220
Warfield, B. B., 154
Watson, Thomas E., 127, 137, 144, 178, 178n. 208, 187, 210, 213–214
Wayland, Francis, 233
Williamson, G. I., 142–147, 169
Wilmot, John, 35–36
Wilson, Douglas, 17n. 76, 102n. 156, 115–118, 178–181
Witsius, Herman, 223

Y
Young, E. J., 45

Subject Index

A
Abraham
  children of, 84n. 138, 166
  descendants of, 215
  promise to, 138–139. *See also* Abrahamic Covenant
  seed of, 8–9, 70, 72, 74, 97–100, 110, 120–121, 139
  seed promises to, 54–55
Abrahamic Covenant, 8–9
  application today, 72–73
  breaking of, 59
  Christ's coming, references to, 64–65
  circumcision in, 111–112, 119–120
  conditions of, 66
  covenant breakers, 114
  as Covenant of Grace, 248
  fulfillment of, 54, 98, *140–141*
  as God's promise to Abraham, 61
  infants included in, 5n. 30, 9–10
  organic element of, 68
  parties to, 214–215
  physical elements of, 73–74
  replacement with New Covenant, 74
  signs of, 66, 119–120, 256
  Sinai Covenant and, 53
Adam, 52
Adult missionary baptism, 128
Akatharta (unclean), 144–145
Andrew, baptism of, 158
Annual Atonement, 96
Apostates, 101–102, 106–109, 114
  locus classicus of, 106–109
Apostles
  baptism of, 4–5
  knowledge of baptisms, 211–212
Apostolic tradition, 188–189
  silence on infant baptism, 191–193
Argument from silence, 165–166
  erroneous nature of, 191–193
  for infant baptism, 38, 148–149, 163
  as normative principle, 168
  rejection of, 167–171
Association of Reformed Baptist Churches of America Web site, 203n. 228
Augustine, 189

B
Baptism. *See also* Credobaptism; Infant baptism
  as act of confession, 210
  adult missionary baptism, 128
  of apostles versus later Christian baptism, 4–5
  baptizo, etymology of, 234–235
  baptizo, verb forms, 235–236
  church and, 6–9
  circumcision and, 14, 120–124
  of disciples alone, 38, 55. *See also* Credobaptism
  efficacy of, 16–18
  household baptisms, 11–12, 12n. 55, 13, 26, 127, 260–262. *See also* Household baptisms
  import of, 4–6
  infant baptism. *See* Infant baptism
  intelligent remembrance of, 15n. 68
  of John versus later Christian baptism, 4. *See also* John the Baptist
  mode of, 6, 150, 205–208, 223–244. *See also Baptizo*
  New Testament evidence for, 95
  normative principles of application, 170
  oath of allegiance to God in, 210
  prerequisite for, 196
  principles of interpretation, 44–47
  profession of faith requirement for, 13–14
  for purification, 5
  records of, 212–214
  regulative principle, governance by, 169
  repentance as condition of, 15n. 68, 157–158, 164–165
  as retrospective sign of heart circumcision, 125
  as seal of Covenant of Grace, 246
  as sign and seal of church membership, 8
  as sign and seal of New Covenant, 109–110, 119–120
  subjects of, 208–221
  as union with Christ, 5
  of unworthy, 211
  water baptism, 99, 123–124, 190
Baptist churches, building of, 201–203
Baptist faith
  on circumcision, 257–258
  differences with paedobaptists, 253–254
  on holiness of children, 258–260
  on infant baptism, 260–265
  on ordinances allowed for children, 258–260
  precept, sanctioning of worship from, 255–258
  repentance requirements for baptism, 255
  service to God, 254, 265
  worship of God, 254
Baptizo, 205–207, 224–227
  definition of, 232
  etymology of, 234–235
  figurative uses of, 237–243

272

Subject Index

grammatical forms of, 225–232
Josephus, use by, 224–225
meaning of, 6
New Testament, use in, 229–232
Old Testament, use in, 225–229
root of, 227–229
verb forms of, 235–236
Bapto, 227–229
Barnes, Albert, 141
Believers
 determination of, 6–7
 as disciples of Christ, 197
 ministry to, 196
 priesthood of, 197
 as subjects of baptism, 208–209
Believers' seed, 261–263. *See also*
  Covenant children
 condition of, 216–217
 covenant promises to, 174–182
 election by God, 183–184
 God's promises to, 182–185
 regenerate nature of, 177
 salvation of, 178–179
Berith, meaning of, 56
The Biblical Doctrine of Infant Baptism
  (Marcel), 3, 245–251
 confusing language in, 249–251
 exegetical errors in, 246–248
 hermeneutical errors in, 248–249
Born-again Christians, 45
Burial of bodies, 237–239
By Oath Consigned (Kline), 73

C

Case laws. *See* Mosaic case laws
Catechumens, baptism of, 189–190, 193.
  See also Credobaptism; Disciples-only
  baptism
Chantry, Walter, 27, 192n. 225
Charismatic theology, 181
Children. *See also* Believers' seed;
  Covenant children
 as believers, 262–263
 of believers, 142
 blessing by Jesus, 153–154
 blessings of, 28, 173–185
 condition of, 216–217
 as covenant breakers, 182, 250
 in Covenant of Grace, 214–217
 Covenant of Works, removal from, 181–182
 election by God, 183–184
 of faith confessors, baptism of, 16
 faithfulness of, 179–181
 false assurance of salvation, 177–178
 gospel heritage of, 146–147, 149
 holiness of, 11, 141–149, 258–260
 Jesus' attitude toward, 151–155
 Lord's Supper, participation in, 14–16, 26–28
 of mixed marriages, 141–149, 219

obedience to parents, 262
parental relations of, 11
Passover, participation in, 23–26
Peter's promises to, 12
receiving kingdom of heaven as, 151–153
regeneration of, 218
repentance of, 181–182
as saints, 11
salvation of, 174–176, 180–181, 184–185
Children of the Promise (Booth), 57
Christ-seed children, 54–55
Christian baptism. *See also* Baptism
 and baptism of Jesus, 159–160
 earliest reference to, 232
Christian Baptism (Murray), 3–18
Christian Nurture (Bushnell), 217
Christians
 faith-lives of, 93
 first called in Antioch, 160–161
Church
 admission to fellowship, 7–8
 autonomy of versus denominationalism, 196–197
 baptism and, 6–9
 biblically regulated worship of, 198
 circumcision and, 117–119
 as disciples, 195
 disciples of, 160–161, 197–198
 as generically one, 8–9
 invisible aspect of, 6–7
 membership in, 215–216
 of New Testament, 84n. 138, 112n., 168
 regenerate and unregenerate members of, 8
 visible aspect of, 7–8
Church fathers, misinterpretation of, 188–191
Church history, mode of baptism throughout, 232–233
Church in the wilderness, 8n., 44, 32–33
 baptism in, 149–150
 circumcision and, 112, 112n., 168
Church tradition, 187–191
Circumcision, 5n., 30
 Abrahamic Covenant and, 9–10, 111–112
 antitype of, 123–124, 218–219. *See also*
   Baptism; Holy Spirit regeneration
 baptism, parallel sign and seal with, 111, 119–120
 baptism and, 14, 54, 120–124
 carry over into New Covenant, 54
 of Christians, 165–166
 church and synagogue membership and, 117–119
 in church in the wilderness, 112n., 168
 divine institution of, 218
 fulfillment of, 116, 247–248
 God's institution of, 171
 heart circumcision. *See* Heart circumcision
 as Holy Spirit's work in the heart, 120–121

infant baptism, parallel to, 9, 44
interpretation of, 36
for justification, 114–115
in New Testament, 114–119
in Old Testament, 111–114
physical versus spiritual, 115–117. *See also* Heart circumcision
as prospective sign of need of heart circumcision, 125
religious significance of, 115–116
salvation and, 165–166
in Sinai Covenant, 112–113
Circumstances of worship, 169
Commandments, 41–42
Communion, for baptized believers, 263
Concerned Presbyterians, 202
Conversion, 151–152
Cornelius, 145
Cornelius' household baptism, 131
Counsel of Redemption, 59, 63
Covenant(s)
believers included in, 63
bond-in-blood element, 56n., 113
conditional nature of, 57–58
content of, 66
covenant breaking, 58, 182
covenantal Baptist definitions of, 60–65
covenantal Baptist views of, 59–66
covenantal paedobaptist definitions of, 56–57
covenantal paedobaptist views of, 55–59
definition by erroneous inference, 62, 64
diversity of, 66–78
genealogical elements of, 69–70
as promises, 61
revelation, definition by, 59, 61
seals of, 123, 256–257
as sovereign bond, 62
suntheke (Greek for), 56n., 111
unity of, 66–78
Covenant children, 75n. 133, 250. *See also* Believers' seed
blessings of, 28, 173–185
communion of, 26
expanded blessings for, 173–185
salvation, promises of, 182
Covenant family, 28
salvation of, 175
salvation within, 181
Covenant of Grace, 52–53, 59
Abrahamic Covenant as, 248
baptism as sign and seal of, 10, 246
for believers and their seed, 63, 68
children in, 214–217
definition of, 68
dual definition of, 62–63
members in, 96, 214–215
organic seed in, 248
purpose of, 64
unifying corporate idea of, 69–70

Covenant of Redemption, 52
definition of, 67
fulfilled in the New Covenant, 82–83
Covenant of Works, 52–53, 64
infants in, 9–10n., 47, 96
members in, 96
removal from, 181–182
Covenant parents
responsibilities of raising children, 173, 175–176, 178
unfaithful children of, 179–181
Covenant theology, 51n., 105
on fulfillment of Old Testament prophecies, 32
of paedobaptists, 51. *See also* Covenantal paedobaptist views
Covenantal Baptist views, 52–55
agreements and disagreements with paedobaptists, 52–55
on children, God's promises to, 182–185
on covenants, 59–66
on covenants, unity and diversity of, 67, 71–78
Covenantal paedobaptist views, 52–55
on covenant seed, salvation of, 182
on covenants, 55–59
on parental efforts, blessing of, 182
Covenants of promise, 53
Covenant of Grace, equating with, 64
fulfillment of, 83
oikos formula in, 129
organic elements of, 98
Creative worship practices, 37
Credenda Agenda, 180
Credobaptism, 78, 95, 199. *See also* Baptism; Disciples-only baptism
evangelism and, 196
as Jesus' instruction, 160
practical implications of, 195–198
Crispus' household baptism, 133

D

Decrees of God, 52
Deductive reasoning versus inferential reasoning, 19
Denominationalism, 197
Diatheke, 56n., 111, 61–62
meaning of, 56
Didache
reference to baptism in, 232
silence on infant baptism issue, 189–191
Disciple(s)
baptism of, 158, 209
believers as, 197
as church visible, 160–161
definition of, 103, 159
mode of baptism of, 229–230
New Testament church as, 195
rebaptism of, 158–159
teaching of good news, 209

Subject Index

Disciples
  baptism of, 189–191
Disciples-only baptism, 220–221. *See also* Baptism; Credobaptism
  evidence for, 133
Discipling, 209–211
Dispensationalism, 84n. 138, 88–89
Dispensationalist views
  on church in the wilderness, interpretation of, 33
  New Testament priority, violation of, 35–36
  on Old Testament prophecies, fulfillment of, 32
Doctrine of organic unity, 217–218
Drama in worship, 39–40

E

Early church
  apostolic tradition, 188–189
  silence on infant baptism, 191–193
Effectual calling, 185
Elders
  children of, 179–180
  qualifications of, 179–180
Elect people, 69
Election of grace, 104–105
Elements of worship, 168
Eternal life, 94
Evangelicalism, hermeneutics of, 28–34
Eve, 53
Ezra, 264

F

Faith
  analogy of, 30
  confessions of, 9
  invisibility of, 6
  justification by, 188n., 218
  professions and confessions of, 7–8
  seal of, 217–218
Faith-lives, 93
False believers, determination of, 6–7
False profession, by children, 180
Feast of Tabernacles, 264
Females
  extension of baptism to, 14n. 64
  extension of privilege to, 14
Fifth Commandment, 11n., 53
Figurative language, interpretation of, 149–150, 225–226, 237–243
Founders Ministries Web site, 203n., 228

G

Generic unity, 8–9
Gentile Christians, 89
  circumcision of, 114, 117–118, 121–122
  status of, 144–145
  uncleanness of, 144–145
Gentile Roman church, 104
Gentiles, faith of, 104–105

God
  believers' seed, promises made to, 182–185
  children of by faith, 216
  decrees of, 52
  election of grace of, 104–105
  individual's responsibility to, 75
  and inspiration of Scripture, 29
  saving through covenant relations, 18, 18n., 77
  sovereignty of, 181
Good and necessary inference
  application of, 20
  authority of, 27
  binding power of, 21
  infant baptism and, 18–22
  limits to, 20–22
  misapplication of, 1, 20–21, 198
Grace
  election of, 104–105
  inheritability of, 216
  through baptism, 16–18
Grammatical interpretation of Scripture, 29
Great Commission, 4, 4n., 28, 5, 5n., 30, 42
  Christian baptism, institution of, 157–158, 160
  disciples-alone baptism command, 159
  mode of baptism, 230
  teaching of, 196

H

Heart circumcision, 5n., 32, 46, 85–86, 100, 113–114, 116–117, 119–122, 183–184
  God's promise of, 183–184
  as New Covenant seal, 119–120
  signs of, 125
Hermeneutics
  of baptism, inconsistencies in, 23–26
  biblical, 44–47
  for Christian baptism, 44–47
  context, accounting for, 107
  errors of, 1
  Evangelical, 28–34
  guidelines for application of, 33–34
  of infant baptism, 34–44
  inferences from Scripture, 19
  paedobaptist violations of, 101–109
  Reformed, 28–34
  of typology, 123
  unclear text, building doctrines on, 107
Historical interpretation of Scripture, 29
Hodge, Charles, 36
Holy Spirit
  promise of, 138–140, 138n., 186
  as seal of New Covenant, 110
Holy Spirit regeneration, 119–120, 122–124. *See also* Heart circumcision
Household baptisms, 127–135, 260–262
  Cornelius' household, 131
  Crispus' household, 133

infants and children present in, 128
Lydia's household, 132
Philippian jailer's household, 132–133
Stephanas' household, 134
Humility, 151–152

I

Immersion, 205–207, *224. See also Baptizo*
  as preferred practice for baptism, 232–233
Infant baptism, 7n., 37, 9–12, 40
  as apostolic tradition, 188–189
  argument from silence for, 38, 163, 165–171
  basis of, 14n., 61
  and biblical Christianity, decline in, 202n., 227
  as carry over of Abrahamic circumcision, 54
  case for, 3
  circumcision and, 9–10, 14, 44
  comfort derived from, 17–18
  command prohibiting, 163–164
  of confessors of Christ, 16
  as continuation of Old Testament economy, 10
  corroborating evidence supporting, 10–12
  efficacy of, 16–18, 16n., 71
  evidence for, 18
  evils of, 178n., 208
  example from Old Testament, 149–150
  existence of, 219–220
  failed lives of recipients of, 14
  females, extension to, 14n., 64
  as good and necessary inference, defective use of, 20
  good and necessary inference as evidence of, 13, 18–22
  hermeneutics, inconsistent application to, 34–44
  mention in writings of early church, 188–189, 193
  New Covenant and, 109–110
  normative principles of application, 40
  objections to, 12–16
  obscure texts, use in support of, 236–237
  oikos formula theory for, 127, 134
  parental duty of, 30n. 88
  versus participation in Lord's Supper, 14–16
  precepts for baptism and, 163–165
  Presbyterian explanation for, 174
  profession of faith requirement for, 13–14
  proof-texts for, 137–150
  proselyte baptism as support for, 187–188
  regulative principle of worship and, 169–171
  Scripture verses supporting, 101–109
  selection of individuals for, 16
  significance of, 10
  silence regarding, 148–149
  universal practice of, 191–192

Infant blessing, 153–154
Infants
  death of, 184–185, 250
  effectual calling of, 185
  election by God, 177
  holiness of, 177
  regeneration of, 177
Inferences. *See also* Good and necessary inference
  plausible versus necessary, 20
  in Scripture, 19–20
Inferential reasoning versus deductive reasoning, 19
Invisibility of regeneration and faith, 6
Irenaeus, 189
Israel
  antitypical, 90
  baptism in cloud and sea, 206
  in New Covenant, 88–89
  of Old Testament, heirs of, 106
Israel of God, 45n., 102, 55n., 110, 75, 77, 104–105
  children of, 166
  Christ's faith-seed as, 98n. 154
  elect as, 105n., 159

J

Jerusalem Council, 114
Jesus Christ
  baptism, institution of, 11n., 52
  baptism, instructions concerning, 159–160
  baptism of, 4, 4n., 27, 5, 157–159
  baptism of, and Christian baptism, 159–160
  baptism of disciples alone, 129–130
  burial and resurrection with, 240–241
  children, attitude toward, 11, 151–155
  children, blessing of, 261–262
  circumcision of, 121, 124–125
  death and resurrection of, 121
  disciples of, 103
  faith-seed of, 99
  individual knowledge of, 94
  as Mediator of New Covenant, 85, 91, 94–97, 100, 138
  New Covenant, establishment of, 82
  personal relationship to, 74
  as representative of people, 83
  sacraments instituted by, 170–171
  sacrifice of, 95–97
  seed of, 74
  as seed of Abraham, 98–100
Jesus Christ's commission, 208–213
  order of activities, 209–211
Jewish Christians, 89
  circumcision of, 114–115, 117–118
  unbelieving, 104–105
Jewish proselyte baptism, 128–130, 135, 148, 187–188, 188n., 217
  mode of, 207

Subject Index 277

Jewish Talmud, 218
John the Baptist
  baptism of, 4–5, 157–159, 206, 211–212, 243
  baptism of disciples alone, 129–130
  individuals greater than, 95
Josephus, 235
baptizo, use of, 224–225
Judah, 84n. 138
  in New Covenant, 88–89
Judaizers, 114–115, 165–166
Justification
  circumcision as means of, 114–115
  by faith, 188n. 218

K

Kingdom of God, 77
  humility and conversion as conditions of entering, 151–152
  unregenerate members in, 103, 105, 247

L

Larger Catechism, 141
Literal-grammatical-historical method of interpretation, 29–30
  of *baptizo,* 234–235, 243
Literal interpretation of Scripture, 29
Locus classicus, 106–109
Lord's Supper
  children's participation in, 14–16, 26–28
  entrance to, 164
  infants' participation in, 14–16
  recipient's understanding of, 15
  as sign of New Covenant, 110
  women's participation in, 166
Luke, 132
Lydia's household baptism, 132

M

Manasseh, 76
Ministry for people of faith, not seekers, 196
Mixed marriages, 143
  children of, 141–149
Moral Law, continuance of, 44
Mosaic case laws, 41n. 99
  application in New Covenant era, 88
  continuance of, 41–43
  practice of, 115
Mosaic Covenant, application of, 115–116
Mosaic food laws, rejection of, 118–119
Moses, circumcision and, 112

N

Naaman, 226–227
Nehemiah, 264
New Covenant, 53
  Abrahamic covenantal relations, change in, 71–74
  as administration in force, 54
  administration of, 27–28, 71–78
  baptism and, 55
  better promises of, 62
  blessings, for children, 173–185
  blessings, individual, 91–95
  blessings, potential, 89
  blessings, realization of, 88–91
  children in, 95
  conditions of, 58–59
  covenant breakers of, 100–103, 102n., 156, 105–109
  definition of, 81–88
  diversity of, 71–78
  divinity of, 84–86
  false professors of, 100–102
  as fulfillment of Abrahamic Covenant and Covenant of Grace, 53
  heart circumcision in, 113–114, 119–120
  infant baptism and, 109–110
  infants in, 96–97
  interpretation of, 36
  Jesus Christ and His Seed of faith in, 98–100
  mediation through blood, 96
  membership in, 97–100. *See also* New Covenant members
  newness of, 86–88
  promises of, 58
  as prophecy, 82–84
  as pure Covenant of Grace, 64–65
  as replacement of Abrahamic Covenant, 74
  seal of, 5, 5n., 31, 110, 119–120
  unbreakable nature of, 58–59, 85, 100–101
  unconditional nature of, 58, 84–86
  uniqueness of, 71
  unregenerate individuals in, 103, 105
New Covenant Israel, 55n., 110, 75n., 133, 84n., 138
New Covenant members, 84–85, 91
  baptism of, 109
  blessings of, 88–91
  children as, 95
  forgiveness of sins of, 91–92, 94–95
  hearts of, 77
  individual covenantal responsibility of, 74–78
  infants as, 96–97
  inheritance of, 72–73
  Jesus Christ and His Seed of faith as, 98–100
  knowledge of God, 91–92, 94
  law written in hearts of, 85–86, 88, 90, 92–93
  regenerate nature of, 73n., 131
  root and branch metaphor, 102–106
  sacrifice for, 95–97
  sanctification of, 106–108
  signs of, 109–110

278 Subject Index

unregenerate individuals as, 103, 105
water baptism of, 125
New Geneva Study Bible, 102–103
New Testament
  authority of, 46–47
  baptism, express command and clear example of, 13
  baptism, precepts for, 163
  baptizo, use of, 229–232
  church, form of, 8–9
  circumcision in, 5n., 32, 114–119
  clarity of, 31
  as complement to Old Testament, 30
  distinction from Old Testament, 30
  finality of, 31
  priority of, 31–32, 34, 43–44
  prophecies, fulfillment in, 35–36
  revelation of versus Old Testament revelation, 36
  on Sabbath, 166
  sacraments, express commands and explicit institution of, 19
  unity with Old Testament, 44–45
New Testament church, 84n. 138. *See also* Church
  identity of, 112n. 168
Newton, B. W., 35–36
Noahic Covenant, 60–61
  unbreakable and unconditional nature of, 66
Normative principle of worship, 27, 148–149, 168
  additions to worship made under, 168–169
  baptism, application to, 170
  New Testament priority, violation of, 37–40

O

Obscure texts, use in support of paedobaptism, 236–237
Oikos formula theory, 127–130, 134, 140
  baptism, Jesus' application of, 155
Old Covenant administration, 27–28
Old Testament
  authority of, 44
  baptizo, use of, 225–229
  case laws, continuance of, 41–43
  church, form of, 8–9
  circumcision, fulfillment of, 122–124
  circumcision in, 5n. 32, 111–114
  as complement to New Testament, 30
  distinction from New Testament, 30
  erroneous inferences from, 37
  interpretation of, 31–32, 45
  law, interpretation and qualification of, 46
  prophecies, fulfillment of, 32, 35–36, 46
  unity with New Testament, 44–45
Ordinances of church, importance of, 195

Organic unity, doctrine of, 217–218
Origen, 189

P

Paedobaptism Examined (Booth), 38–39
Paedobaptist churches, life cycle of, 202
Paedobaptists
  baptism, inconsistency in dispensing, 14–15
  baptismal regeneration and presumptive regeneration properties, 10n. 50
  child salvation, views of, 174–182
  on Covenant of Grace, 245–246
  covenant theology of, 51
  covenants, belief in unity and diversity of, 67–71
  covenants, hermeneutical error in defining, 62–63
  hermeneutic errors of, 34
  hermeneutical disagreements among, 25
  hermeneutical errors of, 36, 39
  household baptism, divided opinions on, 127
  on John the Baptist and Jesus' baptisms, 4
  on Lord's Supper, participation in, 164
  on mode of baptism, 223, 232–244
  New Covenant, broad definition of, 90
  New Covenant and Abrahamic Covenant, belief in similarities of, 54
  obscure texts, use in support of paedobaptism, 236–237
  parable of wheat and tares, misinterpretation of, 8n., 42
  regulative principle, adoption and violation of, 38
  Scripture verses supporting infant baptism, use of, 101–109
  typological exegesis, disregard of, 32–33
Paedocommunion, 15, 23, 25, 28, 164
Paedoglossalalia, 131
Parents
  failure in responsibilities of raising children, 249
  faithfulness of, and grace bestowed on children, 17, 17n., 76
  responsibilities of raising children, 173, 175–176, 178
Particular Baptists, interpretation of good and necessary consequence, 20
Particular redemption, 95–97
Passover, children's participation in, 23–26
Passover Lamb, 96
Paul, 93
  on baptism, 165–166
  on circumcision, 114–116, 165–166
  circumcision, definition of, 121–122
  law of Moses, keeping of, 116
  Mosaic food laws, rejection of, 118–119

preaching of gospel, 132
on unbelieving husbands, 143
PCA Book of Church Order, 174–175
Pentecost
  baptism before and after, 158
  baptisms at, 130–131
  Gentiles, extension to, 131
Peter
  discipling and baptizing on Pentecost, 212
  law of Moses, keeping of, 116
  Mosaic food laws, rejection of, 118–119
Pharisees, erroneous deductions of, 20
Philip, baptism of, 206
Philippian jailer's household baptism, 132–133
Precept
  sanctioning of worship from, 255–258
  weight of, 163–165
Presbyterian Church of America (PCA), position on infant baptism, 25
Presbyterianism, 167
Pride, 151
Profession of faith as requirement for baptism, 13–14, 255
Progressive revelation, 31
Promise of Holy Spirit, 138–140, 138n. 186. *See also* Holy Spirit regeneration
  children in, 140–141
Proof-texts for infant baptism, 137–150
  1 Corinthians 7:12–16, 141–149
  1 Corinthians 10:1–14, 149–150
  Acts 2:38–39, 137–141
Prophecies, fulfillment of, 32, 35–36, 46
Purification by baptism, 5

R

Redemption
  apostates in, 108–109
  false teachers in, 108–109
  particular redemption, 95–97
  proof-text for, 108
Reformed Baptists, 128n. 178
  building church of, 201–203
  elements of worship, 168
  hermeneutics of, 28–34
  resurgence of, 201
Regenerate individuals, 76–77
Regenerate remnant, 139
Regeneration, 146. *See also* Heart circumcision
  baptism based on, 14
  of children, 218
  by Holy Spirit, 119–120, 122–124
  invisibility of, 6
Regulative principle of worship, 10n., 49, 13n. 58, 19, 27, 37–39, 149, 167–171
  circumstances of worship, 169
  compromise of, 202
  definition of, 167–169
  elements of worship, 167–168

infant baptism and, 169–171
recommitment to, 171
violation of, 249
Religious liberty, 220
Repentance, as condition of baptism, 157–158, 164–165, 255
Repentant individuals, 77
  baptism of, 130
Roman Catholics, 20
  church tradition, authority of, 21
  theological inference, authority of, 21
Root and branch metaphor, 102–106

S

Sabbath, 93, 166
Sacraments
  baptism as, 169
  as elements of worship, 168
  good and necessary consequence and, 20
  instituted by Christ, 199
  as positive precepts, 39
Sacrifice for New Covenant members, 95–97
Salvation
  of children, 184–185
  of children, false assurance of, 177–178
  of covenant family members, 174–175
  God's choice for, 181
  by grace, 53
  through water, 241–242. *See also* Water baptism
Satan, 53
Scripture
  on circumcision and baptism, link between, 121–124
  diversity of, 31, 45–46
  examples in versus deductions made from, 19
  hermeneutical principles, application to, 33–34
  inerrancy of, 29
  inspiration of, 29
  as interpreter of Scripture, 30
  on Jesus' interaction with children, 151–155
  literal-grammatical-historical method of interpretation of, 29–30
  literal interpretation of, 29n. 87
  perspicuity of, 30
  records forbidding infant baptism, 219–220
  records of baptism in, 212–214
  silence on infant baptism, 219–220
  as support for infant baptism, 130–135
  typology of, 32–33
  unity of, 30, 44–45
  warning passages in, 101–102
Seal of faith, 217–218
Seed of the woman, 53
Seed promises to Abraham, 54–55
Self-examination precept, 164

Septuagint, use of *baptizo,* 225–229
Silas, preaching of gospel, 132
Sinai Covenant, 53, 66
  blessing-cursing formula in, 85
  circumcision in, 112–113
  conditional nature of, 86
  temporal nature of, 87n. 146
Sins, forgiveness of, 94–95. *See also* Salvation
1689 London Baptist Confession, 7, 201
  appendix of, 253–265
  covenantal Baptists, agreements and disagreements with paedobaptists, 52–55
  on holiness of children, 145–146
  on infant death, 185
  regulative principle, definition of, 167
Sovereign election, 139–140
Spirit, baptism of, 206
Sprinkling and pouring versus immersion. *See* Baptism, mode of; *Baptizo*
Stephanas' household baptism, 134
Suntheke, 62
Synagogue membership, circumcision and, 117–119
Systematic theology, 88n. 147

T
The Teaching of the Twelve Apostles, reference to baptism in, 232
Ten Commandments, 92–93, 166
  moral case laws based on, 41n., 99
Tertullian, 188–189, 220
Theonomists, hermeneutical error of, 41–43
Theonomy, 43n. 101, 87–88
Timothy, 263
  circumcision of, 114
  conversion to Judaism, 114
Tradition, church, 187–191

Trinitarian baptism versus John's baptism, 4
Typological exegesis, 32–33
Typology, type and antitype, 123

U
Unbelieving spouses, 143–144
  sanctification of, 144, 146
Universal church, 55n., 110
Unregenerate individuals, 103, 105

V
Visible church, paedobaptist churches in, 191–192

W
Water baptism, 99. *See also* Baptism
  for confessors of faith, 123–124
  Didache instruction for, 190
  of New Covenant members, 125
Westminster Confession of Faith
  on baptism, meaning of, 9n., 46
  on good and necessary inference, 18–19
  on infant death, 185
  on regulative principle of worship, 37, 167
  on Scripture, clarity of, 30
  on Scripture, warning against adding to, 20
  on traditions of men, interpretation of, 190
Wheat and tares parable, 247
Women, participation in Lord's Supper, 166
Worship
  circumstances of, 39
  elements of, 37, 39
Worship in Spirit and Truth (Frame), 39–40

Scripture Index

A
Acts
 1:4, 138
 1:15, 160
 2:17, 242
 2:29–32, 238
 2:33, 138
 2:37–39, 177
 2:37–42, 125, 158, 181
 2:38, 141, 176, 183–184
 2:38–39, 12, 24, 137–141, 138n. 186, 143, 248
 2:38–41, 95, 97, 119, 130, 139–140, 163
 2:38–42, 7
 2:39, 65, 138, 140–141, 151, 183–184
 2:39–41, 86
 2:41, 11n. 52, 12n. 56, 13n. 59, 79, 118, 128n. 178, 140, 184, 192
 6:1, 160, 246
 6:1–7, 195
 7:38, 112
 8:13, 7
 8:35–38, 7
 9:19, 160
 9:26, 160, 195, 246
 9:28, 160
 9:38, 246
 10:22, 131
 10:28, 145
 10:34–38, 7
 10:44–48, 131
 10:47–48, 11
 11:12, 131
 11:14, 11, 128, 131
 11:17, 131
 11:18, 131
 11:26, 55, 160, 195, 246
 11:29, 119, 160, 246
 13:47–48, 104
 13:52, 160, 246
 14:20, 160, 246
 14:22, 160, 246
 14:28, 160, 246
 15, 10n. 49, 165, 197
 15:1 ff., 114
 15:10, 160
 16:1, 144
 16:3, 114
 16:14, 7
 16:15, 7, 11, 128, 132
 16:30–34, 132
 16:31–33, 7
 16:33, 128
 16:33–34, 11
 17:19, 87
 17:26–31, 64
 17:30, 11n. 53
 17:30–31, 181
 18:8, 128, 133
 18:23, 160
 18:24–28, 158
 18:27, 160
 19:1–7, 158
 19:4, 212
 19:9, 160
 19:30, 160
 20:1, 160
 20:7, 160, 166
 20:28, 97
 20:30, 160
 21:4, 160
 21:16, 160
 21:18–25, 115
 21:20–21, 114
 26:18, 144, 146

C
Colossians
 2:8–11, 115–117
 2:9–12, 121–124
 2:9–14, 124
 2:11, 5, 70, 116, 124, 218
 2:11–12, 5n. 32, 14, 45, 85, 115, 122–123, 240–241, 247
 2:12, 5, 70, 124, 226, 232
 2:13–14, 122
 3:20–21, 11
1 Corinthians
 1:2, 150
 1:16, 11, 128, 134
 3:16–17, 35, 45
 7:4, 258
 7:12–16, 141–149
 7:14, 11, 144, 147–149, 177, 188n. 217, 248
 7:19, 218, 257
 7:34, 143
 9:19–23, 114
 10:1–13, 44
 10:1–14, 149–150
 10:2, 226, 231–232, 239–240
 10:32, 114
 11, 164, 166
 11:28, 25
 12:13, 124
 16:15, 134
2 Corinthians
 1:21–22, 119
 1:22, 5n. 31, 110, 123
 5:17, 87
 6:16, 32, 35

D
Deuteronomy
 4:13, 85
 5:33, 86
 10:16, 85, 92, 113
 22:8, 87
 23:2, 145
 24:5, 87
 30:6, 69, 81, 85, 113, 183–184

281

E

Ephesians
 1:1, 147
 1:3–14, 52, 63
 1:13, 5n. 31, 110, 123, 147–148
 1:13–14, 119, 125, 246
 2:12, 54, 62, 74
 2:12–20, 8
 2:15, 42, 116
 2:19–22, 35
 2:19ff., 45
 2:20, 32, 35
 4:1–6, 148
 4:30, 110, 119, 123, 246
 5:25, 96
 6:1, 11
 6:1–4, 147
 6:4, 11

Exodus
 1:8, 87
 12, 24, 26
 12:19, 23–24
 12:24, 23–24, 26
 12:26, 23–24
 12:28, 23–24
 12:29, 23–24
 12:43–51, 23, 26
 12:49, 257
 20:6, 17

Ezekiel
 3:25 ff., 183
 18:1–9, 76
 36:24–27, 77
 36:25, 231
 36:25–27, 242
 36:26, 85, 87
 36:26–27, 92, 138
 37:26–28, 32, 35

Ezra
 2:62–63, 254
 9, 143
 10:2–3, 143–144

G

Galatians
 1:9, 115
 3, 45, 54, 98
 3–6, 118
 3:2, 165
 3:2–5, 55
 3:3, 124, 165
 3:7, 83, 99
 3:8–9, 55
 3:9, 8, 83, 99
 3:14, 8, 55, 83, 89, 99, 121, 131, 138, 166
 3:14–15, 137
 3:16, 9n. 45, 53, 70, 98
 3:16–19, 87n. 146
 3:17, 8, 65
 3:19, 9n. 45, 53, 70, 74, 83, 112, 116
 3:21, 53
 3:22, 99, 138
 3:26, 83
 3:27, 99
 3:28–29, 84n. 138, 98, 121
 3:29, 55, 70, 75, 83, 99, 124, 138, 166
 4:19, 210
 5:2, 114, 165
 5:3, 165
 5:19, 93
 6:12–14, 114
 6:14–16, 166
 6:15, 115–116, 166, 218
 6:15–16, 5n. 32, 10n. 49, 75
 6:16, 45, 73, 84n. 138, 90–91, 105, 166
 6:16–17, 84n. 138

Genesis
 3:15, 53, 68, 83, 98
 6:18–22, 61
 9:8–17, 61, 66
 17, 111–112, 258
 17:7, 176, 214
 17:11, 119
 17:14, 59, 66, 114, 182
 17:27, 72
 35:8, 238

H

Hebrews
 2:10, 107
 3–4, 150
 3:1, 97, 102, 106
 3:2–4, 240
 3:16, 240
 4:14, 102, 106
 5:7–9, 107
 6:4, 102
 6:4–6, 92, 101
 6:4–8, 100–102
 6:13–18, 248
 6:13–20, 61
 8:8, 87
 8:8–12, 36, 54, 82, 84n. 138, 89, 91, 103, 107
 8:10, 85
 8:10–12, 177
 8:11, 89
 9, 32, 96
 9:10, 231, 236–237
 9:11–12, 107
 9:13, 236
 9:15, 83, 96
 9:19, 236
 9:21, 236
 10:1–17, 45
 10:10, 95
 10:11–22, 95
 10:12, 95
 10:14, 95, 143
 10:16, 95
 10:16–17, 36, 82, 89, 94, 107
 10:23, 102, 106
 10:26–31, 92
 10:29, 100, 106–109
 11:6, 216
 11:29, 240
 12:23, 97

Hosea
 6:7, 52, 83

I

Isaiah
 11:1–12, 77
 21:4, 226
 44:3, 141
 53:10, 54
 54:9–10, 61
 55:11, 184
 59:21, 141, 176
 66:22, 87

J

James
 2:2–4, 117
 2:26, 93

Jeremiah
 4:4, 92
 6:9, 76
 6:14–16, 65
 23:1–6, 76
 26:23, 238
 31, 76–77
 31–34, 82
 31:7–8, 76
 31:27–30, 76
 31:27–34, 58, 70, 74, 91, 102n. 156, 103, 248
 31:29–31, 75
 31:31, 86–87
 31:31–34, 32, 36, 45, 66, 84n. 138, 87–88, 90, 92, 94, 166, 183–184
 31:33, 75, 89, 152
 31:33–34, 94
 31:34, 75, 89, 94, 152
 32:37, 76
 32:37–41, 113
 32:39, 69, 114
 32:40, 36, 58, 85, 109, 248
 33:20, 62

Scripture Index 283

Joel
  2:28, 85
  2:28–29, 138
  2:28–30, 242
John
  1:35, 158
  1:40, 158
  2:27, 94
  3:1–7, 103
  3:5, 77
  3:5–6, 125
  3:22, 212
  4:1, 212, 246
  4:1–2, 78, 119, 155,
    157–158, 196, 230, 237
  4:1ff., 4n. 27
  4:2, 212
  4:21–24, 32, 35
  6:44, 94
  6:45, 94
  8:31, 6
  10:14, 94
  13:34, 42, 87
  14:15, 42, 93
  15, 102–103
  15:1–8, 6, 100
  15:1–17, 102
  15:2, 102–103
  15:6, 102
  15:8, 103
  17:3, 94
  17:19, 107
Joshua
  3:13, 228
  3:15, 228
  5:2–7, 112
Jude
  24–25, 109

K
2 Kings
  5:14, 227
  21:11–15, 76
  23:6, 238
  23:26–27, 76

L
Leviticus
  14:6, 228
  14:51, 228
  16, 96
Luke
  2:23, 177
  2:25, 147
  7:11–17, 238
  9:46–48, 151
  11:44, 238
  18:15–17, 11, 152–154
  22:20, 82, 96
  24:47, 43
  24:49, 138

M
Malachi
  2:15, 77
Mark
  1:1, 159
  1:4, 158
  1:5, 212, 229
  1:8–9, 237
  1:9, 6n. 33, 229, 235
  2, 166
  7:4–5, 236–237
  9:33–37, 151
  10:13–16, 152–154
  14:24, 96
Matthew
  1:21, 83, 95
  3:6, 157
  3:11, 235, 242–243
  3:11–12, 231
  3:12, 243
  5–7, 44
  5:17–20, 41–42
  5:21ff., 42
  7:22–23, 197
  7:23, 93, 101
  8:12, 77
  8:27, 210
  9:17, 87
  11:11, 95, 152
  11:27, 94
  12, 93, 166
  13:24–30, 8n. 42
  13:38, 8n. 42, 77,
    103, 247
  15:1–10, 20
  16:16–18, 125
  16:16–19, 159
  16:24–26, 159
  17:14, 210
  18:1–6, 11
  18:1–10, 151–152
  18:15–17, 197
  19:13–14, 11
  19:13–15, 152–154
  19:17, 42
  22:36–40, 42
  22:37–39, 93
  23:35, 76
  23:36, 76
  26:28, 82
  27:7, 238
  27:60, 87
  28:18–20, 42, 93–94,
    119, 160, 165, 190,
    232, 246
  28:19, 89, 125
  28:19–20, 4, 78, 197,
    230
  28:20, 32, 35

P
1 Peter
  3:18–22, 241–242
  3:21, 226, 231–232, 242
2 Peter
  2:1, 108
Philippians
  1:5–7, 7n. 37
  3:1–3, 45
  3:3, 5n. 32, 73, 84n.
    138, 85, 90, 92, 115,
    120, 123, 166, 218
  3:15–16, 254
Psalms
  33:3, 87
  77:17, 240
  103:17, 17
  103:17–18, 176
  103:18, 17

R
Revelation
  1:10, 166
  2–3, 197
  20:4–5, 237
Romans
  2:1–16, 11n. 53, 182
  2:14–15, 93
  2:14–16, 181
  2:20–23, 93
  2:25–29, 116, 120–121
  2:28, 218
  2:28–29, 5n. 32, 115
  2:29, 45, 84n. 138, 85,
    90, 92, 218
  3:19–20, 53
  3:26, 84
  3:31, 93
  4, 98–99
  4:9–25, 119
  4:11, 119, 123, 257
  4:11–12, 99
  4:12, 55
  4:12–13, 99, 120
  4:13, 139
  4:13–16, 55
  4:16, 70, 83, 99, 138
  4:23, 120
  5, 250
  5:1–6:14, 109
  5:12, 83
  5:12–19, 83–84
  5:12–21, 52
  5:12 ff., 74, 182
  5:12ff., 53, 58

6:3, 124, 210
6:3–4, 122, 226, 232, 237–239
6:4, 124, 231
6:14, 53, 96
6:17, 93
7:7, 93
7:8, 42
7:12, 93
7:14–8:4, 92
7:22, 93
7:25, 93
8:1, 96
8:4, 166
8:9, 99
8:14–17, 99
9, 17n. 76, 175, 181, 250
9–11, 104–106
9:1–5, 147
9:6–8, 120, 138

11, 147
11:1–11, 104
11:5, 105
11:11–24, 100
11:16, 147
11:16–21, 8
11:17–24, 104
11:26, 104
12:23, 254
13:8–10, 93
13:9, 42
13:10, 93
13:11ff., 44
14:4–10, 254
15:27, 104

S
1 Samuel
  6:7, 87
  14:27, 228

2 Samuel
  12:23, 185

T
1 Thessalonians
  4:9, 94
1 Timothy
  3:4, 179
  4:5, 143
  6:14, 42
2 Timothy
  1:8–10, 53–54, 68
  1:9, 52, 69
  1:9–10, 63, 82
  3:15–17, 44
  3:16–17, 254
Titus
  1:1–3, 63, 69
  1:6, 179